OLD TESTAMENT THEOLOGY
IN A CANONICAL CONTEXT

BREVARD S. CHILDS

OLD TESTAMENT THEOLOGY
IN A CANONICAL CONTEXT

FORTRESS PRESS   PHILADELPHIA

Library of Congress Cataloging in Publication Data

Childs, Brevard S.
  Old Testament theology in a canonical context

  Bibliography: p.
  Includes indexes.
  1. Bible. O.T.—Theology. I. Title.
BS1192.5.C38 1986   221.6   85–45503
ISBN 0-8006-0772-3 (cloth)
ISBN 0-8006-2772-5 (paper)

Manufactured in the U.S.A.   1-2772

                                    9   10

To John and Vicky

with much affection

CONTENTS

    (i) The modern debate   175
    (ii) A theological interpretation of Israel's institutions 177
        (a) Civil institutions   178
        (b) Class structure   181
        (c) Legal institutions   182
        (d) Military institutions   184
        (e) Family Institutions   185

16 MALE AND FEMALE AS A THEOLOGICAL PROBLEM   188

    (i) Male and female in Genesis 1–3   189
    (ii) Male and female in the Song of Songs   192

17 THE THEOLOGICAL DIMENSION OF BEING HUMAN   196

    (i)   Introduction   196
    (ii) Canonical indices within the tradition   197
    (iii) Theological reflections on Old Testament anthropology 199

18 THE SHAPE OF THE OBEDIENT LIFE   204

    (i)   A review of some theological approaches   204
    (ii) Canonical guidelines to Israel's response   207
        (a) The Psalter   207
        (b) Wisdom   210
        (c) The Pentateuch   212
    (iii) Theological reflections in a canonical context   214
        (a) The Psalter   214
        (b) The prophets   217
        (c) The histories and the writings   217
        (d) The patriarchal narratives   218
    (iv) Summary   220

19 LIFE UNDER THREAT   222

    (i)   The primaeval threat, Genesis 1–11   222
    (ii)   Covenant and curse   226
    (iii) Prophets   228
    (iv)   Daniel and apocalyptic   230
    (v)   The Psalms, *de profundis*   231
    (vi)   Wisdom   232
    (vii) The limits of the threat   232
    (viii) Summary   234

PREFACE

Modern Old Testament study is at present undergoing many changes of direction. To a new generation the older approaches often appear less than convincing; however, the newer models have not yet established a firm course. For this reason I have chosen to develop my understanding of Old Testament theology in a less technical form than my earlier commentary and introductions. The most pressing need within the contemporary scene seems to be in suggesting a new manner of theological reflection rather than once again rehearsing in detail the familiar lines of earlier research.

I recall with gratitude the privilege of having heard lectures on Old Testament theology from my unforgettable teachers, W. Eichrodt, G. von Rad and W. Zimmerli. In those places where I have been forced to register my disagreement, it is done in the spirit of honest theological inquiry which is a concern first learned from them. In the end, my sense of continuity with these great scholars of the church exceeds that of rupture.

New Haven,
April 1985

ABBREVIATIONS

AbTANT	Abhandlungen zur Theologie des Alten und Neuen Testaments, Zürich
AnBibl	Analecta Biblica, Rome
BGBE	Beiträge zur Geschichte der biblischen Exegese, Tübingen
BibB	Biblische Beiträge, Fribourg
BSt	Biblische Studien, Neukirchen-Vluyn
BWANT	Beiträge zur Wissenschaft von Alten und Neuen Testament, Leipzig, Stuttgart
BZAW	Beihefte zur *Zeitschrift für die alttestamentliche Wissenschaft*, Giessen, Berlin
EJ	*Encyclopaedia Judaica*, Jerusalem 1971–2
ET	English translation
EvTh	*Evangelische Theologie*, Munich
FRLANT	Forschungen zur Religion und Literatur des Alten und Neuen Testaments, Göttingen
FS	*Festschrift*
GA	*Gesammelte Aufsätze*
GSAT	*Gesammelte Schriften des Alten Testaments*
HTR	*Harvard Theological Review*, Cambridge, Mass.
Interp	*Interpretation*, Richmond, Va.
JAAR	*Journal of the American Academy of Religion*, Boston
JBL	*Journal of Biblical Literature*, Philadelphia, Missoula, Chico
JNES	*Journal of Near Eastern Studies*, Chicago
JSOT	*Journal for the Study of the Old Testament*, Sheffield
JSOT Suppl	*Journal for the Study of the Old Testament, Supplements*, Sheffield
JSS	*Journal of Semitic Studies*, Manchester
KuD	*Kerygma und Dogma*, Göttingen

NJPS	The Jewish Publication Society translation, Philadelphia
OBeO	Orbis Biblicus et Orientalis, Freiburg, Göttingen
SBS	Stuttgarter Bibelstudien, Stuttgart
SBT	Studies in Biblical Theology, London and Naperville
SJLA	Studies in Judaism in Late Antiquity, Leiden
StBib	*Studia Biblica et Theologica*, Pasadena
StTh	*Studia Theologica*, Lund, Aarhus
SVT	*Supplements to Vetus Testamentum*, Leiden
TDNT	*Theological Dictionary of the New Testament*, ET of *TWNT*, Grand Rapids 1964–1976
TDOT	*Theological Dictionary of the Old Testament*, ET of *TWAT*, Grand Rapids 1974ff.
ThB	Theologische Bücherei, Munich
ThBl	*Theologische Blätter*, Leipzig
TRE	*Theologische Realenzyklopädie*, Berlin, New York
TWAT	*Theologisches Wörterbuch zum Alten Testament*, ed. G. J. Botterweck and H. Ringgren, Stuttgart 1970ff.
TWNT	*Theologisches Wörterbuch zum Neuen Testament*, ed. G. Kittel, Stuttgart 1932ff.
VuF	*Verkündigung und Forschungen*, Munich
WdF	Wege der Forschung, Darmstadt
WMANT	Wissenschaftliche Monographien zum Alten und Neuen Testament, Neukirchen-Vluyn
ZAW	*Zeitschrift für die alttestamentliche Wissenschaft*, Giessen, Berlin
ZTK	*Zeitschrift für Theologie und Kirche*, Tübingen

1

INTRODUCTION TO OLD TESTAMENT THEOLOGY

(i) *The present task*

Although most biblical scholars no longer share the traditional position that the theology of the Old Testament stands as the crown of the entire discipline, a strong case can still be made for the basic importance of this theological enterprise. Of course, its importance is matched by its difficulty. To write an Old Testament theology requires, first of all, a construal of the whole, which is an awesome task. Then again, theological judgments need to be made regarding the primary or secondary significance of disparate features of the literature, and decisions rendered in respect to the nature of its coherence. Finally, because the discipline is not bound to a text in the same manner as in a commentary on a biblical book, the ensuing freedom offers its author an unusual challenge for interpretation which includes a high level of promise as well as threat.

It should come as no surprise to learn that great differences of opinion exist among contemporary scholars as to how the task of writing an Old Testament theology should proceed. Not least of the disagreement turns on how theological reflection on the Old Testament relates to the prior, analytical study of the biblical text which is generally subsumed under the rubric of the historical-critical study of the Bible. It is my thesis that a canonical approach to the scriptures of the Old Testament opens up a fruitful avenue along which to explore the theological dimensions of the biblical text. Especially in the light of the widespread uncertainty at present as to how best to pursue the discipline, to try a different approach to the material would seem appropriate.

(ii) *A survey of the history of the discipline*

In order to gain a perspective on the present debate regarding Old Testament theology, a brief review of the history of the discipline is called for. The survey can be brief because the history has been frequently rehearsed at length within recent years (cf. Dentan, Kraus, Reventlow, Clements, Hayes).

A separate discipline of Old Testament theology as distinct from New Testament theology or dogmatic theology was unknown in the Christian church during the ancient, mediaeval and Reformation periods of its history. The Old Testament, of course, was studied and used, but in combination with the other disciplines. Significantly, the Jewish synagogue did not develop a special discipline either, but joined the study of the Bible with the rabbinic traditions.

For several reasons there developed in the post-Reformation period a discipline of Old Testament theology as a distinct area of study which at first was considered a part of the larger field of biblical theology. On the one hand, a major force toward developing a theology based on the Bible arose from within German pietistic circles as a protest against the use of largely philosophical concepts and terminology in scholastic theology. On the other hand, at the other end of the theological spectrum was the rationalist's attempt to give a closer descriptive historical and philological investigation to theology by a direct appeal to the Bible which would be unencumbered by traditional ballast. The famous lecture of J. P. Gabler in 1787 articulated in an illuminating fashion a precise conceptual theory for effecting a sharp separation between biblical and dogmatic theology. He distinguished the analytical task of describing what the biblical writers themselves thought from the constructive task of interpreting how the church later sought to appropriate and use the Bible.

At first the theology of the two Testaments was treated together, but increasingly by the early nineteenth century Old Testament theology emerged as a separate discipline from the New Testament even among those writers who still felt competent to write on both Testaments (e.g. de Wette, Ewald). This development towards specialization can be explained in part by the growing mass of literary, historical, and philological material associated with each Testament, but also in part by a new sense of the great differences between the two Testaments, which had become increasingly difficult to relate. During the first half of the nineteenth century, under the influence of German idealistic philosophy, several impressive construals of the Old Testament were attempted (Vatke, Ewald). However, during the latter part of the nineteenth century the discipline became more and more occupied with defending its concept of theology in the light of the new impact from the literary-critical analysis associated with Wellhausen and his school. The changing shape of the two standard nineteenth-century German Old Testament theologies (Oehler, Schultz), and the unresolved tension within the much used English Old Testament theology of A. B. Davidson, are characteristic signs of the growing uncertainty within the discipline.

The effect of the new critical approach to the Old Testament by the end of the nineteenth century was to threaten the very integrity of the theological discipline itself. Regardless of how one finally overcame the problems, there was a widespread consensus regarding the nature of the Old Testament literature which had emerged from 'the assured results of criticism'. These included, first, the recognition of the enormous variety of perspectives within the text, with respect both to the various parts of the Old Testament and to the different layers represented with a single literary entity, such as the Pentateuch. Secondly, the historical time-conditioned quality of the literature had been firmly established and a wide variety of cultural influence from outside Israel widely accepted. Thirdly, the problems of development and growth in the changing forms of Israel's religion had become a major issue, whether in the form of J. C. K. von Hofmann's *Heilsgeschichte* or of Wellhausen's documentary hypothesis. Finally, the new sense of the differences between the Old Testament and the New arose as a major obstacle to the traditional theological handling of the two Testaments in any sense as a unified religious corpus. When many writers chose to substitute the title of the 'religion of Israel' for Old Testament theology by the beginning of the twentieth century, they were quite logically drawing the implications of the shift in perspective which had overtaken much of the critical research of the last part of the nineteenth century.

Although H. Gunkel and his *religionsgeschichtliche* school are often assigned a decisive role in effecting an alteration in the literary-critical model, no significant change for the theological perception of the Old Testament emerged from this quarter. Rather, the decisive reaction set in during the 1920s in Germany largely in response to an awakening of confessional theology, and to the new political threat to the church caused by the rise of National Socialism in the 1930s. Some very creative, if often inadequate, attempts at reuniting Bible and theology emerged in the aftermath (Barth, Girgensohn, Vischer), which did serve to prepare the way for a new period in Old Testament theology.

The era between the 1930s and 1960s has been called 'a golden age' of Old Testament theology (Dentan, 72). After years of virtual inactivity, a steady stream of Old Testament theologies began to appear which were associated with some of Europe's leading scholars (Köhler, Eichrodt, Vriezen, von Rad, Zimmerli). Of these, the volumes of Eichrodt and von Rad marked major methodological advances and dominated the scholarly discussion for decades. Unfortunately, British and American scholarship continued to limp along even in this period with some weak imitations of continental scholarship. Of these, probably H. Wheeler Robinson's posthumous work was the most significant.

Several important gains emerged from this great period which cannot be gainsaid. First, the full legitimacy of the discipline of Old Testament theology as distinct from history of religion established itself again firmly within the field. Secondly, the ability to exploit historical-critical scholarship in a positive fashion for the theological enterprise seemed largely realized, especially by the broad circle of strongly confessional scholars who were associated with von Rad and his circle. Thirdly, it became increasingly clear that the revived interest in Old Testament theology was in turn exerting a force on the exegetical enterprise by posing fresh questions and expanding the horizons of the interpreters. Particularly, von Rad's Old Testament theology, much like Bultmann's New Testament theology, provided a focus for much of the critical work throughout the entire field.

(iii) *Continuing problems*

In spite of the significant advances during these years, a whole set of unresolved problems has remained. At first these seemed only to gnaw at the peripheries, but increasingly they have begun to undermine the structures of the discipline (cf. Reventlow's survey). Some of the issues can be briefly summarized.

(*a*) The fundamental problem of whether the discipline is

conceived of as a theology of the Old Testament or as a history of Israel's religion, or both, has never been successfully resolved. Closely akin is the issue whether the discipline strives in some sense for theologically normative appraisals of the biblical literature for the life of the church, or whether the discipline entails primarily an objectively historical description of an aspect of ancient culture whose method of research is shared with the study of any ancient Near Eastern religion. Both Eichrodt and von Rad introduced normative categories without adequate acknowledgment or methodological clarity.

(b) The problem of handling theologically a literature whose enormous variety and multi-layered growth had been convincingly demonstrated, has resulted in a deep erosion of any attempt to bring coherence into an ever-changing collage. Eichrodt, von Rad and Westermann – to name but a few – reflect a very diverse understanding of how to accommodate theologically the elements of religious development. The various attempts to isolate the theologies of 'J' or 'P' have only exacerbated the problem.

(c) Clements has signalled a significant problem in pointing out that the discipline of Old Testament theology has not engaged the question of how the biblical text was heard and appropriated in practice by concrete communities of faith. Rather, under the guise of hard-nosed historical study, the meaning of the literature has been sought apart from its actual historical reception. When the history of exegesis is occasionally introduced, it serves only as a foil for a modern author's new proposal.

(d) Finally, the relation of Old Testament theology to both Judaism and to the New Testament remains confusing and ill-defined. Eichrodt largely shared Wellhausen's low estimate of the late post-exilic period, and assumed that in some fashion the New Testament had recovered from prophetic religion what Judaism had lost. Nor has Gese resolved the problem when he envisions a traditio-historical trajectory uniting the Old Testament with the New, a process which he sharply sets apart from the development of rabbinic Judaism.

In sum, it seems neither unfair nor an exaggeration to conclude that the field has run into a stalemate. In spite of the impressive legacy from the last generation for which one can only be grateful, the need is acute for a fresh proposal which can at least begin to point in a direction for overcoming the present impasse.

(iv) *A canonical approach to Old Testament theology*

My concern in the succeeding pages of this chapter is to outline a canonical approach to Old Testament theology which, in my judgment, not only presents a fresh approach to the discipline by resolving many of the crucial methodological issues at stake, but also opens an avenue into the material in order to free the Old Testament for a more powerful theological role within the life of the Christian church.

The initial point to be made is that the canonical approach to Old Testament theology is unequivocal in asserting that the object of theological reflection is the canonical writing of the Old Testament, that is, the Hebrew scriptures which are the received traditions of Israel. The materials for theological reflection are not the events or experiences behind the text, or apart from the construal in scripture by a community of faith and practice. However, because the biblical text continually bears witness to events and reactions in the life of Israel, the literature cannot be isolated from its ostensive reference. In view of these factors alone it is a basic misunderstanding to try to describe a canonical approach simply as a form of structuralism (*contra* Barton). Moreover, one of the enduring confusions within the discipline is that of maintaining the formal canonical categories implicit in the term 'Old Testament' theology, but in practice developing the discipline as an allegedly objective science without any true reference to the canonical form and function of the literature. The canonical approach which I am suggesting is explicit in developing an approach which is consistent in working within canonical categories.

The discipline of Old Testament theology derives from theological reflection on a received body of scripture whose formation was the result of a lengthy history of development. The process began in the early pre-exilic period of Israel's history and extended through the final structuring by the Jewish synagogue during the Hellenistic era. Central to its history was a hermeneutical activity which continued to shape the material theologically in order to render it accessible to future generations of believers. Canonization proper, which was the final stage in the process, established the scope of the authoritative literature. Although scholars differ as to whether the final fixing of the scope of the canon was effected largely from the side of the Jewish synagogue (Leiman), or whether it stemmed from

Christianity's cutting off the old process in order to contrast it with its own new tradition (Gese), both Jews and Christians agree that the canonical process of the Hebrew scriptures, or Old Testament, came to an end, and a different canonical process began for both faiths in the growth of the rabbinic and evangelical traditions. The decisive point is that the Christian church recognized the integrity of the Old Testament for its own faith within its canon of authoritative scripture. It neither incorporated the Old Testament within the framework of the New nor altered its shape significantly. In sum, the Christian church accepted the scriptures of the synagogue, as previously shaped, as part of its own canon, and sought to interpret them according to various Christian construals. Of course, for numerous historical reasons the church generally used the Greek form of the Hebrew scriptures, but it should not be forgotten that the Septuagint was a Jewish translation, not a Christian one.

Although the subject of this biblical discipline is theological reflection on the Hebrew scriptures, it is highly significant that the discipline bears the title of theology of the Old Testament. The term 'Old Testament' correctly recognizes that the discipline is part of Christian theology, and that the Jewish scriptures as they have been appropriated by the Christian church within its own canon are the object of the discipline. However, because of the highly controversial nature of this formulation, there is need for a further elaboration.

It is my contention that the discipline of Old Testament theology is essentially a Christian discipline, not simply because of the Christian custom of referring to the Hebrew Scriptures as the Old Testament, but on a far deeper level. Basic to the discipline is a concept of how the Old Testament is interpreted and appropriated, which, in spite of the great differences in its execution, shares certain features stemming from Christian theology. First, the biblical text is viewed as a completed entity which is set at a distance in some sort of dialectical relationship with the New Testament and the ongoing life of the church. Secondly, it remains a feature of Old Testament theology even when unexpressed, that a relation of some sort is assumed between the life and history of Israel and that of Jesus Christ. Thirdly, the various attempts to designate certain parts of the Old Testament as its 'heart' or 'centre', often by the use of various philosophical construals of the whole (idealism, existentialism, *Heilsgeschichte*), confirm a basically Christian stance even when highly secularized.

Moreover, it is not by accident that Jewish scholars have not participated in the writing of biblical theologies. (The occasional exception serves to confirm the rule.) The purpose of making this point is not to mount an apologetic for Christianity, nor to imply an inherent superiority of understanding. Rather, it is to suggest that Jews have appropriated the Hebrew scriptures in a different fashion without the need of biblical theology. First of all, the Hebrew scriptures are not viewed as a closed entity in a dialectical relation to the later rabbinic tradition, but rather there is an unbroken continuity between scripture and tradition which results in a different understanding of how its authority functions. Secondly, the Jewish understanding of the role of oral tradition as an authoritative commentary on the written tradition effects a very different dynamic (midrashic) from that of Christianity. Finally, for the Jew the heart of the Bible is Torah, which also establishes a different relationship to the present community of faith from that of Christianity whose relation to the Bible remains christologically conceived.

In my opinion, much of the confusion in the history of Old Testament theology derives from the reluctance to recognize that it is a Christian enterprise. Yet the presence of Christian assumptions is implicit in virtually every modern Old Testament theology and even in the allegedly objective religions of Israel, a fact which Jewish scholars readily point out.

However, once the point has been established that Old Testament theology is a discipline of Christian theology, it still remains a highly complex and controversial issue to determine the exact shape of the discipline. Certain classic solutions have been proposed which, in my opinion, have not only been unsuccessful in illuminating the biblical text, but run in the face of a genuinely canonical method. For example, the approach of much mediaeval theology in shifting the entire semantic range of the Old Testament to a non-literal, metaphorical level, in order to retain a reference to Jesus Christ, destroyed the integrity which the Christian canon had assigned to this portion of scripture. Or again, to force the entire Old Testament within a fixed schema of prophecy and fulfilment absolutized one relationship to the detriment of many other options which even the New Testament employs.

Conversely, to suggest that the Christian should read the Old

Testament as if he were living before the coming of Christ is an historical anachronism which also fails to take seriously the literature's present function within the Christian Bible for a practising community of faith. Similar theological objections obtain for the frequent proposal that Christians read the Old Testament as Jews and only the New Testament as Christians, which of course destroys the theological meaning of the canonical terminology of the Old Testament within the Christian Bible.

I would suggest that careful attention to the shape of the Christian canon provides some initial guidelines for overcoming this dilemma. The Christian canon maintains the integrity of the Old Testament in its own right as scripture of the church. However, it sets it within a new canonical context in a dialectical relation with the New Testament. In my judgment, the task of biblical theology is to explore the relation between these two witnesses, whereas the task of Old Testament theology is to reflect theologically on only the one portion of the Christian canon, but as Christian scripture.

To use an analogy, the Gospel of Mark recounts the gospel from the theological perspective of the post-resurrection period. Both the writer of the Gospel and his audience confess that Jesus is the risen Lord. Nevertheless, the New Testament writer feels constrained to bear a theological witness to Christ by recounting the pre-resurrection traditions of Jesus and viewing him largely through the eyes of those for whom his true identity was still hidden. For Mark no true understanding of the resurrected Christ was possible, even in the post-resurrection era, without the testimony to the suffering and death of the Son of man.

In a similar manner, I would argue that the Old Testament functions within Christian scripture as a witness to Jesus Christ precisely in its pre-Christian form. The task of Old Testament theology is, therefore, not to Christianize the Old Testament by identifying it with the New Testament witness, but to hear its own theological testimony to the God of Israel whom the church confesses also to worship. Although Christians confess that God who revealed himself to Israel is the God and Father of Jesus Christ, it is still necessary to hear Israel's witness in order to understand who the Father of Jesus Christ is. The coming of Jesus does not remove the function of the divine disclosure in the old covenant. Needless to say, for an Old Testament theology to avoid dogmatism on the right and historicism on the left requires both skill and wisdom.

The profile of the discipline of Old Testament theology which I am suggesting can perhaps be made more precise by briefly sketching its relationship both to Judaism and to biblical theology. I have emphasized that Old Testament theology is a Christian discipline which reflects on the scriptures held in common with the synagogue. One of the main reasons for the Christian use of the Hebrew text of the Old Testament rather than its Greek form lies in the theological concern to preserve this common textual bond between Jews and Christians. Historically, Christianity confronted first-century Judaism through the Greek form of the Jewish scriptures, and thus the New Testament is stamped indelibly by the Septuagint. Yet the theological issue of how Christians relate to the Jewish scriptures cannot be decided biblicistically by an appeal to New Testament practice, but must be addressed theologically. The debate transcends the historical moment of the first-century encounter, and turns on the church's ongoing relation to the authoritative scriptures which Israel treasured and continues to treasure in the Hebrew. A canonical approach takes the Hebrew scriptures seriously because of its confession that Israel remains the prime tradent of this witness. It remains an essential part of the church's theological reflection on the Old Testament to continue in dialogue with the synagogue which lives from the common biblical text, but often construes it in a very different manner. The goal of the dialogue is that both religious renderings be continually forced to react to the coercion of the common text which serves both to enrich and to challenge all interpretations.

The discipline of Old Testament theology also differs from biblical theology in several important ways. Biblical theology provides a disciplined reflection on the scriptures of both Old and New Testaments. Its emphasis differs because of the overriding problem of relating the witnesses of the two different Testaments. Moreover, because of its concern to interpret the entire Christian Bible theologically, it tends to be in dialogue more with the traditions of dogmatic theology than with the discrete problems which arise from the separate Testaments. However, the theological approaches to the text of both Old Testament theology and biblical theology do not differ hermeneutically. Both are disciplines arising from within

Christian theology and both involve the application of descriptive and constructive tools in order to execute the task.

It is a basic tenet of the canonical approach that one reflects theologically on the text as it has been received and shaped. Yet the emphasis on the normative status of the canonical text is not a denial of the significance of the canonical process which formed the text. The frequently expressed contrast between a 'static' canonical text and a 'dynamic' traditio-historical process badly misconstrues the issue. Similarly, to claim that attention to canon elevates one specific historical response to a dogmatic principle utterly fails to grasp the function of canon. Rather, the basic problem turns on the relationship between text and process. The final canonical literature reflects a long history of development in which the received tradition was selected, transmitted and shaped by hundreds of decisions. This process of construing its religious tradition involved a continual critical evaluation of historical options which were available to Israel and a transformation of its received tradition toward certain theological goals. That the final form of the biblical text has preserved much from the earlier stages of Israel's theological reflection is fully evident. However, the various elements have been so fused as to resist easy diachronic reconstructions which fracture the witness of the whole.

The controversy with the traditio-historical critics is not over the theological significance of a depth dimension of the tradition. Rather, the issue turns on whether or not features within the tradition which have been subordinated, modified or placed in the distant background of the text can be interpreted apart from the role assigned to them in the final form when attempting to write a theology of the Old Testament. For example, to seek to give theological autonomy to a reconstructed Yahwist source apart from its present canonical context is to disregard the crucial theological intention of the tradents of the tradition, and to isolate a text's meaning from its reception.

Even more controversial is the usual method of reconstructing an alleged traditio-historical trajectory which does not reflect actual layers within Israel's tradition, but is a critical construct lying outside Israel's faith. To draw an analogy, it is one thing to trace the different levels within the growth of the New Testament parables. It is quite another to reconstruct putative earlier levels apart from their reception and transmission within the community of faith. The canonical approach to Old Testament theology is insistent that the critical process of theological reflection takes place from a stance within the circle of received tradition prescribed by the affirmation of the canon.

The canonical approach to Old Testament theology rejects a method which is unaware of its own time-conditioned quality and which is confident in its ability to stand outside, above and over against the received tradition in adjudicating the truth or lack of truth of the biblical material according to its own criteria. Of course, lying at the heart of the canonical proposal is the conviction that the divine revelation of the Old Testament cannot be abstracted or removed from the form of the witness which the historical community of Israel gave it. In the same way, there is no avenue open to the Jesus Christ who is worshipped by the Christian church apart from the testimony of his fully human apostles. To suggest that the task of theological reflection takes place from within a canonical context assumes not only a received tradition, but a faithful disposition by hearers who await the illumination of God's Spirit. This latter point has been developed so thoroughly by Calvin as to make further elaboration unnecessary (*Institutes*, I, ch. VII).

Then again, a canonical approach envisions the discipline of Old Testament theology as combining both descriptive and constructive features. It recognizes the descriptive task of correctly interpreting an ancient text which bears testimony to historic Israel's faith. Yet it also understands that the theological enterprise involves a construal by the modern interpreter, whose stance to the text affects its meaning. For this reason, Old Testament theology cannot be identified with describing an historical process in the past (*contra* Gese), but involves wrestling with the subject-matter to which scripture continues to bear testimony. In sum, Old Testament theology is a continuing enterprise in which each new generation must engage. An important implication of the approach is that the interpreter does not conceive of Old Testament theology as a closed, phenomenological deposit – Eichrodt spoke of a 'self-contained entity' (*Theology* I, 11) – whose understanding depends on the discovery of a single lost key. Much of the recent discussion of the so-called 'centre of the Old Testament' seems to have arisen from a concept of the discipline which views it simply as an historical enterprise (cf. Reventlow).

One of the important aspects within the shaping process of the

Old Testament is the manner by which different parts of the canon were increasingly interchanged to produce a new angle of vision on the tradition. The canonical process involved the shaping of the tradition not only into independent books, but also into larger canonical units, such as the Torah, Prophets and Writings. For example, law was seen from the perspective of wisdom; psalmody and prophecy were interrelated; and Israel's narrative traditions were sapientialized (cf. Sheppard). The canonical process thus built in a dimension of flexibility which encourages constantly fresh ways of actualizing the material.

There are some important implications to be drawn from this canonical process for the structuring of a modern Old Testament theology. This canonical structuring provides a warrant for applying a similar element of flexibility in its modern actualization which is consonant with its shape. In other words, a new dynamic issues from the collection which maintains a potential for a variety of new theological combinations. Even though historically Old Testament law was often of a different age and was transmitted by other tradents from much of the narrative tradition, a theology of the Old Testament according to the proposed canonical model seeks to exploit a theological interaction. Therefore, regardless of the original literary and historical relationship between the Decalogue and the narrative sections of the Pentateuch, a theological interchange is possible within its new canonical context which affords a mutual aid for interpretation. Of course, there are rules which control and govern the interaction which derive from the literature's structure, content, and intertextuality, but these can be best illustrated in practice. The recognition of this dimension of a canonical approach further sets it apart from the usual descriptive method which is bound to original historical sequence.

One of the hallmarks of the modern study of the Bible, which is one of the important legacies of the Enlightenment, is the recognition of the time-conditioned quality of both the form and the content of scripture. A pre-critical method which could feel free simply to translate every statement of the Bible into a principle of right doctrine is no longer possible. Of course, it is a caricature of the history of Christian theology to suggest that such a use of the Bible was universal in the pre-Enlightenment period. Augustine, Luther and Calvin – to name but a few – all worked with a far more sophisticated understanding of the Bible than the term 'pre-critical' suggests. Nevertheless, it is still true that the issue of the Bible's time-conditioned quality became a major hermeneutical problem in the wake of the Enlightenment and the rise of the historical-critical method.

Modern Old Testament theologians have applied various hermeneutical approaches to the text in order to accommodate the problem. One sought critically to abstract the 'abiding truth' or 'elements of lasting value' from the literature. Or a history of moral progress was discerned which slowly sloughed off its primitive inheritance in order to reach its ethical goal, often found in the Sermon on the Mount. Finally, some mode of consciousness, egalitarian ideology, or elements of liberation were discovered and assigned a normative theological function. However, in spite of the tendentious nature of many of these proposals, it is significant to observe that a concern was always expressed to retain at least some understanding of biblical authority for the modern church, and to resist its complete relativity.

The hermeneutic implied in a canonical understanding of the Old Testament moves in a strikingly different direction in seeking its resolution to the problem. The emphasis on scripture as canon focuses its attention on the process by which divine truth acquired its authoritative form as it was received and transmitted by a community of faith. Accordingly, there is no biblical revelation apart from that which bears Israel's imprint. All of scripture is time-conditioned because the whole Old Testament has been conditioned by an historical people. There is no pure doctrine or uncontaminated piety. Any attempt to abstract elements from its present form by which, as it were, to distinguish the kernel from its husk, or inauthentic existence from authentic expression, runs directly in the face of the canon's function.

Moreover, to take seriously a canonical approach is also to recognize the time-conditioned quality of the modern, post-Enlightenment Christian whose context is just as historically moored as any of his predecessors. One of the disastrous legacies of the Enlightenment was the new confidence of standing outside the stream of time and with clear rationality being able to distinguish truth from error, light from darkness.

In conscious opposition to this legacy of the Enlightenment, the canonical approach seeks to approach the problem with a different understanding of how the Bible functions as a vehicle of God's truth. By accepting the scriptures as normative for the obedient life of the church, the Old Testament theologian takes his stance within the circle of tradition, and thus identifies himself with Israel as the community of faith. Moreover, he shares in that hermeneutical process of which the canon is a testimony, as the people of God struggled to discern the will of God in all its historical particularity. Its shaping of the biblical tradition indicated how it sought to appropriate the tradition as a faithful response to God's word. In an analogous context of a received witness, the modern biblical theologian takes his stance within the testimony of Israel and struggles to discern the will of God. Fully aware of his own frailty, he awaits in anticipation a fresh illumination through God's Spirit, for whom the Bible's frailty is no barrier. Although such understanding derives ultimately from the illumination of the Spirit, this divine activity functions through the scriptures of the church; that is to say, completely within the time-conditioned form of the tradition. There is no one hermeneutical key for unlocking the biblical message, but the canon provides the arena in which the struggle for understanding takes place.

(v) *Canonical approach and the modern debate*

Space is too limited for a lengthy discussion with many of the classic issues which currently agitate the field. However, I would like briefly to suggest ways in which a canonical approach seeks to overcome some of the major problems at present under debate (cf. Reventlow).

(*a*) In respect to the disagreement between Eichrodt and von Rad, among others, as to whether an Old Testament theology should be organized 'systematically' or 'traditio-historically', I suggest that both of these alternatives arise from a view of a closed body of material which is to be analysed descriptively. Both writers have worked hard to discover inner-biblical categories, which is an effort not to be disparaged. Nevertheless, when Old Testament theology is viewed in its canonical context as a continuing interpretative activity by that community of faith which treasures its scriptures as authoritative, the issue of organization is sharply relativized. At times the shaping process introduced systematic features; at times it structured the material historically. However, even more significant, there are innumerable other options within the theological activity of interpreting scripture which are available for grappling with the material. The real issue lies in the quality of the construal and the illumination it brings to the text.

(*b*) A canonical approach once again attempts to overcome the sharp polarity in the debate whether the object of an Old Testament theology is a faith-construal of history (*Geschichte*), according to von Rad, or based on a reconstructed scientific history (*Historie*), according to Hesse and others. It reckons with the fact that Israel bore witness to its encounter with God in actual time and space, and yet registered its testimony in a text through a complex multi-layered manner which far transcends the categories of ordinary historical discourse. The canonical approach views history from the perspective of Israel's faith-construal, and in this respect sides with von Rad. However, it differs in not being concerned to assign theological value to a traditio-historical trajectory which has been detached from the canonical form of the text. To put the issue in another way, the canonical approach seeks to follow the biblical text in its theological use of historical referentiality rather than to construct a contrast between *Geschichte* and *Historie* at the outset. At times, the nature of an Old Testament passage has been so construed as to register little which is accessible to objective historical scrutiny. At other times, an event which is grounded in common historical perception, such as the destruction of Jerusalem in 587 BC, is of central importance for the theological task. In sum, although different dimensions of history are freely recognized, by focusing on Israel's historical role as the bearer of the traditions of faith, these two aspects of Israel's experience are held together in a subtle balance within the shape of the canon, and should not be threatened by some overarching theory of history.

(*c*) Finally, in respect to the position of Pannenberg which has sought to identify history with revelation, the canonical approach looks with suspicion on any view of history as a bearer of theological value which is divorced from the concrete reality of historical Israel. Far more is at stake here than simply making an academic point. Rather, scripture serves as a continuing medium through which the saving events of Israel's history are appropriated by each new generation of faith. Thus God's activity of self-disclosure is continually being extended into human time and space, which lies at the heart of the debate over the nature of revelation through scripture.

(vi) *The importance of Old Testament theology*

Lastly, a word is in order to justify the importance of the discipline of Old Testament theology even when it is conceived of as a modest and restricted enterprise within the larger field of biblical theology.

(*a*) First, in terms of strategy, to focus solely on the Old Testament in theological reflection allows one to deal with the subject in much more detail and depth than if one sought to treat the entire Christian canon at once. It seems wise at some point to focus primary attention on the Old Testament before coming to grips with the sheer mass of material and the overwhelming complexity of issues which arise when the New Testament is also included.

(*b*) Attention to the Old Testament within a theological discipline provides a major check against the widespread modern practice of treating it solely from a philological, historical or literary perspective. The inability of most systematic theologians to make much sense of the Old Testament stems in part from the failure of the biblical specialists to render it in such a way which is not theologically mute.

(*c*) It is a major function of Old Testament theology to treat the Old Testament in such a manner as to guard it from being used simply as a foil for the New Testament. Rather, it is theologically important to understand the Old Testament's witness in its own right in regard to its coherence, variety and unresolved tensions.

(*d*) Finally, theological reflection on the Old Testament makes possible a more correct hearing of the New Testament by clarifying the effect of the Hebrew scriptures on the Jewish people from whom Jesus stemmed, to whom he preached, and from whom the early church was formed. As the history of exegesis eloquently demonstrates, a Christian church without the Old Testament is in constant danger of turning the faith into various forms of gnostic, mystic, or romantic speculation.

Bibliography

(*a*) *A selection of Old Testament theologies*

R. E. **Clements,** *Old Testament Theology. A Fresh Approach*, London 1978; A. B. **Davidson,** *The Theology of the Old Testament*, Edinburgh and New York 1904; W. **Eichrodt,** *Theology of the Old Testament*, ET London and

Philadelphia, I, 1961; II, 1967; G. H. A. **Ewald**, *Die Lehre der Bibel von Gott*, 4 vols., Leipzig 1871–76; P. **van Imschoot**, *Theology of the Old Testament*, ET London 1965; E. **Jacob**, *Theology of the Old Testament*, ET London and New York 1958; W. C. **Kaiser**, Jr, *Toward an Old Testament Theology*, Grand Rapids 1978; G. A. F. **Knight**, *A Christian Theology of the Old Testament*, London and Richmond 1959; L. **Köhler**, *Old Testament Theology*, ET London 1957; K. **Marti**, *The Religion of the Old Testament*, ET London and New York 1907; J. L. **McKenzie**, *A Theology of the Old Testament*, New York and London 1974; G. F. **Oehler**, *Theology of the Old Testament*, ET Edinburgh 1874 and New York 1883; O. **Procksch**, *Theologie des Alten Testaments*, Gütersloh 1950; G. **von Rad**, *Old Testament Theology*, ET Edinburgh and New York, I, 1962; II, 1965; H. W. **Robinson**, *Inspiration and Revelation in the Old Testament*, Oxford 1946; H. **Schultz**, *Old Testament Theology*, ET 2 vols., Edinburgh 1892; B. **Stade**, *Biblische Theologie des Alten Testaments*, ed. A. Bertholet, Tübingen I, 1905; II, 1911; W. **Vatke**, *Die biblische Theologie wissenschaftlich dargestellt*, I. *Die Religion des Alten Testamentes*, Berlin 1835; T. C. **Vriezen**, *An Outline of Old Testament Theology*, ET Oxford and Boston 1958; C. **Westermann**, *Elements of Old Testament Theology*, ET Atlanta 1982; W. **Zimmerli**, *Old Testament Theology in Outline*, ET Atlanta and London 1978.

(b) *The critical debate*

J. **Barr**, *The Bible in the Modern World*, London and Philadelphia 1973; C. **Barth**, 'Grundprobleme einer Theologie des Alten Testaments', *EvTh* 23, 1963, 342–72; J. **Barton**, *Reading the Old Testament. Method in Biblical Study*, London and Philadelphia 1984; F. **Baumgärtel**, *Verheissung. Zur Frage des evangelischen Verständnisses des Alten Testaments*, Gütersloh 1952; F. F. **Bruce**, 'The Theology and Interpretation of the Old Testament', in *Tradition and Interpretation*, ed. G. W. Anderson, Oxford 1979, 385–416; W. **Brueggemann**, 'A Convergence in Recent Old Testament Theologies', *JSOT* 18, 1980, 2–18; R. C. **Dentan**, 'The Nature of Old Testament Theology', *Preface to Old Testament Theology*, New York ²1963, 87–125; S. J. **DeVries**, *The Achievements of Biblical Religion. A Prolegomenon to Old Testament Theology*, Lanham, Md. and London 1983; L. **Diestel**, *Geschichte des Alten Testamentes in der christlichen Kirche*, Jena 1869; W. **Eichrodt**, 'Zur Frage der theologischen Exegese des Alten Testamentes', *ThBl* 17, 1936, 73–87; 'Excursus: The Problem of Old Testament Theology', ET *Old Testament Theology*, I, 512–20; J. P. **Gabler**, '*Oratio de justo discrimine theologiae biblicae et dogmaticae regundisque recte utriusque finibus*' (1787), reprinted *Opuscula Academica* II, Ulm 1831, 179–94; ET *SJT* 33, 1980, 133–58; K. **Girgensohn**, *Die Inspiration der Heiligen Schrift*, Dresden 1925; J. **Goldingay**, *Approaches to Old Testament Interpretation*, Leicester and Downers Grove 1981; M. H. **Goshen-Gottstein**, 'Christianity, Judaism and the Modern Bible Study', *SVT* 28, 1975, 69–88; A. H. J. **Gunneweg**, *Understanding the*

Old Testament, ET London and Philadelphia, 1978; ' "Theologie" des Alten Testaments oder "Biblische Theologie"?' *Textgemäss, FS E. Würthwein*, ed. A. H. J. Gunneweg and O. Kaiser, Göttingen 1979, 39–46; H. **Gunkel**, 'Ziele und Methoden der Erklärung des Alten Testaments', *Reden und Aufsätze*, Göttingen 1913, 11–29; F. **Hahn**, *The Old Testament in Modern Research*, Philadelphia ³1970; G. F. **Hasel**, *Old Testament Theology. Basic Issues in the Current Debate*, Grand Rapids ²1975; J. H. **Hayes** and F. C. **Prussner**, *Old Testament Theology. Its History and Development*, London and Philadelphia 1985; F. **Hesse**, *Das Alte Testament als Buch der Kirche*, Gütersloh 1966; J. C. K. **von Hofmann**, *Weissagung und Erfüllung*, 2 vols., Nördlingen 1841; R. **Knierim**, 'The Task of Old Testament Theology', *Horizons in Biblical Theology*, VI, 1984, 25–57; H.-J. **Kraus**, *Geschichte der historisch-kritischen Erforschung des Alten Testaments*, Neukirchen 1956, ³1982; *Die Biblische Theologie. Ihre Geschichte und Problematik*, Neukirchen-Vluyn 1970; R. B. **Laurin** (ed.), *Contemporary Old Testament Theologians*, Valley Forge 1970; N. **Lohfink**, *The Christian Meaning of the Old Testament*, ET London 1968; K. H. **Miskotte**, *When the Gods are Silent*, ET London 1967; W. **Pannenberg**, *Revelation as History*, ET New York 1968 and London 1969; G. **von Rad**, 'Postscript', *Old Testament Theology*, II, 410–29; R. **Rendtorff**, 'Zur Bedeutung des Kanons für eine Theologie des Alten Testaments', *Wenn nicht jetzt, wann dann? FS H.-J. Kraus*, ed. H. G. Geyer et al, Neukirchen-Vluyn 1983, 3–11; H. Graf **Reventlow**, *Problems of Old Testament Theology in the Twentieth Century*, ET London and Philadelphia 1985; S. **Schechter**, *Some Aspects of Rabbinic Theology*, New York 1923; W. F. **Schmidt**, 'Theologie des Alten Testaments vor und nach Gerhard von Rad', *VuF* 17, 1972, 1–25; G. T. **Sheppard**, 'Hearing the Voice of the Same God through Historically Dissimilar Traditions', *Interp* 36, 1982, 21–33; R. **Smend**, 'Theologie im Alten Testament', *Verifikationen, FS G. Ebeling*, ed. E. Jüngel, J. Wallmann, W. Werbeck, Tübingen 1982, 11–26; D. G. **Spriggs**, *Two Old Testament Theologies. A Comparative Evaluation of the Contributions of Eichrodt and von Rad to our Understanding of the Nature of Old Testament Theology*, SBT II. 30, 1974; W. **Vischer**, *The Witness of the Old Testament to Christ. I. The Pentateuch*, ET London 1949; G. E. **Wright**, *God Who Acts*, SBT I.8, 1952; *The Old Testament and Theology*, New York 1969; W. **Zimmerli**, 'Biblische Theologie. I. Altes Testament', *TRE* VI, 426–55.

2

THE OLD TESTAMENT AS REVELATION

Throughout much of its history Christian theology has made use of the term 'revelation' to describe the content of the Bible. However, for a variety of reasons – historical, philosophical, theological – it can no longer be simply assumed that the term is an appropriate one. Several major attacks on the whole concept of revelation have been launched within the modern period. It seems important, therefore, briefly to review some of the major objections before seeking to redefine its use within my canonical construal.

I am aware that the larger philosophical and theological issues involved in the term far exceed the boundaries of an Old Testament theology. Indeed, the problem touches on a host of important questions which relate to the entire enterprise of Christian theology such as its use of the Bible, the nature of the knowledge of God, and how faith is appropriated. Moreover, the use of the term is far from uniform and varies greatly depending on whether it is viewed propositionally or existentially. My concern is much more narrowly conceived and relates specifically to the use of the term within biblical studies. Two major attacks have been recently launched which I shall address in turn. The first arises from the side of analytical philosophy, the second from the side of sociological analysis.

(i) *The criticism of analytical philosophy*

The problem of using the term 'revelation' in relation to the Old Testament (and the Bible in general) has received an incisive criticism from James Barr. In several articles he argues that it is unwarranted and meaningless to continue to use the term in reference to the Bible. His attack focuses initially on the theological model of Karl Barth, but is broader in scope. He makes the following points:

(a) The term revelation arose in modern theology as an appositional pair to 'reason' or to 'religion'. The term lumps together everything learned of God other than through direct intervention as 'reason' and reserves 'revelation' for special encounters. He concludes that this polarity cannot be sustained by the modern study of the Bible.

(b) The Bible's use of the terminology of revealing functions in a different fashion. There is little basis in the Bible for considering it to be a blanket concept for man's source of the knowledge of God. In fact, the lack of revelatory terminology is striking. Rather, when it does appear, it has a specific role, for example, in eschatological discourse to denote that which is now hidden but will in the future be revealed. Usually the knowledge of God proceeds on a continuum with Israel's experience and is communicated through traditions, institutions and stories. What matters is the question of whether more will be added to that which is already known.

(c) Finally, to use the term revelation as a major concept is to run the danger of returning to a pre-critical understanding of the Bible. The term has its origin in a dogmatic stance which conceived of the Bible as a collection of timeless propositional truths about God, whereas historical critics now see the full time-conditioned quality of the Bible as it has been filtered through a long development and reflects both truth and error.

Barr's attack on the use of the term revelation has received major support of a biblical and philosophical nature from F. G. Downing's book, *Has Christianity a Revelation?* Downing begins by defining revelation as 'the removing of some obscurity to make clear, visible, and comprehensible, what had up to that point been befogged' (10). He then analyses the varied biblical terminology and concludes that it functions in a different way from the concept of revelation. God comes out of hiding by acts on Israel's behalf, but there is no connection made between his alleged activity and his own character. Moreover, the Old Testament is explicit that God remains hidden. Thus, Downing concludes: 'The Old Testament writers do not pretend that the relation of God and man is close enough and clear enough for God to be said to have revealed himself' (47). According to Downing, the term revelation only became important when

Christianity began unduly to emphasize the role of the intellect in the service of God (249).

Clearly Barr and Downing have raised several significant issues. Indeed, the traditional use of the term has been overladen with a variety of philosophical connotations which often reflect former theological battles without contemporary significance. However, I am far from convinced that the basic theological issues respecting the Bible have been adequately treated.

(a) Both Barr and Downing begin by defining the term revelation according to common parlance. Barr stresses that revelation implies hitherto unknown information, Downing that it effects a removal of obscurity. On the basis of these proposed definitions it is easy to show that the features of the Bible do not conform to the modern usage. The knowledge of God is not outside a historical continuum, nor does it remove all obscurity. Yet the point to be made is that the knowledge of God in the Old Testament (and the New) involves a great variety of things far transcending the simple, common-sense definitions offered. It includes events which both disclose and conceal, which are experiential and also cognitive, which are directed to the past and the future. The theological term 'revelation' is, in other words, an inadequate shorthand expression which seeks to encompass an enormous range of activities related to God's relation to his people. Much like the Reformers' use of the phrase 'the Word of God', which far exceeded the connotations of its normal grammatical components, the term revelation is also a theological construct. That its use involves certain dangers of misconstrual is evident from the history of theology. Yet it seems clear from the essays of both Barr and Downing that no better term has emerged which even begins to convey the full range of meanings associated with the disclosures of God in the Bible. Downing's hypothesis that the term appeared only when Christians began unduly to emphasize the role of the intellect in the service of God is unsupported and highly questionable.

(b) The interpretation of the Old Testament offered by both Barr and Downing which seeks to demonstrate that the term revelation has a different function in the Bible from its subsequent theological usage fails to deal adequately with the Bible's role as authoritative canonical literature. Their exegesis suffers from being flat and reductionistic in quality. The canonical process often assigned a function to the literature as a whole which transcended its parts.

The collection acquired a theological role in instructing, admonishing and edifying a community of faith, and that altered its original semantic level. Frequently a particular story was deemed paradigmatic of God's ways with his people. Thus even though the knowledge of God communicated through a traditional narrative was not a revelation in its strictly linguistic sense of disclosing hitherto unknown information available to God, in its new role as scripture it served a unique religious role. It disclosed God for the community in a way which was transmitted only through this corpus of literature.

This analysis is not to suggest that canonization changed profane literature into sacred by rendering it qualitatively different from its origins. The religious function of the biblical material was communicated in numerous ways on all the various levels of composition, but with a view to continuing to address the future generations with the reality of God – his presence, his saving activity, his will. Various theophanies could depict the outward form of a divine appearance by means of a restrictive use of certain Hebrew verbs (e.g. *gālāh, rā'āh*), but the whole context of these stories in their canonical shape was directed to providing a vehicle by which Israel could learn to know and obey its God. Even the superscriptions point to a theological rendering of narrative which moved it beyond its original limited function (cf. Gen. 18.1; Ex. 3.2).

An essential feature of the Old Testament is its great variety of ways of portraying God's relation with Israel, by means of narrative, psalm and prophetic oracle. These genres are usually retained in all their original specificity. The use of the term revelation within a canonical context is not set in an appositional relationship to tradition, reason or experience. Indeed one of the central goals of emphasizing the role of the canon is to stress the horizontal dimension of the reception, collection and ordering of the experiences of the divine by a community of faith. A canonical approach would be equally critical of a stance which stressed only the vertical dimension of divine truth, as if word and tradition were always in tension. In sum, when the term revelation is construed in such a way as to do justice to its function within the canon, its continued use seems to be fully warranted.

(ii) *The criticism of sociological analysis*

A second major attack on the use of the term revelation has been recently launched by N. Gottwald in a sociological approach which he describes as a cultural-materialistic reading of the Old Testament (*The Tribes of Yahweh*).

At the outset Gottwald sets forth clearly his working assumptions. Religion is to be interpreted as a social phenomenon in relation to all other social phenomena, and is only one aspect of an interconnected network of social reality. Theology (ideology) is a particular form of symbolic language which seeks to give expression to these social realities in traditional conventions in terms either of rationalizations of cultural phenomena or of the empowering of socio-political organizations. The dynamic of his approach is to move from given social phenomena to secondary ideological formulations. Specifically the task of writing a sociology of Israel is to take its religious ideology and render it into material equivalents in order to establish the correlatives within the social system. This hermeneutical process enables one to see how the historical religion of Israel served sociologically to express the needs of the historically mutant community of Israel.

In a later chapter I shall examine in detail Gottwald's specific application of his sociological analysis of one period of Israel's history, 1250–1000 BC. Here my concern is with the hermeneutical assumptions and their effect on the use of the term revelation. The great service of Gottwald lies in his spelling out in an impressive manner the radical implications of a consistent sociological approach to the Old Testament. Although in recent years many other biblical scholars have toyed with the sociological method, the credit belongs to Gottwald for exploiting the full implications of a method which lies at the opposite extreme to the canonical approach which I am suggesting.

Gottwald immediately establishes his hermeneutical stance. He reads the biblical text as a symbolic expression of certain underlying primary social realities which he seeks to uncover by means of a critical sociological analysis. He assumes that there is a cultural material equivalent to each aspect of biblical ideology which can be rendered by means of a direct correlation to a social system. Obviously in Gottwald's approach there is no place for the traditional term revelation. He rejects as 'idealistic' any attempt even to distinguish religious beliefs from social realities. Of course in so doing he is making enormous epistemological assumptions regarding the nature of reality. Regardless of how Israel articulated its faith, Gottwald, taking his stance fully outside the tradition, assumes that it can be 'demythologized' to recover the real force behind the confession which is a cultural phenomenon.

In my judgment, Gottwald's position results in a massive theological reductionism. Certainly lying at the heart of Christian theology is the confession that God has brought into being a new reality which is different in kind from all immanental forces at work in the world (Isa. 65.17; Rom. 4.17). With the widest possible variety of terminology – new creation, new birth, new Jerusalem, life in the Spirit – the Bible bears testimony to a divine activity which breaks into human society in countless unexpected ways. To claim that these confessions are simply symbolic expressions of common social phenomena not only renders the uniquely biblical witness mute, but destroys the need for closely hearing the text on its verbal level. The sociologist has a privileged access behind the text to those forces really at work, and from his superior vantage point knows better than the tradition.

Of course, theologians have long been aware that there is no easy separation between theology and culture, and that no theological formulation stands apart from its time-conditioned quality. The failure of various forms of idealistic philosophy to resolve the issue is well known. Yet to propose that theology and social reality can be simply identified destroys any possibility of doing justice to the complex tensions within the Bible between the ways of God and the world. Gottwald's attempt to replace biblical theology with biblical sociology by offering examples of his method of demythologizing the tradition only illustrates the high level of reductionism at work. In my judgment, the least which one can demand of a modern critical interpreter is that some dialectical tension is maintained between theology and culture. How well one integrates the two will largely determine the success of the enterprise.

In sum, the use of the term revelation within the context of the canon reflects the concern to be open to the theological dimensions of the biblical tradition which can never be either separated from or identified with the life of empirical Israel. The term revelation is integral to the task of Old Testament theology, but only as a shorthand formula pointing to the whole enterprise of theological reflection on the reality of God. The insistence on placing the term firmly within a canonical context seeks to prevent misconstruals of interpretation which derive from over-emphasizing the cognitive, experiental, or historical elements.

Actually the use of the term revelation in respect of the Bible entails a far greater threat than that envisioned by any of its recent critics. It is constitutive of human sinfulness to turn the witness to God through the scriptures into a manageable object and thus fail to reckon with revelation as a means of encountering the living God on his own terms. The theological issue is not resolved by positing a sharp contrast between pre-critical and modern historical interpretation. Both Barth and Bultmann tried to teach us that lesson in the 1920s. The threat of domesticating the Word is equally present on both the right and left of the spectrum. If the canonical approach is conceived of as a closed system by which to handle biblical revelation, it is also doomed to failure and should rightly be rejected. However, if it can serve as a means for taking seriously the human form of the witness to divine revelation which God continues to bring alive for each new generation through his Spirit, it may serve as a useful tool for grappling with the real issues at stake in the theological enterprise.

Bibliography

J. **Barr**, 'Revelation through History in the Old Testament and in Modern Theology', *Interp* 17, 1963, 193–205; 'Revelation', *Dictionary of the Bible*, ed. James Hastings, rev. ed. F. C. Grant and H. H. Rowley, Edinburgh and New York 1963, 847–9; *Old and New in Interpretation*, London and Philadelphia 1966; K. **Barth**, *Church Dogmatics*, I/1–2, ET Edinburgh 1936, ²1975; 1956; R. **Bultmann**, 'The Concept of Revelation in the New Testament' (1929), ET *Existence and Faith*, New York 1960, 58–91; 'What Does it Mean to Speak of God?', ET *Faith and Understanding*, London and New York 1969, 53–65; F. G. **Downing**, *Has Christianity a Revelation?*, London 1964; N. K. **Gottwald**, *The Tribes of Yahweh*, Maryknoll, NY 1979 and London 1980; R. **Knierim**, 'Offenbarung im Alten Testament', *Probleme biblischer Theologie*, FS G. *von Rad*, ed. H. W. Wolff, Munich 1971, 206–35; R. **Rendtorff**, 'The Concept of Revelation in Ancient Israel', *Revelation as History*, ed. W. Pannenberg, New York 1968 and London 1969, 23–53; G. **Stroup**, *The Promise of Narrative Theology*, Atlanta and London 1981; T. C. **Vriezen**, *An Outline of Old Testament Theology*, ET Oxford and

Boston 1968, 118–25; W. **Zimmerli**, 'Knowledge of God According to the Book of Ezekiel', in *I Am Yahweh*, ET Atlanta 1982, 29–98.

3

HOW GOD IS KNOWN

(i) *Introduction*

I would like to start talking about God in the Old Testament, but how do I do this? Do I try to start at the beginning of Israel's tradition and trace the earliest witnesses in the Old Testament to God in a history of development? Do I try to sketch all the varieties of tradition (prophetic, priestly, sapiential), and describe the religion of each group of tradents? Do I seek to explore a system of symbols and discern the psychological and sociological forces which gave rise to these forms of expression? Or conversely, as a Christian theologian reading the Old Testament, do I begin with the confession that there is no full knowledge of God apart from his revelation in Jesus Christ, and then seek to view the Old Testament material in some fashion from the light of this faith perspective? How does a canonical context alter these usual perspectives?

I do not come to the Old Testament to learn about someone else's God, but about the God we confess, who made himself known to Israel, to Abraham, Isaac and to Jacob. I do not approach some ancient concept, some mythological construct akin to Zeus or Moloch, but our God, our Father. The Old Testament bears witness that God revealed himself to Abraham, and we confess that he has also broken into our lives. I do not come to the Old Testament to be informed about some strange religious phenomenon, but in faith I strive for knowledge as I seek to understand ourselves in the light of God's self-disclosure. In the context of the church's scripture I seek to be pointed to our God who has made himself known, is making himself known, and will make himself known.

I do not come to a hitherto unknown subject, but to the God whom we already know. I stand in a community of faith which confesses to know God, or rather to be known by God. We live our lives in the midst of confessing, celebrating and hoping. Thus, I cannot act as if I were living at the beginning of Israel's history, but as one who already knows the story, and who has entered into the middle of an activity of faith long in progress.

I belong to a community of faith which has received a sacred tradition in the form of an authoritative canon of scripture. There is a rule of faith and practice which has been formed because God is known. The Old Testament assumes the reality of God. Because he has established a relationship with his creation, the Old Testament never speculates on the possibility of what Israel testifies already to have experienced.

However, it is also the case that the nature of this relationship and the quality of knowledge varies in the Old Testament. Genesis 4 speaks of the time 'when men first began to call upon Yahweh', which indicates a change of relationship. Clearly the understanding of God and his will varies within the life of Israel, the nations, and in an individual. The Old Testament is fully aware of varying degrees of knowledge, from an indifferent, superficial relationship to an intense, all-encompassing closeness (Ps. 77). Indeed, there is a beginning (Gen. 1) and an ending (Dan. 12), but these termini have to do with God's purpose and the mystery of his will, and do not present a point at which either historical Israel or the present worshipping community can stand to contemplate its relation to God.

In sum, there is no place in time, either Israel's or our own, from which one begins from scratch to develop an understanding of God. Rather, we, as they, enter into a history of God with his creation which has already begun. Of course, this stance is no different from the education of each new generation into the faith. There is no correct point at which to enter, as if a child would be confused unless he or she entered the faith at Advent. Rather, one shares in a life already confessed, and seeks through growth to understand the grounds of that faith which has been received and experienced. Of course, it remains possible not to believe. The Psalmist speaks of the fool who says in his heart that there is no God (Ps. 14.1). However, it is clear from the context that the issue of God's existence is not at stake, but rather a manner of living which is without attention to his will.

Up to this point, I have argued that to reflect on the Old

Testament theologically in the context of the Christian canon establishes a perspective from which the enterprise is engaged. It rules out a stance which distances itself from Christian faith and tries merely to describe the development of Israel's faith in God or to picture different concepts of an ancient deity. But then does not this canonical context imply that a reflection on the Old Testament faith in God be immediately related to Christian faith in Jesus Christ? The very fact that the Christian canon treasures a portion of the scripture in which the name of Jesus is not mentioned offers an initial warrant for seeking another theological option. The implication of the Old Testament canon, both on a formal and material level, is that the Christian life is still lived between promise and fulfilment, not as a unilinear *heilsgeschichtliche* pattern, but as a description of the essential eschatological dimension of divine redemption. To reflect on God's revelation in the Old Testament is not a pre-Christian stage which has been rendered inoperative by the full revelation in Jesus Christ. Rather, it belongs to the nature of the Christian faith that the perception of God through the witness of the old covenant remains a constitutive stance for Christian theology. The struggle to perceive God in the testimony of the Hebrew scriptures is not an historical anachronism, but a consciously Christian understanding of the continuing, authoritative function of the Old Testament for the church. Although the ultimate task of biblical theology is to hear the witness of both Testaments, such an enterprise does not call into question the legitimacy, even necessity, of serious theological reflection on the old covenant in its own right as scripture of the church.

(ii) *God is known through creation*

The Old Testament can speak of God because he has made himself known. The Psalmist testifies that God has set for himself a witness: 'He has established a memorial to his mighty works' (111. 4). How, then, has God disclosed his nature and purpose? The entire Old Testament responds in concert: above all, through his creation.

The Psalmist bears eloquent testimony to this truth. 'The heavens are telling the glory of God and the firmament proclaims his handiwork . . . day to day pours forth speech and night to night declares knowledge' (19. 1). Similarly, in Ps. 8 the psalmist views the immensity of the heavens, which he acknowledges as the work of God's fingers – 'the moon and the stars which thou hast established' – and breaks forth into praise for God's mercy in such a creation: 'What is man that thou art mindful of him . . . that thou dost care for him?' Finally, in Job 38, God reviews the wonders of his creation:

> Where were you when I laid the foundation of the earth?
> Tell me, if you have understanding . . .
> when I made clouds its garment,
> and thick darkness its swaddling band . . . (vv. 4–9)

Before the sheer mystery and awesome power, Job confesses his inability to argue with God. Where were you when I made the hippopotamus?

To say that God reveals himself in his creation is not to say that God is known through nature. To try to discover God by scanning the sun and the moon can just as easily lead to idolatry and superstition. Rather, the confession of the biblical writer is that God reveals himself as creator. To suggest that no act of faith was involved, but only an assumption without an alternative (Westermann), seems to me an unfortunate misconstrual of the biblical witness.

Genesis 1 presents the basic biblical testimony to what is involved in this confession. 'In the beginning God created the heavens and the earth.' The text does not speak of a God who first was, and then who acted, but of a God who makes known his nature and will in his action. God brought into being 'the heavens and the earth', in an act unique to him, as it were, out of nothing. He did not merely transf rm something into something else, but the emphasis falls on the completely new beginning, before which there was no time of earthly being. He brought forth a reality which was distinct from himself, over which he had complete freedom.

The further elaboration in Ps. 33 rightly emphasizes the role of God's speaking in creating the world: 'By the word of the Lord the heavens were made, and all their host by the breath of his mouth.' There is no hiatus between his will expressed in his word and its accomplishment. 'God said, "Let there be light," and there was light. God said, "Let the waters be gathered together . . . and it was so".' Genesis 1 emphasizes the absolute freedom and power of God over his creation. Likewise, Isa. 45 testifies to God's absolute sovereignty over his creation:

I am the Lord, and there is no other,
    besides me there is no God . . .
I form light and create darkness,
I make weal and create woe,
I am the Lord, who do all these things (vv. 5–7).

The claim of divine sovereignty in the exercise of control of the creation is often expressed in the Old Testament in the familiar imagery of God's kingship. A whole set of psalms (93, 95–99) rings the changes on the theme of God's rule as king. Several important features of the Old Testament's witness to creation emerge from these psalms, which are widely represented elsewhere as well. First, God's rule expressed in creation is continuous. It is not something which relates only to the past; it persists. 'The world is established; it shall never be moved' (Ps. 93.1). Secondly, God's act of creation is set against opposing powers. Genesis 1.2 pits creation against chaos rather than non-being. So too does Ps. 93.3: 'The floods have lifted up . . . the floods lift up their roaring.' When God's creation is continually celebrated in Israel's worship, it reflects Israel's faith that its life is sustained by God's watchful care against the persistent forces of destruction. Belief in God's powers was not simply a philosophical option for Israel or an assumption to be taken for granted, but an existential belief which undergirded all of life.

Genesis 1 stresses that God's work consisted of an ordering of his creation. He did not create the world a chaos (Isa. 45.18). In a closely honed succession of acts, light is separated from darkness, the dry land formed, and the world inhabited. Then God pronounced it good with a blessing. Creation implies that God's work was towards an end. It was not done for divine amusement. Thus the world was created in order that 'salvation may sprout forth . . . and righteousness spring up also' (Isa. 45.8).

Some fifty years ago von Rad inaugurated a heated debate by suggesting that creation was a subordinate theme in the Old Testament in respect to redemption ('The Theological Problem', 53ff.). His theory was contested by others who sought to show that the widespread presence of creation motifs in the ancient Near East made its late appearance in Israel unlikely (Schmid, 'Creation'). In my judgment, these two questions have often been confused in the debate. It is possible that the creation theme developed secondarily within Israel's tradition. However, it is a different issue to determine on the basis of the intertextuality of scripture the present theological function of the two themes. By suggesting that they function as correlatives, I allow for numerous kinds of creative interaction between these closely joined themes, but it is highly questionable whether creation was subordinated in principle.

Old Testament commentators differ as to what extent a covenant theology is already implicit in Gen. 1–3. Certainly it is not present with the fully developed terminology of Deuteronomy. Nevertheless, the witness of Gen. 1–3 makes it abundantly clear that the creation of mankind was not an afterthought, but the goal of the divine purpose from the start. Moreover, Barth (*CD*. III/1) is certainly correct in seeing in the relation between two once independent creation stories a close interaction between the outer and inner dimension of creation as a gracious act of divine mercy. Some of the elements of joy as a suitable response to divine grace are reflected in Gen. 2, but this note is sounded unequivocally and repeatedly in the psalms (100. 1).

Although creation in the Old Testament is often viewed as a continuous providential support, there is another way of seeing its function which emerges especially in the prophets and psalms. The imagery is of a new creation. Israel's reflections on God's creative power are continually made in a context of suffering and defeat. The enormous tension within the Psalter arises from the fearful contrast between Israel's memory of what God once did and her present situation of grief. 'I remember the years long ago . . . when the waters saw thee, they were afraid . . . Has God forgotten to be gracious? Has the right hand of the Most High changed?' (Ps. 77.5–9). At times the prophet speaks of the creation of new heavens and a new earth in which the former things are forgotten (Isa. 65.17), and all of Israel's sorrow is removed as a world according to God's original plan is ushered in. At other times, the old and new creations are viewed as one unified eschatological act, spanning all of human history which encompasses God's single purpose of redemption. In Isa. 51.9ff. the original act of creation flows together imperceptibly with the new act of redemption from Babylon and continues the single song of joy.

An essential witness of Gen. 1 is that God also created mankind (*'ādām*), male and female, in his own image. He left his special stamp on this particular part of his creation, a mark which the recipient could not erase (Gen. 5.1). Old Testament scholars continue to wrestle with the full meaning of this concept which has played such an important role in Jewish and Christian theology, but which remains obscure in the Genesis text (cf. Chapter 8 below). However, in spite of its unclarity, at least one can say that it denotes a special relation between God and mankind which is unique among all the creatures. Only *'ādām* receives the image. Moreover, it is not an individual stamp, but functions as an analogy between the creator and the human species. To what extent the dual form of human sexuality, male and female, is an essential part of the image, remains contested.

In different ways Israel's sages and psalmists also testified to the special quality of man's creation. Ecclesiastes speaks of God's planting eternity in man's mind (3.11), which evokes man's restlessness to overcome his strange alienation. The psalmist writes of his inability to escape the presence of God – 'Whither shall I flee from thy presence' – and turns to reflect on the wonders of his own creation:

> For thou didst form my inward parts,
> Thou didst knit me together in my mother's womb.
> I praise thee, for thou art fearful and wonderful . . .
> That my soul knoweth right well . . . (139.13–14).

(iii) *Revelation through wisdom*

There is another major avenue of God's revelation in the Old Testament which is found in wisdom. 'The Lord has founded the earth in wisdom, and established the heavens in understanding' (Prov.3.19). There is a divine mystery of creation which escapes human ingenuity and defies his diligent search. This knowledge cannot be wrested away from God. It lies concealed within the divine purpose and planted within his creative works:

> Man does not know the way to it,
> and it is not found in the land of the living . . .
> Whence then comes wisdom?
> And where is the place of understanding?
> It is hid from the eyes of all living . . .
> God understands the way to it,
> and he knows its place (Job 28.13–23).

At the beginning of his creation – 'when he established the heavens and drew a circle on the face of the deep' – God implanted in his work a divine stamp which continues to bear witness to the wisdom of its creator. This imprint is not an impersonal world order like the Egyptian *maat*, but an active voice of wisdom seeking to guide humanity into paths of true life.

This revelation of God in his creation in the form of wisdom actively seeks to engage his creatures. Wisdom is a force which saves one from the way of evil and perverted speech (Prov. 2.12). By it kings reign and rulers decree what is just (Prov. 8.15). Von Rad speaks of this order as the form of 'self-revelation' of creation. 'Creation not only exists, it also discharges truth' (*Wisdom in Israel*, 165). As an essential witness to God's purpose in his creation, wisdom is built into the very structure of reality, and in this role seeks to guide humanity to the way of truth. However, it cannot be found through reason nor by human cleverness. The way to wisdom is in the fear of the Lord. Because wisdom invites all to come – 'I love those who love me and those who seek me will find me' (Prov. 8.17) – the promise of finding God's will in wisdom bears a striking resemblance to that offered by the prophet: 'You will seek me and find me, when you seek me with all your heart' (Jer. 29.13).

Similarly, the psalmist praises the wonders of God's creation:

How manifold are thy works!
In wisdom hast thou made them all (Ps. 104.24).

Thou dost cause the grass to grow for the cattle,
and plants for man to cultivate,
that he may bring forth food from the earth . . . (Ps. 104.14–15).

Thus, creation in God's great wisdom causes both himself and man to rejoice (Ps. 104.32–34). Little wonder that the psalmist seems overcome by the mercy of God and breaks forth in a resounding blessing: 'Praise the Lord.' From a canonical perspective it is highly significant to see how the wisdom themes have been fully incorporated into Israel's worship, and in spite of originally very different origins have been tightly interwoven together in a unified response of praise by the worshipping community.

(iv) *Revelation through history*

God also reveals himself in Israel's history. The revelation of himself in history is not seen as being different in kind from that of his creation. The psalmist can move with the greatest ease from praising God in the creation and preservation of the world to one who made his deeds known among the people (Ps. 105.1), who is ever mindful of his covenant with Abraham and promise to Jacob (vv. 7ff.). The book of Exodus explicitly connects the creation with the sabbath as a sign of the perpetual covenant between God and the people of Israel (31.12ff.; cf. 20.8ff.).

One of the great themes running throughout the book of Genesis is God's making known his will and purpose to the patriarchs as he breaks into their lives. All the narratives of Genesis serve to illustrate this activity of divine self-disclosure. He appeared to Abraham by the oaks of Mamre (18.1), to Jacob at the top of a ramp reaching up to heaven (28.12ff.), and to Hagar in the wilderness (21.17). Similarly, Moses thought that he was discovering the divine, only to experience that he was being discovered (Ex. 3.5ff.).

The psalmist never fails to recount the great favour of God through his wonderful works on Israel's behalf (105. 1ff.), and the intensity of the plea for help (126. 1ff.) is predicated on the firm conviction that God could again intervene in salvation (77.5ff.). The lengthy prayer of Daniel 9 continues the same pattern of confession of sin followed by a plea for God to reveal himself once again in salvation according to the promises of the covenant.

However, the theme of God's revealing his righteous will and redemptive plan for Israel through the events of history is developed most completely by the prophets. Especially clear is the sense of the divine control of history in Isaiah. Mighty Assyria is the 'rod of my anger, the staff of my fury', whom God sends against his own people. When his purpose is completed (14.24ff.), then he will cut down the boastful tyrant. Again, Jeremiah's use of the theme of the 'enemy from the north' (ch. 5–7) whom God beckons from the ends of the earth to wreck havoc on Israel portrays the demonic dimension of divine judgment which enters, but fully transcends, history. Conversely, the revelation of God as Israel's redeemer (*gô'ēl*) emerges most powerfully in II Isaiah's words:

> Thus says the Lord, your Redeemer, the Holy One of
> Israel: 'For your sake I will send to Babylon and

break down all the bars . . . behold I am doing a new thing . . . do you not perceive it?' (Isa. 43.14–19).

Moreover, the theme that God also reveals himself in the history of the nations extends throughout the Old Testament. When Pharaoh taunted Moses, saying: 'Who is Yahweh? . . . I do not know him' (Ex. 5.2), then the Lord made himself known to the king of Egypt in great acts of judgment causing him to confess: 'Yahweh is in the right and I . . . in the wrong.' Similarly, before the arrogance of Nebuchadnezzar, the God of Israel revealed himself in judgment, driving him from his throne until he confessed before the Most High:

. . . his dominion is an everlasting dominion,
and his kingdom endures from generation to generation . . .
and none can stay his hand or say to him,
'What doest thou?' (Dan. 4.34f.).

Again, Yahweh contests the alleged power of the idols in the metaphorical form of a law suit. He challenges them to do something in history: 'Do good or do harm that we may be dismayed and terrified' (Isa. 41.23). Then Yahweh alone is able to explain the past and predict the future. He alone can stir up kings and bring down kingdoms, that all who see must bear testimony: 'He is right' (41. 26).

When Israel grows proud and lays unrightful claim to special privilege, then Amos reminds the chosen people of God's similar concern for the nations as well:

Are you not like the Ethiopians to me, O people of Israel . . .
Did I not bring up Israel from the land of Egypt,
and the Philistines from Caphtor and the Syrians from Kir?
(Amos 9.7).

And Malachi assures the sinful nation that 'from the rising of the sun to its setting my name is great among the nations' (1.11). Ultimately, for the Old Testament the revelation of God extends to all nations, and the great eschatological portrayals of the end-time are painted in terms of all the nations of the earth assembling to be taught by the word of God (Isa. 2.1ff.).

Nevertheless, the revelation of God in history remains in an arena in which God both reveals and conceals his footprints (Isa. 45.15).

Particularly the prophet Isaiah wrestles hard with the strangeness of God's purpose. Indeed, God has a purpose which he will surely execute:

> The Lord of hosts has sworn
> as I have planned so shall it be,
> as I have purposed so shall it stand . . . (14.24ff.).

But it is a work which the prophet then characterizes as strange and alien.

In Isa. 28.23 the prophet uses a parable of the farmer to clarify his argument. Just as the work of the farmer is suited to the seasons – he ploughs, levels and sows – so also God's purpose varies according to his own time and will: 'He does not thresh for ever . . .' One needs wisdom, therefore, to perceive the hand of God moving on the plane of human history in both judgment and redemption.

Certainly the Hebrew prophets were consistent in their claims of a moral dimension in history. To this extent prophetic interpretation stands in stark contrast to all those theories of post-Enlightenment historians who view history as a complex nexus of purely immanental forces. Yet it is a serious misunderstanding of the Old Testament to infer that the Bible is concerned chiefly in constructing a history of morality in order to contrast good and bad behaviour. Actually one of the disturbing features of the Old Testament for many modern readers is precisely its lack of interest in this area which runs roughshod over questions of ethics. Rather, it is only at a far deeper level and growing out of a profoundly theological reflection on God's purpose in the world that the prophets see the mysterious hand of God ruling and over-ruling human folly.

(v) *Revelation through the name*

Finally, God reveals his identity through his name. In the Old Testament the name is not simply an arbitrary label, but testifies to the reality behind the name. When a person's character is changed, so his name must change. To the patriarchs God revealed his peculiar relationship by means of different names. He was 'Eternal God' (*El Olam*), or 'God Almighty' (*El Shaddai*). Each new dispensation within God's economy received a different revelation of his name. However, the name of God revealed to Moses, Yahweh, made clear the continuity of the divine revelation between the past and the future. According to Ex. 6.2 God said to Moses: 'I am YHWH. I appeared to Abraham, to Isaac and to Jacob as God Almighty (*El Shaddai*), but by my name YHWH I did not make myself known to them.' Rather, by the name YHWH the covenant God established his eternal relationship with his people through Moses: 'This is my name for ever, and thus I am to be remembered through all generations' (3.15).

Moreover, the significance of the name Yahweh was carefully explained to Moses: '*Ehyeh asher ehyeh*' ('I am who I am', or 'I will be who I will be'). God's being is not a static entity, but God makes known to Moses how he would learn of his true nature through his acts of redemption. Israel would understand who he was by what he did on her behalf. Therefore, his name was to be celebrated in worship ever after.

The revelation of God's will in his name continues to play a major role, especially in the book of Ezekiel. The refrain 'that you may know that I am Yahweh' (7.1, 27; 12.16; 20.38) points to the acts of God which reveal the true knowledge of his being. He acts in the history of Israel that all may know who he is, namely Yahweh. The prohibition of taking the name of God in vain is to prevent an abuse of this knowledge which is offered for Israel's redemption and cannot be usurped for an illegitimate end.

(vi) *Is the God of the Old Testament a male deity?*

From time to time in the history of interpretation the God of the Old Testament has been portrayed as a bloodthirsty, 'macho', male deity. Ironically, the same profile has recently reappeared in some feminist literature. How do Christians know that the God of Israel is not a male deity? We know it because the canonical scriptures of the Old Testament reveal to us his true nature! How is it possible to make such a claim when the Old Testament itself consistently refers to God with a male pronoun, and describes him fully in the context of Ancient Near Eastern culture as king, father and husband? Is not the Bible the source of the problem rather than its solution?

Of course one can easily respond by pointing out that much feminine imagery is also used of God in the Old Testament, who as a mother comforts her suffering children (Isa. 66.12), who cries out in the labours of birth (Isa. 42.14), and who gathers her dispersed as a hen. Still, this observation, even when true, does not strike to the heart of the hermeneutical problem, which operates on a far deeper level of understanding.

The basic theological confusion arises by failing to see that the meaning of scripture for a community of faith is not buried in a lifeless book which requires 'purification' in order for it to function as a religious norm. Rather, meaning derives from the use which a religious community makes of a sacred text and from the text's coercion in a particular context of faith. The major thrust of the entire biblical witness is in portraying the God of Israel as different in kind from his creation, which he brings into being and sustains by grace. The Old Testament leans over backwards in emphasizing the difference. God is not a mortal, who vacillates, who grows weak and dies; the God of Israel inhabits eternity. He watches over Israel without slumber and in him there is no shadow from turning. To fail to see what God is like because of the use of linguistic conventions, often peculiar to Hebrew, is to misunderstand completely the quality of the intertextuality of scripture. To read the Old Testament with no sense for its kerygmatic intentionality is to be guilty of the worst kind of literalism.

The point is that the Bible functions in such a way that such terms as 'father' and 'king' gain their theological content from the character of God, who continues to be worshipped in the conventions of a language which believers have always understood as inadequate for rendering the full divine reality. When such biblical terms to designate God become stumbling blocks, the hermeneutical question must be raised whether the problem lies with the imagery, or with a generation which no longer possesses the needed 'reader competence' to render the Bible as scripture of the church.

Still, I judge it quite appropriate in the contemporary actualiz-ation of the Old Testament through preaching and teaching to make explicit the universal nature of God's invitation to salvation by the use of so-called 'inclusive language'. Any good translation accommodates itself to its concrete historical audience. However, such a rendering of the biblical message reflects a totally different hermeneutic from one which seeks to 'liberate' the Bible from its time-conditioned flaws.

(vii) *Characteristic features of God's self-disclosure*

In spite of the great variety of emphases within the Old Testament as to how God is known, there are certain characteristic patterns which emerge: (*a*) The God of the Old Testament consistently takes the initiative in his pursuit of mankind. 'Adam, where art thou?' He takes the lead, whether in patriarchal narrative or prophetic oracle, to bring a new and fresh dimension of wonder.

(*b*) God is not limited to any one means of revelation, but his coming is one of surprise. He spoke to Moses in the fire and thunder, but then chose to disappoint Elijah in not repeating the fireworks. Instead, he let his presence be known in the still, small voice (1 Kings 19.12). The frequent use of irony in this context seems almost to suggest a form of divine humour (cf. the stories of Balaam, Naaman, Jonah).

(*c*) God both reveals and conceals his identity to Israel. What first seems to be the divine form itself soon emerges as only his outward manifestation: his 'glory', 'messenger' or 'face'. Moses is permitted to converse with God 'face to face', but what he sees is only his fleeting back (Ex. 33.23). When the prophet Isaiah sees the Lord as king, only the smallest tip of his robe engulfs the temple (Isa. 6.1).

(*d*) It is characteristic of the Old Testament revelation of God's presence to move quickly from the vision to that which is spoken. Jacob, terrified before the awesome theophany, receives a verbal promise (Gen. 28.13ff.), as do Abraham and Moses. Because God speaks, his primary medium is his word. He communicates to the patriarchs by calling them by name. If at times his voice is in the thunder, the *qôl YHWH* soon becomes an interpreted word which Israel can understand. In the prophetic literature the vision is usually subordinated to the all-encompassing force of the word of God: 'Thus saith the Lord.'

(*e*) The God of the Old Testament is never viewed as a monolithic, unchanging entity. The elements of his eternity are held in tension with the imagery of great movement and action (Ezek. 1.4ff.). His transcendence does not undercut his immanence, nor his mysterious otherness his gracious presence. It was not by chance that the Christian church felt constrained to respond to this biblical witness of the Old Testament in trinitarian terminology.

Bibliography

B. W. **Anderson,** *Creation versus Chaos,* New York 1967; B. W. **Anderson** (ed.) *Creation in the Old Testament,* London and Philadelphia 1984; K. **Barth,** *The Doctrine of Creation, Church Dogmatics,* ET III/1–4, Edinburgh 1958ff.; R. C. **Dentan,** *The Knowledge of God in Ancient Israel,* New York 1968; L. **Gilkey,** *Maker of Heaven and Earth,* New York 1959; H.-J. **Hermisson,** 'Observations on the Creation Theology in Wisdom', in B. W. Anderson (ed.) *Creation,* 118–34; C. J. **Labuschagne,** *The Incomparability of Yahweh in the Old Testament,* Leiden 1966; G. **von Rad,** 'The Theological Problem of the Old Testament Doctrine of Creation', in Anderson (ed.) *Creation,* 53–64; *Wisdom in Israel,* ET London and Nashville 1972, 144–76; J. **Reumann,** *Creation and New Creation,* Minneapolis 1973; J. C. **Rylaarsdam,** *Revelation in Jewish Wisdom Literature,* Chicago 1946; H. H. **Schmid,** 'Creation, Righteousness, and Salvation: "Creation Theology as the Broad Horizon of Biblical Theology" ', in Anderson (ed.), *Creation,* 102–17; S. **Terrien,** *The Elusive Presence,* New York 1978; C. **Westermann,** *Creation,* ET Philadelphia and London 1974; *The Elements of Old Testament Theology,* ET Atlanta 1978, 9–34; W. **Zimmerli,** *I am Yahweh,* ET Atlanta 1982; *Old Testament Theology in Outline,* ET Atlanta and London 1978, 17–58.

4

GOD'S PURPOSE IN REVELATION

It seems an obvious question to inquire about God's motivation in revealing himself to Israel and the nations? Why did God make himself known?

(i) *The goal of self-disclosure*

Surprisingly, the Old Testament is virtually silent regarding divine motivation. One searches in vain to see this issue treated in any direct fashion. It is evident that divine revelation is never grounded in some need of God, as if he were lonely. There is no hint that God required some fulfilment, or even sought fellowship with mankind in order truly to express his Godhead. Such a move is simply foreign to the Old Testament.

Even to suggest that the motivation behind his revelation in creation was to establish a covenant with Israel is to misconstrue a theme which functions in a different way within the Pentateuch. Certainly an explicit connection is made in Ex. 31.12ff. between the creation and the establishment of a covenant. Also, there is an implicit connection in Gen. 1 between the successive acts of creation which culminate in the sabbath and the history of the generation of mankind which begins in ch. 2. Yet this connection does not provide the motivation for God's revelation of himself. Rather, the covenant is a means of revelation whose major function is to demonstrate God's faithfulness to his word, as we read in Ps. 89 respecting the covenant with David:

> . . . I will not remove from him my steadfast love,
>   or be false to my faithfulness.
> I will not violate my covenant,
>   or alter the word that went forth from my lips (vv. 33f.).

The truth is that the Old Testament is consistently theocentric. It assumes that God's primary action lies in revealing himself, and it never attempts to penetrate behind this initiative. Thus, Israel's understanding of God is grounded in divine disclosure, and there is never any attempt to locate it in his being or existence *per se*.

To be sure, Israel pondered the divine motivation behind different aspects of God's self-disclosure and sought to understand the meaning of strange or conflicting acts within the divine purpose. For example, Isaiah marvelled at the incomprehensibility of the divine plan: 'strange is his deed – alien is his work' (28.21), and resorted to comparing it with the farmer's changing activities in accordance with the seasons (28.27). Again, Deut. 7 sought to explain the election of Israel by appealing ultimately to the mystery of God's love for his people:

> It was not because you were more in number than any other people . . . for you were the fewest of all people, but it is because the Lord loves you . . . (vv. 6ff.).

In both cases the mystery of God's purpose is grounded on God's own counsel, which he has unveiled partially in order to suit his own ends. Whenever this claim for absolute sovereignty is challenged, God disavows the challenge with uncompromising authority:

> Woe to him who strives with his Maker,
>   an earthen vessel with the potter!
> Does the clay say to him who fashions it,
>   'What are you making?' or 'Your work has no handles'?
> Thus says the Lord, the Holy One of Israel, and his Maker:
>   'Will you question me about my children,
>   or command me concerning the work of my hands?
> I made the earth, and created man upon it;
>   it was my hands that stretched out the heavens
>   and I commanded all their host . . .'
> Truly, thou art a God who hidest thyself,
>   O God of Israel, the Saviour (Isa. 45.9–15).

Or recall the divine sarcasm when Job sought to establish his own integrity at God's expense:

Where were you when I laid the foundation of the earth?
Tell me, if you have understanding (38.4).

Nevertheless, God has a purpose, an *ēṣah*. Whatever he does is not executed in caprice or by whim. The psalmist renders praise to God because, 'The counsel of the Lord stands for ever, the thought of his heart to all generations' (33.11). Or again, he breaks into praise when contemplating the gracious providence and extreme care by which the world is sustained:

O Lord, how manifold are thy works!
In wisdom, thou hast made them all (104.24).

Likewise, Isaiah makes much of God's counsel:

As I have planned, so shall it be,
As I have purposed, so shall it stand (14.24).

Finally, II Isaiah argues that creation itself involves an ordered plan. He did not create the earth as a chaos – indeed a contradiction in terms – but he formed it in order for it to be inhabited (45.18).

If one asks what was God's purpose, that is, his *motivation* in revealing himself, the Old Testament is silent. However, if one asks what was God's purpose, that is, his *goal* toward which his self-disclosure pointed, then the Old Testament is eloquent in its response. God revealed himself that all may see and know who God is:

I am Yahweh, and there is no other;
    besides me there is no God;
I gird you, though you do not know me,
    that men may know, from the rising of the sun
    and from the west, that there is none besides me;
I am Yahweh, and there is no other . . .
I am Yahweh, who do all these things (Isa. 45.5–7).

Or again, the prophet Ezekiel never wearies of grounding God's purpose with the formula: 'that you may know Yahweh' – and thus have life.

The disclosure of who God is emerges from his activity. To know his deeds is to understand who he is. There is no hiatus between his acts and his being. The world is the theatre in which God's purpose is demonstrated. To the psalmist it appears as fully self-evident that God's intention is abundantly manifest in his deeds. Hence the constant appeal: 'Come, and behold the works of the Lord' (Ps. 46.8). 'Be still and know that I am God . . . I am exalted in the earth' (46.10). One can see his handiwork in the heavens (Ps. 8.3) or his wondrous deeds in the deep (Ps. 107.23f.).

Therefore, the only proper response is one of praise before the manifest glory of God's presence in his works:

Say to God, 'How awe-inspiring are thy deeds!
So great is thy power that thy enemies cringe before thee.
All the earth worships thee; they sing praises to thee . . .
Come and see what God has done . . . Come and hear . . .
and I will tell you what he has done for me' (Ps. 66.3–16).

(ii) *The obscuring of God's will*

Yet the Old Testament is fully aware that God's gracious purpose which he has manifested in his deeds is not seen nor understood by all. There is a massive disruption which has obscured God's will in making himself known to humanity. It does not do justice to the diversity within the Old Testament canon to suggest that the doctrine of the 'fall', as testified to in Gen. 3, provides the framework in which the entire Old Testament functions. This particular formulation of human alienation in terms of Adam's original transgression is very restricted in its use. Moreover, there is a striking difference between Jewish and Christian interpretation of the role assigned to these early chapters. Nevertheless, that there has been a major disruption between God and his creation recurs throughout the entire Old Testament, albeit in differing forms.

The prophet Isaiah describes this alienation as a major theme of his preaching:

Sons have I reared and brought up,
but they have rebelled against me.
The ox knows its owner,
and the ass its master's crib;
but Israel does not know,
my people does not understand (1.2–3).

Or again, the words of II Isaiah:

> Hear, you deaf, and look you blind, that you may see!
> Who is blind but my servant,
> Or deaf as my messenger whom I send?
> He sees many things, but does not observe them;
> his ears are open, but he does not hear (42.19–20)

Israel worships the creatures rather than the creator:

> . . . they sin more and more,
> and make for themselves molten images,
> idols skilfully made of their silver . . .
> 'Sacrifice to these,' they say. Men kiss calves! (Hos. 13.2).

As a result,

> they exchanged the glory of God
> for the image of an ox that eats grass,
> they forgot God, their Saviour,
> who had done great things in Egypt (Ps. 106.20–21).

Therefore,

> there is no faithfulness or kindness,
> and no knowledge of God in the land;
> there is swearing, lying, killing, stealing, and adultery . . .
> and the land mourns (Hos. 4.1–3).

In a similar fashion, but often with different imagery, the psalmist testifies to Israel's rebellion and lack of memory (106.7). The nation became wicked and proud. Everyone utters lies to his neighbour (52.2ff.), until there is no knowledge, but all have gone astray (14.3). Likewise, the sages reflect on how man has lost the way to wisdom, and stumbles as a sleepwalker without direction, or walks as a naive child unaware of all danger (Prov. 7.6ff.).

The understanding of the purpose of God in his deeds is therefore inextricably tied to the condition of the one viewing God's works. There is need for God's grace, the gift of a true perception, in order to see what God is doing in the world. God reveals himself in salvation to those who love him, to the humble and contrite. 'You will seek me and find me, when you seek me with all your heart' (Jer. 29.13). To the broken of heart, God fulfils his purpose

(Ps. 138.8), not to the proud and arrogant. The knowledge of God is inseparably bound to a knowledge of oneself.

(iii) *The eschatological restoration of his purpose*

In the light of human ignorance and blindness to the truth of revelation it is not strange that the major biblical testimony of God's ultimate purpose is not set forth at the beginning of the biblical story, but at the end. Moreover, the sense of the end is such that the entire Old Testament has an eschatological quality about it.

Of course, the Genesis account of creation in chapters 1–2 pictures the goodness and grace of God's intention in providing a fruitful world of harmony and beauty in which to live in fellowship with the creation. However, the portrayal is one of great restraint and functions as a backdrop for man's search for false knowledge and arrogant independence of God's domain.

Rather, it is in the prophetic testimony to the gracious restoration of the divine purpose by divine intervention that the true goal of God's revelation appears in its clearest form. The world is portrayed in restored harmony with no hurt, exploitation, or violence, 'for the earth shall be full of the knowledge of the Lord as the waters cover the sea' (Isa. 11.9). Again, in that day 'nation shall not lift up sword against nation, neither shall they learn war any more' (Isa. 2.4). Jeremiah speaks of the new covenant in which 'all shall know from the least to the greatest' (31.31). The restored Jerusalem, the city of God, will again be called 'city of righteousness' (Isa. 1.26). The creation of the new heavens and the new earth will result in a rejoicing reminiscent of the first creation when 'the morning stars sang together and all the sons of God shouted for joy' (Job 38.7), or when wisdom was with God 'rejoicing in his inhabited world and delighting in the sons of man' (Prov. 8.30f.).

Finally, just as the knowledge of God's purpose is dependent on the condition of the receiver, so the goal of God's salvation for his creation results inexorably in the participation of the redeemed:

Is not this the fact that I choose:
. . . to let the oppressed go free,
and to break every yoke?
Is it not to share your bread with the hungry,
and bring the homeless poor into your house . . .

Then shall your light break forth like the dawn
and your healing shall spring up speedily . . .
The glory of the Lord shall be your rear guard . . .
And the Lord will guide you continually
and satisfy your desire with good things . . . (Isa. 58.6ff.)

The goal of God's revelation of himself points to the fulfilling of a
hope which was only adumbrated in the first creation, but which
yearns for the final reconciliation, for the new Jerusalem, and for a
transformed world.

In conclusion, I would argue that the most suitable biblical term
for God's purpose with his creation is 'salvation' or 'redemption'.
These are much to be preferred to the much-abused term 'liberation'. Of course, the word liberation has the initial advantage of
including the dimension of social and political amelioration which is
indeed part of the biblical connotation. Certainly God's intervention
cannot be restricted merely to a spiritual, internal exercise.
However, the contemporary use of liberation is seriously marred by
its dominantly political and economic connotations with heavy
ideological overtones, which have robbed the word of its rich
religious connotations. The term liberation, as currently used in
theological circles, fails to treat seriously those features basic to
the Old Testament's understanding of God's intention, namely
forgiveness of sin, response of faith, and the basic inability of all
human schemes to accomplish genuine freedom. The hope of the
biblical writers is not anchored to a human social programme,
regardless of how well-meaning or pious, but to God's salvation
which he is already bringing to fruition according to his eternal
purpose. To make use of the biblical term 'kingdom of God' as an
equivalent to salvation – his rule over all that he created – will
perhaps serve to prevent any restriction of God's work to the
individual human soul, but also point to the divine initiative of
bringing his cosmic will to completion, which is an eschatological
force energizing the world.

Bibliography

J. **Fichtner**, 'Jahwes Plan in der Botschaft des Jesaja', *ZAW* 63, 1951,
16–33; J. **Jeremias**, *Die Reue Gottes. Aspekte alttestamentlicher Gottesvorstellung*,
BS 65, 1975; C. **Westermann**, *Elements of Old Testament Theology*, ET

Atlanta 1982, 35–84; G. E. **Wright**, *God Who Acts*, SBT I. 8, 1952; W. **Zimmerli,** *Old Testament Theology in Outline*, ET London and Atlanta 1978, 43–8.

5

THE LAW OF GOD

(i) *The knowledge and will of God*

To know God is to know his will. In the Old Testament to know God
is not a mystical experience or merely an inter-personal relationship.
Nor is it a feeling of spirituality. Rather, the knowledge of God is
defined throughout as obedience to his will which has a content.
When God reveals himself in his name, 'I am Yahweh', he also
reveals his will (Ex. 20.2ff.). Just as the knowledge of God is based
on his disclosure, so also his will is made known simultaneously.
Israel does not first know God, and then later discover what God
wants. Knowledge of his person and will are identical, and both
are grounded in his self-revelation. To lack knowledge of God is
described as disobeying his will and therefore it evokes his anger.

Isaiah speaks of a disobedient people dying for lack of knowledge
(5.13), and Hosea describes the consequences of the failure of
knowledge as lawlessness (4.1). The latter condemns a people who
have broken the covenant, transgressed the Law, and yet cry, 'My
God, we, Israel, know thee' (8.2). Conversely, God is present and
known where the oppressed are freed, and the naked are covered
(Isa. 58.6ff.).

(ii) *The divine imperative*

God has expressed his will from the beginning: 'The Lord God
commanded the man saying. "You may freely eat of every tree of
the garden; but of the tree of the knowledge of good and evil, you
shall not eat . . ." ' (Gen. 2.16). For the writer of Gen. 2, to be
human consists in living in freedom, within a community, and
under the divine imperative. Again, God commanded Abraham,

saying, 'Go from your country and your kindred . . . to the land
that I will show you' (Gen. 12.1). Or to Jacob, 'Return to your
country, and to your kindred and I will do you good' (Gen. 32.9).
God also charged Moses, 'Come, I send you to Pharaoh that you
may bring forth my people . . . out of Egypt' (Ex. 3.10). When
Moses then resisted the command, God was willing even to negotiate
for his plan until the real grounds for Moses' resistance emerged as
unbelief. In sum, God appears throughout the Old Testament as a
person with a will which he freely communicates.

Conversely, it is a divine judgment of the severest sort when the
word of God becomes 'rare' in the land (I Sam. 3.1). Amos pictures
the judgment of God:

> not a famine of bread, nor a thirst for water,
> but of hearing the words of the Lord.
> They shall wander from sea to sea,
>   and from north to east;
> They shall run to and fro to seek the word of the Lord
>   but they shall not find it (8.11–12).

Saul despairs of his life because 'God has turned away from me and
answers me no more' (I Sam. 28.15). It is a deep biblical conviction
that when God withdraws his presence, man does not know what to
do!

(iii) *God's will and its realization*

The creation account of Gen. 1 bears clearest witness that there is
no hiatus between the will of God and his action. When God said,
'let it be', it was. It therefore belongs to the divine attribute of
grace when there is a temporal distinction between prophecy and
fulfilment. God delays his decision of judgment in order to give his
people every chance for repentance.

One of the truly remarkable chapters on this topic consists of a
dialogue between God and Abraham before the destruction of
Sodom (Gen. 18.22ff.). God takes Abraham into his confidence and
reveals to him his decision to destroy Sodom because of its great
evil. Then God allows Abraham to persuade him to refrain from his
judgment for the sake of ten righteous inhabitants. In the course of
the dialogue, Abraham implies a distinction between God's will
and his action: 'Shall not the judge of all the earth do right?'

However, the tension is only an apparent one – it serves as a literary device in the chapter – and is resolved by God's matching his will for justice with his acts of mercy by accepting Abraham's compromise. In a similar vein, the Hebrew idiom of God's 'repenting of his resolve' retains the integrity of the divine will, but allows for decision and flexibility in relation to a genuine human history (cf. Jeremias).

(iv) The canonical shape of the Sinai witness

The fullest and most direct expression of the will of God in the Old Testament is found in the revelation of the Law at Sinai. In a real sense the book of Genesis is its prologue and the book of Deuteronomy its epilogue, but the heart of the Pentateuch lies in the tradition of Sinai contained in the middle books of Exodus, Leviticus and Numbers.

The usual procedure of critical commentaries and Old Testament theologies is to begin any discussion of the theology of the Law by rehearsing the many literary problems within this complex of tradition which stretches from Ex. 19 to Num. 10. The various discrete units, such as the Decalogue, Covenant Code, Holiness Code, and Priestly legislation are distinguished and separately evaluated. However, in spite of much evidence that these chapters have indeed undergone a complex history of development, in my opinion it is methodologically a mistake to make the writing of an Old Testament theology directly dependent on its historical reconstruction. Rather, the approach being proposed is to describe the theology of the Old Testament according to the intertextuality of its canonical shaping and to seek to understand how this corpus of material was ordered and rendered within the context of scripture. To the extent that a depth dimension illuminates the canonical text, and is not viewed as a rival construal, its use can be often a great help.

Certain broad interpretative lines become immediately apparent. The revelation of Sinai (Ex. 19) is integrally connected with the deliverance from Egypt. The giving of the Law (Ex. 20ff.) and the sealing of the covenant (Ex. 24) form the climax of the formation of the people of God (19.4–6). Moreover, the Decalogue has been assigned a special place within the Old Testament tradition, which is apparent by its form, terminology and position within the narrative. The commandments of the Decalogue are tied closely to the divine revelation at Sinai, and bear witness to a direct, unmediated communication from Yahweh himself: 'God spoke all these words, saying. . . .'

The Decalogue is distinguished from most other legal corpora by having little or no reference to a specific historical period of Israel's history, or to a particular institution such as a central sanctuary. In its canonical role the Decalogue forms a theological summary of the entire Sinai tradition. All the detailed legislation which follows is therefore subordinated to and interpreted by the heart of the Law found in the Ten Commandments. The Book of the Covenant which follows in Ex. 20.21ff. has been assigned a role as additional commandments delivered through the mediation of Moses when the people fled in terror from the divine theophany (20.18ff.). That all this legislation was seen in the context of establishing a covenant is made clear from ch. 24.

The laws of the book of Leviticus, regardless of their prehistory, have been firmly tied to the Sinai event. This connection is made explicit in Lev. 8–9, which forms the literary continuation of Ex. 29, namely, the inauguration of Aaron and his sons. Moreover, the ceremony unfolds according to the exact execution of the will of God, 'as Yahweh commanded Moses' (8.9, 13, 17, 21, 29, etc.). The same intention to bind the laws of Leviticus to Sinai is again made explicit in the concluding subscription to the laws of sacrifice (7.37–38). The editor of Leviticus has structured the material in order to show that the sacrificial system which commenced with the inauguration of Aaron in chs. 8–9 stemmed from a divine revelation at Sinai through Moses (7.38). The sacrifices which Aaron initiated did not derive from mere custom, but in direct compliance with the divine will. Aaron's inauguration became an instantiation of obedience and response in proper worship whereas Nadab and Abihu illustrated judgment on unholy malpractice (Lev. 10.1ff.).

The canonical effect of structuring the book of Leviticus in such a way as to connect all the material directly to the revelation at Sinai is of crucial importance in understanding its role as authoritative scripture for Israel. The laws of Leviticus which stemmed originally from very different periods, and which reflected remarkably different sociological contexts, are subordinated to the one overarching theological construct, namely, the divine will made known to Moses at Sinai for every successive generation. This hermeneutical move is not to be characterized as simply a dehistoricizing of the tradition. Rather, in the book of Leviticus one historical moment in Israel's life has become the norm by means of which all subsequent history of the nation is measured. If a law functions authoritatively for Israel, it must be from Sinai. Conversely, if it is from Sinai, it must be authoritative. Clearly a theological understanding of Sinai is at work in the canonical process which is different in kind from a modern reconstruction of the historical origins of Israel's laws.

Finally, crucial to any understanding of the theological significance of the Sinai material is a correct analysis of the canonical role assigned to the book of Deuteronomy. Once again the canonical approach does not deny that forces from Deuteronomy's long growth have left an imprint on the material; however, the decisive exegetical issue lies in determining how these earlier levels function within the context of a canonical corpus.

The first chapter of Deuteronomy makes it immediately clear that the purpose of Moses' addressing the people is to 'explain the Torah' (v.5). To the new generation who was about to cross into the land, Moses interprets the Sinai covenant. He does not offer a new law, but by means of a rehearsal of the history of Israel since Sinai, seeks to inculcate obedience to the divine law which had once and for all constituted the nation (5.22). Moses applies the divine law to the new situation in which the people would shortly enter. It is, therefore, built into the canonical function of Deuteronomy that a new application of old tradition is being offered. The new interpretation seeks to actualize the traditions of the past for the new generation in such a way as to evoke a response to the divine will in a fresh commitment to the covenant.

The setting forth of the Law is now placed within the context of the new, hitherto unexperienced situation of Israel occasioned by the entrance into the land (18.9; 19.1ff.). Israel is not to continue as before (12.8), but is given a new charter by Moses. This implies that the very different character of the laws of Deuteronomy has been recognized within the canonical process and the change has been accommodated within the framework of the new historical condition of the conquest (cf. 14.24ff.). The effect of the ordering of the laws within chs. 12–26 is to legitimate the principle of change within the Law, and at the same time to subordinate all the various forces at work within the historical development to one theological category. This is to say that the process of canonical ordering worked into the final form of the book a great variety of different laws, but virtually disregarded the specific socio-political forces which produced the new forms of the Law.

The theological implications of the canonical role of Deuteronomy for understanding the Sinai traditions are fundamental. Moses is portrayed as explaining the divine will to a new generation which had not itself experienced the formative events of its religious history. Deuteronomy, therefore, serves as an authoritative commentary on how future generations are to approach the Law and how it functions as a guide for its interpretation. Thus, God's covenant is not tied to past history, but is still offered to all Israel of every generation. Again, the promise of God still lies in the future and Israel can only anticipate in faith the possession of the heritage. Again, Deuteronomy teaches that the Law demands a response of single-hearted commitment. The Deuteronomic writer strives to inculcate the Law into the will of the people. The Law of God remains a dynamic imperative which evokes an active choice to share in the living traditions of God's people. Finally, the ability of Deuteronomy to summarize the Law in terms of loving God with heart, soul and mind is a major check against all forms of legalism. According to Deuteronomy, the whole Mosaic law testifies to the living will of God whose eternal purpose for the life of his people provides the only grounds for life and salvation.

(v) *Theological implications of the Law*

(*a*) In spite of the variety and diversity of the various Old Testament laws, there is a theological coherence to the material as expressing the one will of God to his covenant people. Within the context of the historical covenant, the commandments served different functions in transforming historical Israel into the people of God. One can, therefore, rightly speak of the Law of God, comprising the first part of the Hebrew canon and constituting the covenant relationship.

(*b*) The Law contains both promise and threat. It calls forth decisions which result in either life or death. Commandments which serve the faithful as guides to life similarly work death to the disobedient. The dual side of the Law is highlighted throughout the Pentateuch, both in the ceremony which sealed the covenant (Ex. 24) and in the ritual of blessing and cursing. The execution of judgment announced by the prophets was contained within the Law itself from the beginning.

(c) The Law of God was a gift of God which was instituted for the joy and edification of the covenant people. It was not given as a burden, but as a highest treasure and a clear sign of divine favour. The profoundest testimony to the original intent of the Law is found in Ps. 119:

> How love I thy law,
> It is my meditation all the day . . .
> I will never forget thy precepts,
> for by them thou hast given me life (vv. 97, 93).

(d) The clearest sign of the brokenness of the covenant and of the alienation of Israel from God emerged when his Law became a burden and a means of destroying the nation. This terrifying point was reached in Ezekiel, when the prophet testified that, 'God gave them statutes that were not good and ordinances by which they could not have life . . . I (Yahweh) defiled them through their very gift in making them offer by fire their firstborn that I might destroy them' (20.25f.). However, for the full implications of this understanding of the Law, one has to await the testimony of the apostle Paul.

Bibliography

B. S. **Childs**, *Exodus*, London and Philadelphia 1974, 385–496; R. E. **Clements**, 'The Old Testament as Law', *Old Testament Theology. A Fresh Approach*, London 1978, 104–30; W. **Eichrodt**, *Theology of the Old Testament*, ET, I, 70–97; J. **Ellul**, *The Theological Foundation of Law*, ET New York 1960; H. **Gese**, 'The Law', *Essays on Biblical Theology*, ET Minneapolis 1981, 60–92; Jörg **Jeremias**, *Die Reue Gottes*, BSt 65, 1975; G. E. **Mendenhall**, *Law and Covenant in Israel and the Ancient Near East*, Pittsburgh 1955; M. **Noth**, *The Laws in the Pentateuch and Other Studies*, ET Edinburgh and Toronto 1966, reissued London 1984; G. **von Rad**, 'The Law', *Old Testament Theology*, ET, II, 388–409; S. **Schechter**, *Some Aspects of Rabbinic Theology*, New York 1923, 116–60; E. E. **Urbach**, *The Sages. Their Concepts and Beliefs*, ET, I, Jerusalem 1975, 286–314; W. **Zimmerli**, 'The Theological Relevance of the Law', *The Law and the Prophets*, ET Oxford 1965 and New York 1967, 46–60.

6

KNOWING AND DOING THE WILL OF GOD

(i) *The dialectical poles*

There is another important aspect to the subject of the will of God which must be treated. It lies at the very heart of the theological issue of God's revelation of his will to Israel.

On the one hand, there are numerous passages in the Pentateuch stating that God has made known his will to Israel with the utmost clarity. There is constant reference to the divine imperatives throughout the Old Testament in the narrative, legal, prophetic and wisdom literature. Micah's response is typical of the prophets: 'He has shown you, O man, what is good; and what does the Lord require of you but to do justice, to love kindness, and to walk humbly with your God?' (6.8).

On the other hand, it is equally evident from many Old Testament passages that the knowing of the will of God cannot be simply assumed. Israel still has to 'seek' and 'inquire after' God's will, to discern his ways, and to pursue the path of instruction.

How is one to understand this tension between the different approaches of the Old Testament to the knowing and doing of the will of God? The problem is theological in nature and cannot be resolved by various historical or literary solutions, as if one approach represented an earlier stage of tradition, or as if the legal and prophetic witnesses were at variance. Rather, it appears to be constitutive of how the Old Testament understands the disclosure of God's will for his people.

If one turns to the first affirmation, the Old Testament frequently affirms that the will of God can be articulated in clear formulations. The Decalogue remains the classic expression of the divine law. In spite of the various and different functions of the Law, the unity of the divine will is constant. There is a continuity within the tradition. God does not demand one thing at one period which is countermanded in another. Moreover, the will of God is not an impossible ideal, or merely a 'shared vision', but a claim which can be met. Deuteronomy 30.11ff. formulates it succinctly: 'This commandment which I command you this day is not too hard for you, neither is it far off . . . but the word is very near you; it is in your mouth and in your heart, so that you can do it.'

Yet it is also true that the God of the Old Testament is the living author of his law, and that he continues to address his people throughout their history with his will. There is an active engagement from beginning to end. For Israel the Law could never be distilled into lifeless principles which then functioned independently of God himself. Especially the prophets made the nation aware of the fresh and terrifying dimensions of God's holiness when confronting human sinfulness. Again, the will of God has a specificity directed to concrete historical situations. The imperatives spoken to Isaiah 'in the year that King Uzziah died' were not the same as those addressed to Ezekiel by the river Chebar after the destruction of Jerusalem. The particular application of the divine will consistently took on an unexpected and often radical *ad hoc* form which could never be deduced solely from an ethical principle.

The basic point to be made is that nowhere within the Old Testament – I do not think the New Testament differs – is a system or technique described by which one can translate the general imperatives of the law of God, such as found in the Decalogue, into a specific application within the concrete historical situation. Although the Bible bears eloquent witness to the unchanging eternal will of God, yet at the same time it describes in an inexhaustible variety of ways the surprising and fresh application of God's will to specific individuals and peoples in definite situations. There is a continuity within the divine will, a consistency of redemptive purpose extending from the past to the future. There is a persistent movement from promise to fulfilment. However, the tension remains between this revealed will of God and the struggle for obedience in the concrete moment before a living God. The effort both to know the will of God and to do it remains inseparably joined. In specific acts of obedience one learns to know the will of God, and the knowledge of his will carries with it the imperative for doing it.

Is there anything more than one can say about the move from the revealed will of God in scripture to knowing and doing the will of God in the continuing life of the people of God? Indeed there is. If the Pentateuch serves to set out the major tenets of the will of God for Israel, the other portions of the canon function to instruct God's people in the growth of the knowledge of God.

The term 'to seek' or 'to inquire after God' seems originally to have arisen in a cultic setting and to have designated a worshipper's receiving an oracle at a sanctuary. But throughout most of the Old Testament the term has acquired a new metaphorical sense. God's will has been revealed in his Law, but it also must be discerned afresh. Ezra speaks repeatedly of preparing the heart to seek God (7.10). Chronicles equates 'seeking God' with 'seeking his law' (II Chron. 19.3; 30.19). When the faithful seek God's will 'with one's whole heart', then God 'lets himself be found'. Thus Jeremiah attempts to instruct a confused people living in exile far from Jerusalem: 'If you seek me, you will find me, when you seek me with all your heart. I will be found by you, says the Lord' (29.13).

Particularly the wisdom literature and the psalms make it clear that there is a proper context from which the search for God's will takes place. One must strive for wisdom, discern the way of righteousness anew, but one must start on the right path. 'The fear of the Lord is the beginning of wisdom.' Isa. 26.8 speaks of 'waiting for God', but the moment of anticipation occurs as one proceeds in the 'paths of his statutes'.

Although each generation, each individual, learns to discern the will of God, it is not as a blind leap in the dark. There is a continuity from generation to generation which is recorded in scripture. To the broken in spirit God makes known his presence; from the disobedient, arrogant and proud God hides his face. Israel thus looks both backwards to the experiences of the faithful, and forwards to the promise that if one seeks faithfully, God will be found.

(ii) *Contextual illustrations*

In the context of this set of questions, it is significant to reflect on some of the narratives within the Old Testament. In I Sam. 28 Saul is terrified before the army of the Philistines and does not know where to turn. When he inquires or seeks the Lord, God does not answer. Then Saul tries to force a divine answer by having a medium summon Samuel from the dead. When Saul then begs from

Samuel a word from God as to what he should do, the seer responds: 'Why ask me? The Lord has turned from you and become your enemy.' There was a time when Saul could have heard, but because he had not hearkened to the voice of God, this time has passed. Now there is only a word of judgment.

Again the prophet Amos makes it clear that a nation which has persistently ignored the will of God, can search frantically and never find God:

> They shall wander from sea to sea
>   and from north to east,
> They shall run to and fro and seek the word of the Lord,
>   but they shall not find it (8.12).

In the stories concerning the patriarchs, the issue at stake never turns on the faithful being confused as to what God wants of them. Only the pagan says:

> 'With what shall I come before the Lord
> and bow myself before God on high?
> Shall I come before him with burnt offerings?
> Will the Lord be pleased with thousands of rams?
> Shall I give my first-born for my transgressions,
> the fruit of my body for the sin of my soul . . ?

No! The prophet is adamant:

> He has shown you what is good . . . (Micah 6.6–8).

Rather, the crisis of faith in Israel among the faithful arises from a different threat which assails. Indeed, the whole Psalter is a chorus of agonizing cries: 'Why do the righteous suffer?' 'Why hast thou forsaken me?' 'How can I still live?' Nevertheless, the will of God has been revealed and those who seek him with all their hearts are assured that they will not seek him in vain. Of course, how God runs his world, how he exercises his sovereignty, and what he purposes in his mystery, opens up a different sort of theological question, which is the subject of another chapter.

Bibliography

F. **Büchsel**, V. **Herntrich**, 'Κρίνω', *TWNT* III, 920–54; *TDNT* III, 921–53; G. **Gerlemann**, E. **Ruprecht**, '*drš*, fragen nach', *Theologisches*

Handwörterbuch zum Alten Testament, ed. E. Jenni and C. Westermann, I, Munich and Zürich 1971, 460–67; H. **Greeven,** 'ζητέω', *TWNT* II, 894–8; *TDNT* II, 892–6; J. **Goldingay,** *Approaches to Old Testament Interpretation,* Leicester and Downers Grove 1981, 51–61; S. **Kierkegaard,** *Purity of Heart,* ET London 1961; E. L. **Long,** 'Soteriological Implications of Norm and Context', *Norm and Context in Christian Ethics,* ed. G. H. Outka and P. Ramsey, New York 1968 and London 1969, 265–95; P. S. **Minear,** *Commands of Christ,* Nashville and Edinburgh 1972; G. **von Rad,** *Wisdom in Israel,* ET Abingdon and London 1972, 53ff.; W. **Schrage,** *Die konkreten Einzelgebote in der paulinischen Paränese,* Gütersloh 1962; S. **Wagner,** '*dāraš*', *TWAT* II, 313–29; *TDOT* III, 293–307.

7

THE THEOLOGICAL SIGNIFICANCE OF THE DECALOGUE

The importance of the Decalogue in the history of civilization is abundantly clear. It played a significant role in the development of law, ethics, social theory and philosophy. Within Christian theology it has had a central role, and most of the great theologians of the church have written in some form on the Ten Commandments. Reflection on the Decalogue was also foundational for the synagogue, although in a form differing somewhat from that of the church (cf. Childs, *Exodus*, 431ff.). On what level should Old Testament theology read the Decalogue and in what manner?

Commentators have long observed that this legal corpus has been assigned a special literary place within the book of Exodus. Even though this role appears secondary, its present positioning has raised it to a unique status. Only these words were spoken of God without the mediation of Moses. Only these words have a special name – 'the ten words' – and were repeated in Deuteronomy. In addition, there is a sense of finality: 'he added no more', which sets them apart from the remaining laws.

The Decalogue also reflects a special content. Its imperatives are not addressed to a specific segment of the populace, but to everyone within Israel. They are straightforward and immediate with a comprehensiveness which is unusual. This quality has been achieved historically by a lengthy development which both expanded and contracted the commandments. A certain flexibility can be seen in the different homiletical directions to which the material has been pointed. Yet the Decalogue has not been transformed into eternal, divine principles. It remains an imperative directed to historical Israel, but Israel as the people of God which has been extended both in time and space beyond the first generation of those who experienced Sinai.

In my judgment, it is an important task of an Old Testament theology to sketch the range of interpretation within the whole Old Testament in order to understand how the Decalogue functioned within Israel, and to discern both the dynamics of its movement and the nature of its actualization. For example, the narrative material offers a major commentary within scripture as to how these commands now function within the canon. The story of the temptation of Joseph by Potiphar's wife offers one interpretation of the prohibition of adultery within a concrete situation. The narrative of David and Uriah goes to the heart of the crime of murder. Conversely, biblical law serves an important function in any reading of the narrative material by preventing the reader from simply moralizing the stories and thus failing to see the true nature of human existence with its potential for both good and evil in the light of the divine will.

Similarly, the writings of the prophets, psalmists and sages bear directly on a canonical understanding of the Decalogue. At times certain prophets virtually cite the text of the Decalogue (Hos. 4.2; Jer. 7.9). At other times, the effect of the intertextuality of the canon weaves a prophetic oracle into the larger fabric of the commandments. Likewise, the wisdom literature of Proverbs shows no signs of being historically related to the Sinai tradition in spite of frequent overlap in content, yet it also admonishes its hearers in respect to chastity, honour toward parents, truthfulness, and the like. However, the effect of the canonical collection is to provide a new intertextuality which relates these various witnesses within a literary corpus. To be sure, the exact nature of the parts must be carefully worked out exegetically and theologically.

The prologue

The commandments are introduced by a prologue: 'I am the Lord your God who brought you out of the land of Egypt, out of the house of bondage.' The prologue makes clear from the outset that the imperatives which now follow are understood as the will of God who had already delivered Israel from bondage. Yahweh identifies himself as the redeemer God and establishes his authority to make known his will because of what he had already done on Israel's behalf (cf. the Mekilta on Ex. 20). Israel does not become the people of God by doing the commandments, but because she has been chosen and redeemed, she receives the divine law as the proper response to God's grace.

(i) 'You shall have no other gods before me' (Ex. 20.3)

Regardless of how precisely one renders the Hebrew phrase 'before me' ('al pānay) – in defiance of me, to my disadvantage – an exclusive claim of Yahweh on his people is being made. It is not in the theoretical terminology of monotheism, but as a highly existential demand that the claims of other gods are categorically eliminated as far as Israel is concerned. Verse 5 establishes the context in which the divine imperative is given: 'You shall not bow down to them or serve them for I the Lord, your God, am a jealous God.' Yahweh alone is to be worshipped. The grounds for the commandment go beyond the authority provided by the prologue and rest on the nature of God himself. Because he is a 'jealous God', his passionate love for his people will not tolerate a divided loyalty. Hosea offers an illustration of God's exclusive claim on his bride. He has betrothed himself to Israel in righteousness, love, and steadfast love and now awaits Israel's response: 'Thou art my God' (2.23).

The essence of Israel's idolatry is reflected in Elijah's contest on Mount Carmel (I Kings 18). The issue is not that Israel wanted to reject Yahweh and choose Baal, but rather to serve them both. Elijah called for an either/or decision. 'How long will you go limping between two different opinions? If Yahweh is God, follow him; but if Baal, follow him.' When the fire fell on Elijah's altar, then the people confessed: 'Yahweh, he is God; Yahweh, he is God.' Once again, the commandment was understood in both its positive and negative dimensions.

Another indication of how the reader of the Old Testament canon is guided to interpret the first commandment is offered in Deut. 13. The homilist warns against the temptations of idolatry. Even if a prophet or soothsayer were to entice the people to serve other gods with miraculous signs, that option was to be flatly rejected. Deuteronomy continues: 'For the Lord is testing you, to know whether you love the Lord your God with all your heart and with all your soul. Walk after the Lord – fear him, keep his commandments, serve and cleave to him' (vv. 3–4). Idolatry is prohibited in order that true worship may flourish.

Finally, in the Psalter we have a clear picture of the full dimension of God's exclusive claim. In Ps. 50 God rebukes Israel's imperfect worship. The fault does not lie in the number of sacrifices, nor does God need food from his people. However, he does require praise and thanksgiving to know him aright. Again in Ps. 73, the psalmist wrestles with his own despair. He is envious of the prosperity of the wicked and wonders whether it makes any difference to cleave to God. Then he enters the sanctuary and begins to understand. 'Nevertheless . . .thou dost hold my right hand . . . dost guide me with thy counsel.' Finally, he breaks into praise confessing his sole allegiance to God:

Whom have I in heaven but thee?
And there is nothing upon earth that I desire besides thee (v. 25).

In the light of this rich canonical reflection on the subject of God's sole rule, Luther's paraphrase of the first commandment strikes close to its centre:

'You shall have no other gods before me.' What does this mean? We should fear, love and trust God above everything else (*Larger Catechism*).

(ii) *'You shall not make yourself an image . . .' (v. 4)*

Although this commandment once functioned independently, in its present canonical position it has been subordinated to the first commandment which brackets it (Zimmerli, 'Das zweite Gebot'). This commandment also turns on the proper worship of God, but it makes a different point. The basic issue involves the proper vehicle for worshipping God. The commandment categorically forbids the use of images. However, the central problem is that nowhere is an explicit reason given in Exodus to explain the prohibition. What was it in the image which failed to treat adequately the divine nature?

Perhaps the most helpful parallel is found in the Deuteronomic account of Sinai (4.9ff.). The author argues that because God did not reveal himself in a form, but only in a voice, Israel should beware of making a graven image. Images are a false response to God's making himself known through his word. Von Rad attempts to expand on this idea in a brilliant, but somewhat speculative, line of interpretation. He reasons that God's freedom to relate himself to the world was encroached upon by the image. The image failed to deal with Yahweh's true nature 'by whose hidden action in history Israel was continually held in suspense' (I, 218). Similarly, Zimmerli contrasts revelation through dynamic history with revelation in a static image. These interpretations are stimulating, but I do not regard the evidence as fully convincing. Perhaps it is more important to recognize the parameters of the Old Testament's witness and register carefully where the scriptures are silent.

In many ways, the story of the Golden Calf (Ex. 32) offers the most extended canonical witness regarding the use of images. To be sure, the Decalogue is nowhere cited, and even to assume that it played an implicit role historically is to misconstrue the dynamic of the passage. However, the story has been assigned a crucial canonical function within the Sinai tradition.

The story is recounted with a strange tension. On the one hand, the making of the calf is categorically denounced by God as apostasy: 'The people have corrupted themselves' (v. 7). On the other hand, another perspective is reflected which raises a different set of issues. Aaron's response to the people's demand for a visible sign of their deity interjects a certain ambiguity into the story. He obviously had a different intention from the people when he proclaimed: 'Tomorrow will be a festival to Yahweh' (v. 5). Aaron thought to incorporate the calf within the worship of Yahweh, which he did not interpret as blatant apostasy. Rather, he sought to adjust the faith of Moses to a new historical situation by substituting a new 'creative' form of worship. He thus threw the mantle of religion over the programme of change and bent the faith to the demands of his culture. *Vox populi* and *vox dei* had become identified.

There are several other passages which function canonically to illuminate aspects of the prohibition against making an image by which to worship God. One thinks of the story of Micah's image (Judg. 17), of Jeroboam's setting up a rival cultic sanctuary (1 Kings 12), and of Nebuchadnezzar's call to worship the great image (Dan. 3). In spite of different theological emphases, the issue at stake turns on guarding the purity of God's self-revelation lest Israel confuse its own image with that of God's. In the case of this commandment, the narrative material within the Old Testament did not move in the direction of expounding the negative commandment in such a way as to bring out the positive dimensions of the imperative, but rather continued to probe the full implications of this threat to the divine nature.

(iii) 'You shall not take the name of the Lord, your God, in vain' (v. 7)

The initial problem of this commandment turns on its translation. An important ancient tradition renders the sentence: 'You shall not swear falsely' (cf. Targum, Syriac, NJPS). Moreover, there is good linguistic evidence to support this translation. The lifting up of God's name is identical to taking an oath in Lev. 19.12 and Deut. 6.13. For most references within the Old Testament the issue does turn on a misuse of God's name through false swearing.

Nevertheless, the commandment in its verbal sense seems to carry a wider semantic range of meaning than simply false swearing and thus provides a richer texture for continuing theological reflection. A central part of Israel's worship was the praising of the name of God, the redeemer of Israel (Ex. 34.5). In times of private and public need faithful Israelites called upon God's name for deliverance (II Sam. 22.4). The use of an oath was a more limited practice which grew out of the honouring of God's name. To invoke his name served to confirm the truthfulness of a human word by appealing to divine support. Often as a last court of appeal, when all other means of establishing truth failed, one rested one's case by evoking God's name. The seriousness of this move is made clear immediately in the third commandment of the Decalogue. In itself, the taking of an oath is not forbidden, but God's name is dishonoured when an oath is used to support anything which is untrue or without substance. The commandment is supported by a strong sanction, namely, God will punish the offender.

The heart of the commandment lies in preventing the dishonouring of God. As the source of truth he cannot be linked to falsehood or deception. Nor can God's freedom be infringed by human manipulation. The third commandment is radically theocentric in focus, and thus differs from the concerns of the eighth commandment, which prohibits the injuring of another human being by means of false witness.

The prohibition against a misuse of God's name is to be distinguished from a number of other abuses. Outright blasphemy or insults to God which are incurred by foreigners dishonour God and are punishable by death, but are not regarded as oaths

(Lev. 24.10–23; II Kings 18.19ff.). The distinction is significant in showing the real area of the commandment's concern. It is addressed to those within the covenant – in Christian terminology, to 'believers' – and the dishonouring of God is a much more subtle danger than outright profanation. In a real sense the whole issue of false prophecy turns on the abuse of God's name. Hananiah evokes the name of God, 'Thus saith the Lord', to confirm that his words have God's support. Jeremiah rejects them as lies and brands them as worthless, without substance (Jer. 28.15; cf. 23.16ff.). Interestingly, the Reformers used an extension of the principle of the third commandment in attacking the mediaeval church's claim to divine authority.

There are two other areas in which theological warrants have been sought from this commandment. In what sense does it dishonour God to abuse those things which belong to God as part of his creation? The issue is treated in an indirect fashion within the book of Job (cf. also Jer. 20.14ff). Job does not actually curse God in the dialogue, but ultimately he curses his birth and abandons hope in the wisdom of the creation (20.14). The book does not address the issue directly, but in the context of a canonical intertextuality a subtle relationship is certainly implied.

A second area to evoke theological reflection on the commandment emerges from the narrative corpus, especially in the stories concerning the last days of David. In at least four passages oaths are confirmed by evoking the name of God (1 Kings 1.17; 2.8, 23, 42). The theological issue arises because of the extreme ambiguity of each of the stories, and the basic incongruity of seeking God's confirmation of highly dubious human machinations. Thus, David has sworn by Yahweh that he will not put his enemy, Shimei, to death by the sword. At his death he commands his son, Solomon, to carry out the deed. Although strictly speaking the oath is not broken, David resorts to a form of deception to execute his vengeance. The biblical narrative does not draw any moral implications, but the reader is left to ponder whether God's name has not, in fact, been dishonoured by such human casuistry. The tension arises from a practice which implies great deference towards God's name, but actually represents just the opposite.

(iv) 'Remember the sabbath to keep it holy . . .' (v. 8)

The commandment in the canonical form of Exodus is expressed as a positive command. It is followed by a lengthy elaboration describing the manner by which the sabbath is to be observed, and concludes with a motivation clause which grounds the command in God's resting on the seventh day. As is well known, the Deuteronomic formulation links the command to the redemption from Egypt. Parallel passages offer numerous examples of much shorter formulations which are expressed in either a positive or a negative manner. There is little theological significance in debating which has priority because these are two sides of the same coin.

The command begins with an exhortation to 'hallow' the sabbath. To hallow is not merely to refrain from work, but presumes a positive action of making holy. It assumes the cessation of the normal activity of work in order to set aside this day for something special. Throughout the Old Testament the sabbath is described as being holy (Ex. 16.23; Lev. 23.3; Neh. 9.14; Isa. 58.13); it received this quality when God blessed it (Ex. 20.11). The sabbath is holy both to Israel (Ex. 16.28; Lev. 16.31) and to Yahweh (Ex. 16.23; Lev. 19.3; Deut. 5.14). Therefore, it serves to link Israel's holiness with that of God. The exact nature of its special quality is not spelled out further, but briefly characterized by the phrase: 'The sabbath belongs to Yahweh your God.'

Two traditions are offered in the Old Testament as warrants for observing the sabbath as a day of rest. In Exodus the motivation is grounded on the creative act of God who in six days made the heavens and earth and rested on the seventh. Israel testifies to God's creation of the world by setting apart this day as special. In Deuteronomy the commandment is grounded in God's redemption of Israel from Egypt. The imperative is that 'all Israel' participate in the sabbath. This can only be realized when the slaves also share in its observance. Israel's memory functions to assure the proper celebration of the sabbath by recalling the redemption from Egypt.

Within the context of the canon, the two motivations interpret each other. 'God's creative activity is liberating, and God's activity as liberator is creative. There cannot be one without the other' (Siker, 16). Once again creation and salvation are two aspects of the one theological reality.

Exodus 31 extends the significance of the sabbath even further. It is the sign of the covenant that Israel has been set aside as special (vv. 13, 16–17). However, the sabbath is only a sign as long as Israel responds in faith by keeping it holy. Although the sabbath was originally intended to be a positive sign of Israel's special relation to God, it also proved to be a negative sign of Israel's failure to regard God's commands (Ezek. 20.12). Thus the sabbath became a burden and the blessing was turned to a curse (Ezek. 20.26). To profane the sabbath can only evoke God's just wrath (Neh. 13.17f.). The Old Testament offers only limited answers to the detailed question of what keeping the sabbath entails. In later rabbinic interpretation much attention was given to filling in the details. Leviticus 23.32 specified its observance extended 'from evening to evening', but what exactly were the termini? The sabbath was to be observed 'in all your dwellings' (Lev. 23. 3), and 'for all generations' (Ex. 31.16), but were there situations in which its observance was overruled?

Another difficulty in interpreting this commandment lies in the lack of narrative material which would offer some sort of commentary. Siker makes the interesting point that the command is so pervasive that even the sabbath materials which occur within the context of narratives are presented as commands (Siker, 17; cf. Ex. 16.23–29; 34.31; 35.1–3; Lev. 16.30–31, etc.). Even the narrative in Num. 15 which seems at first so straightforward presents a problem of interpretation. No moral explanation is offered, and the command is assumed. Yet the comment in v. 34 is strange: 'They put him in custody because it had not been made plain what should be done to him.' How is this uncertainty to be understood?

Christians reading the Old Testament moved in a very different direction from the Jewish halachic tradition. The major theological issue lay in determining how far the commandment could be extended beyond the original imperative to observe one particular day in the week as holy. Luther in particular developed his interpretation of the sabbath commandment in the light of the New Testament. Accordingly, the Christian is not bound to a particular day, but is obliged to hold one day sacred in order to be able to hear the preaching of the Word of God.

In contrast, Calvin is much more concerned to find his interpretative key within the Old Testament itself. He argues with considerable cogency that the sabbath was intended to represent for Israel spiritual as well as physical rest, a time in which one could reflect on God's work. Thus the sabbath contained a promise because it was a sign of the covenant that God was at work perfecting, that is, making holy his people. Calvin raises the canonical question within the Old Testament when he seeks to determine to what extent the commandment points beyond the external regulation. He finds two functions operative in the ancient sabbath: (*a*) it served as a stated period for preaching and prayer; (*b*) it gave rest to servants and workmen. He then concludes: 'Who can deny that these two things apply as much to us as to Jews?'

In this subsequent treatment Calvin explores the impact of the New Testament on the Christian observance of Sunday, but his basic study of commandment within the context of the Old Testament is an impressive example of canonical exegesis as he moves from the biblical witness to its theological substance.

(v) *'Honour your father and mother that your days may be long in the land . . .' (v. 12)*

This commandment has often been regarded as providing a bridge between the obligations towards God and towards one's neighbour symbolized by the two tablets. It is one of the few commandments within the Decalogue which has a positive formulation, and is followed by a promise (Eph. 6.2). Most of the parallels in content to this commandment within the Pentateuch are expressed negatively in prohibiting the cursing of one's parents (Ex.21. 15, 17; Lev. 20.9). The seriousness with which a rebellious son was regarded is made clear by the sanctions prescribed in Deut. 21.18ff. Usually it is thought that the concrete setting underlying the commandment was the practice of driving one's parents from the home when they were unable further to work, because of either age or sickness. The commandment requires not only the obeying of one's parents, but the honouring of them, which implies an affection and respect usually reserved for God.

The Reformers extended the commandment to find a warrant for the position that 'degrees of pre-eminence established by God are inviolable' (Calvin). Luther found a major support on which to base the divine authority of the magistrate and the state. Just as one honoured even bad parents because they were given by God, so obedience to the civil governors did not rest on their performance but on divine sanction.

Most modern theologians are agreed that the Reformers' use of the fifth commandment raises serious questions. Especially in the light of four hundred years of political theory, the difficulties have been further exacerbated. The issue at stake is whether the Reformers sought too quickly to justify inherited social structures and ended by defending the political *status quo* as divine in origin. The modern biblical theologian is constrained to ask whether indeed this traditional interpretation has done justice to the entire canonical witness. In my judgment, the Old Testament possesses a dynamic which is far more multi-faceted than traditionally recognized.

Certainly the commandment assigned an authoritative role to the parents, and by joining parental obedience to the promise of long life in the land portrayed parental authority as integral to a divine order of blessing. This same theme is further developed by the wisdom writers of the Old Testament, who continue to interpret honour of parents as part of the wisdom built into the structure of life (Prov. 1.8; 15.5; 19.26).

Nevertheless, the nuances involved in the commandment begin to emerge when one looks at a variety of Old Testament narratives relating to children and parents. Ruth is commended by the narrator for her loyalty to Naomi not only by her immediate reward, but also by the explicit mention of her illustrious posterity (4.17). Likewise, Esther's obedience of Mordecai for the sake of the nation is praised. However, a more complex situation is portrayed by Jonathan's relation to his father Saul. On the one hand, Jonathan emerges as an absolutely loyal son, who suffers abuse from his father's hand, and yet who dies at his side in a hopeless cause. On the other hand, the stories begin to sketch the limits of parental authority. Saul not only misuses his divine authority (I Sam. 20.30ff.), but also seeks to set Jonathan against God's purpose for David and is rightly rebuffed by his son.

Several Old Testament stories reverse the direction of the issue raised by the child's required obedience, and focus on the failure of the parent properly to exercise divine authority. Lot's willingness to sacrifice the honour of his two daughters to satisfy the fury of the men of Sodom is not explicitly condemned by the narrator, but adds to the larger portrayal of his compromise and weakness. Then again, Eli is specifically condemned for his failure to discipline his wicked sons which the narrator implicitly contrasts with the obedience of Samuel to divinely appointed authorities

(I Sam. 2.27ff.). Finally, a major motif in the narrative cycle concerned with Absalom's revolt lies in an indirect criticism of David, who failed to discipline his favourite son when he acted in a completely lawless manner (II Sam. 14.1ff.). As a result, a chain of events was set in motion which brought disaster for David, Absalom and the nation. In the end, David's unrestrained love for Absalom (II Sam 18.33) was used by the narrator in the context of the revolt to depict the weakness rather than the strength of the king.

It is of interest to see how the Jewish tradition interpreted the commandment regarding the disobedient son (cf. Sanhedrin). The Mishnah naturally affirmed the eternal value of the Law, but then hedged it with such restrictions by which to guard the rights of the disobedient son that it is unlikely that the Old Testament sanction of death was ever actually carried out.

In sum, the fifth commandment lends the strongest support for the divinely appointed authority of the parent within the family to provide a training in faith. The commandment, however, offers no warrant for submission to the authority of ruling classes or estates in general, but is directed solely towards the goal of the exercise of God's rule. To find support for the *status quo* or the divine rule of kings is to misconstrue the larger witness of the Old Testament.

(vi) *'You shall not kill' (v.13)*

This commandment appears to pose insurmountable problems for a theology of the Old Testament. Is not the Old Testament itself filled with violence? Beyond this, the Canaanites were put to the sword according to divine instruction (Deut. 13.15), and the ban was instituted as part of Israel's sacred war (Josh. 6.1ff.). Especially offensive to many modern Christians is the persistent warlike description of God (Deut. 32.41–43; Isa. 63. 1–6).

In addition, there is a new sensitivity in the modern world to the issues of violence, which has resulted in a dissatisfaction with much traditional theological reflection on the matter. Recall Luther's interpretation in the *Larger Catechism*: 'We should fear and love God so that we do no harm but rather help and support our neighbour in all of life's trials.' In spite of this powerful formulation of love of neighbour, Luther does not include prohibition against the use of power to kill either by God or the state. Many modern Christians would question whether Luther had too easily imposed limitations on the commandment. Is it so obvious that the commandment does not restrict the state and perhaps even God as well?

Of course, there were other hermeneutical options for resolving the theological issue which have been represented in the Christian tradition in various forms. Some argued that the Old Testament reflected a lower ethical level in principle which had been replaced by Christ's 'law of love'. When in the nineteenth century this ancient Christian bias was joined to a history-of-religions approach, the Old Testament became identified with the early primitive stages of mankind's development toward moral maturity, and thus removed from serious theological discussion. The initial question is whether attention to the sixth commandment in the light of its canonical function can point in a new direction for theological reflection.

The place to begin the discussion is with the literary form of the commandment. It is the first in a series of short, two-word prohibitions which are paralleled elsewhere in the Old Testament with longer descriptions. Passages such as Ex. 21.12; Lev. 24.17; and Deut. 27.24 include other elements such as the condition of the violence or the object of the killing. The shortened form has the effect of broadening the scope of the injunction by removing all restrictions. Lying behind the prohibition is the ancient sanctity of life: 'Whoever sheds the blood of man, by man shall his blood be shed' (Gen. 9.6).

An initial difficulty of the commandment lies in understanding the precise meaning of the verb 'to kill' (*rāṣāḥ*). It has long been recognized that a special type of killing is intended. Often the verb has been translated 'You shall not murder' (NJPS), which appears to reconcile in part the Decalogue's prohibition of killing with the frequent taking of life in the Old Testament. However, the basic distinction between murder and killing, namely, the element of intentionality, cannot be sustained for the Hebrew verb. Rather, the verb denotes a form of illegal killing which threatens the life of the community. The commandment seeks to protect the Israelite within the covenant from illegal violence (cf. Stamm).

Within recent years some further refinement of this interpretation has been put forward which observed that the verb often appears in close connection with blood vengeance. In Israel's early tradition the violent shedding of blood was viewed as an objective act regardless of intention, which called for revenge. Moreover, in the later period the verb became linked with intentional killing which was committed out of enmity, deceit and hatred. In Num. 25 motivation had become a decisive factor and the term was almost equated with murder. Also in the prophets and wisdom literature the verb invariably carries the connotation of intentional and evil violence (Isa. 1.21; Hos. 6.9; Prov. 22.13).

In sum, the verb *rāṣāḥ* at first had an objective meaning describing a type of illegal slaying which called forth blood vengeance. Increasingly the verb came to designate those acts of violence against persons which arose from personal feelings of hatred and malice. The commandment forbids such acts of violence and rejects the right of anyone to take the law into one's own hands out of a feeling of personal injury.

In my opinion, there are few who would question the exegetical significance of a close philological, historical and literary analysis of the commandment. However, the theological task has only begun. It is essential to supplement the initial study of Ex. 20 with passages from the rest of the Old Testament in order to gain an impression of the nuances which the commandment acquired within the larger canonical tradition. The need to take seriously the parallel narrative material is especially acute. Could it be that the canon has established a different agenda by retaining stories which shed a different light on the problem of violence?

(*a*) Exodus 2.11–15 offers a classic example of violence done as a means of obtaining social justice. Moses acts in order to right an injustice, not for his own sake, but for another's. He is motivated to kill out of love for his people, an act which even jeopardizes his own life. Nowhere does the biblical text moralize on the story, or cite the prohibition of the Decalogue against killing. The act is neither explicitly praised nor condemned, but the reader is left to ponder its anomalies.

The ambiguity of the situation is such that the act does not carry only one meaning. Moses' intervention is open to misunderstanding. He supposes that his intentions were obvious, but the Hebrew who was abusing his fellow attributed a totally different motivation, and saw it as a threat. He rebuffed Moses' implied claim of authority, and sought to destroy him by imputing an interpretation which impugned his honesty. The reaction to Moses raises the question whether an act of true justice can ever be done in this way and in these circumstances.

In sum, this biblical story does not provide one clear answer to the complex question of whether violence, even killing, may function for the sake of justice. However, it does raise a whole set of moral questions which are inherent in such action. By uncovering the ambiguities inherent in violence, the Old Testament scriptures force the reader to confront rather than evade the moral issue. In this way, the story in Exodus provides an indirect commentary on the sixth commandment and opens up a fresh dimension of the Law.

(b) The story of David's plot to murder Uriah, the husband of Bathsheba (II Sam. 11), also relates to the commandment. Significantly the narrative touches on the tangle of social, psychological, and political factors which influence all human action. David did not intend to become a murderer. He would gladly have covered over his incontinent affair with Bathsheba. The biblical writer portrays the growth of the web which encircled David. He had first injured Uriah by stealing his wife. Then he abused the power of his divinely appointed office and ruthlessly destroyed his rival. The story brilliantly portrays the murder not simply as one act of violence, but as a nexus of interwoven events, all serving to injure his fellow: lust, deceit, disloyalty and oppression. The irony of the whole event is that David never really hated Uriah. There was no personal anger involved, but the abuse of power by the strong against the weak. The prophet Nathan proclaims David's murder of Uriah to be a blatant offence against God himself. 'You shall not kill.'

Space is too limited to pursue all the significant narratives which continue to nuance the perspectives on the commandment (cf. Judg. 9; 1 Kings 21, etc.). There is, however, one obvious cluster of stories which emerges as a major theological obstacle. The book of Joshua recounts God's command to possess the land of Canaan and to destroy its inhabitants. How can this history of conquest ever be reconciled with the Old Testament's critical stance toward violence?

Two classic modern theological approaches have been frequently used to resolve the ethical problem. One position argues that if such killing is viewed today as wrong, it must have been just as wrong then as now. The difficulty with this approach to theology is that such a non-historical way of thinking is foreign to the Bible, which does not work with abstract, timeless ethical principles. In contrast, the Old Testament recounts the story of God's redemptive history with a sinful, hard-necked people which shares fully the culture of its environment. A dialogue between these approaches to the problem proves unfruitful because the level of discourse is too divergent to communicate meaningfully.

The second approach to the ethical problem of the conquest suggests that Israel simply misunderstood God, and that this portion of the Old Testament needs correction in the light of the rest of the canon, especially the prophets and the New Testament. This position is far more congenial to a canonical reading of the Old Testament as scripture and is certainly to be taken seriously. A major problem, however, is that the canonical process did not understand the issue in this manner. Never once is it suggested that Israel misunderstood God's intention regarding the conquest. Rather, the theological witness of the book of Joshua was rendered in a different fashion. The canonical editors construed the material in the period which extended from the death of Moses to the death of Joshua in such a way as to illustrate a people of God who were obedient to the law of Moses. When Israel obeyed, God fought for Israel and none could withstand. Conversely, the book of Judges illustrated the loss of the blessing when disobedient Israel lost its heritage through its unfaithfulness to the covenant.

The effect of the canonical shaping of the conquest material is that the book of Joshua has been assigned a specific, but time-bound, role in God's economy. The conquest continued to be acknowledged throughout the Old Testament as an integral part of the divine purpose for Israel, but it was never to be repeated. It was theologically rendered inoperative by being consigned wholly to the past. Much like the lost garden of Eden, it functioned canonically as a picture of a forfeited heritage.

When Israel's prophets took up the theme of Israel's conquest, they reversed the imagery of holy war. They portrayed God's fighting against his people because of their disobedience and inner lawlessness (Isa. 10.5.ff.; 5.26ff.; Jer. 5.15ff.). The prophets called for a return to social justice in order to regain the blessings of God, but never exhorted Israel to wage a future holy war. Rather, they envisioned the future according to God's purpose as one of universal peace which God would usher in (Isa. 2.1ff.; 11.1ff.).

The additional witness of the Chronicler and sages confirms this picture. The moving account of the treatment of defeated captives (II Chron. 28.8ff.) illustrated God's fierce displeasure with the folly of war and its cruelty. The narrator warns of God's anger and commends the reversal of roles with the merciful clothing and feeding of the prisoners. Similarly, the instruction of the sages cautions against the sheer madness in the use of violence which always results in the way of death for all involved (Prov. 1.11ff.).

To summarize, the initial commandment prohibited all forms of wanton killing in Israel in order to protect the sanctity of human life which was fundamental to the covenant. The Old Testament narratives provide an extensive commentary on the imperative by illustrating a variety of subtle temptations of self-interest and abuse of power which are inherent in the prohibition. The prophetic hope envisions a world of peace in realizing God's purpose for the world, which is an eschatological goal achieved only by God. Nevertheless, the Old Testament continues to recognize evil as an active and powerful force. The symbol of killing is still reserved for God who 'both kills and brings to life' (I Sam.2.6).

(vii) 'You shall not commit adultery' (v. 14)

The Hebrew verb in this commandment is unequivocal in denoting adultery. The commandment directs its prohibition against any practice which threatens the sanctity of marriage within Israel. Although fornication is condemned throughout the Old Testament as unchastity, it is clearly distinguished from adultery. The holiness of God's people is integrally tied to the sanctity of the institution of marriage, which was assumed by the Old Testament to be both divinely ordained and normative. The issue of celibacy, especially for religious reasons, was never raised in the Old Testament, much less sanctioned. Homosexuality was universally condemned and dismissed as abhorrent (Lev. 18.22).

There are signs in the Old Testament that Israel once accepted a double standard regarding marriage, much like her neighbours. According to the Hebrew linguistic idiom, the husband can only commit adultery against a marriage other than his own, while a woman acts only against her own marriage (Stamm, 100). Again, the seduction of a virgin is compensated for by a money equivalent (Ex. 22.16; Deut.22. 28ff.). Finally, the language of Proverbs implies that sexual temptation derives largely from the side of the woman.

Yet I would argue that close attention must be paid to the whole range of biblical texts on the subject, especially in the context of theological reflection. Material which has now been subordinated into the background or rendered inoperative cannot be reactivated and given an independent life apart from its canonical context. Indeed, the Old Testament is filled with terrifying examples of abuses against women (Gen. 38; Judg. 19; II Sam. 13, etc.). Yet when Phyllis Trible interprets these stories apart from their present canonical intent, she implies that the Bible shares the same universal male prejudice against women, whose true theological significance she seeks to recover as Israel's 'suffering servant' (*Texts of Terror*).

Although the Old Testament does contain many examples of cruelty to women, it has consistently construed these stories as examples of disobedience and sin. The account of the murder of the concubine in Judg. 19 illustrates for the biblical author the utter lawlessness in which Israel lived without a king. The action was in no way condoned, but clearly was judged as a shameful thing. Increasingly within Israel the commandment against adultery was expanded to include all forms of sexual unchastity as being an offence to the holiness of God.

Once again in the narrative tradition one gains a highly nuanced interpretation of the Decalogue's prohibition of adultery. Joseph as a vulnerable slave is tempted to unchastity by Potiphar's wife, but the chief point of the story lies in Joseph's reasons for resisting: 'How then can I do this great wickedness, and sin against God?' (Gen. 39.9). Joseph is not a prude, but a person who rejects a temptation which would show his disloyalty to his master and also be an offence against God.

The story of David's adultery with Bathsheba (II Sam. 11) does not focus on the details of the seduction. The extent to which Bathsheba played an active role is passed over without comment. Rather, the author associates the sin of stealing a man's wife with the ensuing murder of her husband. The offence to God derives from both evils, which should have evoked the punishment by death in Israel had not an exception been made because of David's repentance.

Finally, the rape of Tamar by Amnon (II Sam. 13.1ff.) is presented as a horrifying example of human depravity, and the author exposes the brutality of the act of her subsequent rejection with such power as to expose the full extent of the evil. The helplessness of Tamar to avenge the blatant wrong is pictured with chilling realism. For the biblical author there can be no doubt whatever that it was a shameful act.

The clearest prophetic support for the sanctity of marriage in

Israel is offered by Malachi, who exposes the evil practice of divorce. The prophet interprets marriage as an inviolable covenant between a man and his wife to which God has served as witness. Again the emphasis falls on the divine imperative for a holy people, which is jeopardized by the breaking of the marriage vow (Mal. 2.15).

(viii) *'You shall not steal' (v.15)*

(x) *'You shall not covet your neighbour's house . . . wife . . . or anything that is your neighbour's' (v. 17)*

Scholars differ over how precisely to distinguish between the concerns of the eighth and the tenth commandments. According to one theory, the former originally prohibited the theft of a person, the latter that of property. However, whether or not this interpretation has correctly described the historical development of the tradition, the distinction lies on an earlier, pre-literary level. The final form of the biblical text construes the distinction in a different manner. The eighth commandment, which is now without an object, includes all acts of misappropriation, whereas the tenth commandment functions to address the human impulses which lie behind wrong seizure. Especially in the Deuteronomic parallel (Deut. 5.21), the concern is evident to actualize the command by a form of internalization. Thus, both commandments have expanded the scope of the original traditions, albeit along different interpretative paths.

There is general agreement that these commandments are directed against all attempts to defraud one's neighbour. All forms of violence, deception and dishonesty which would take advantage of another are condemned. The term 'to covet' implies an inner impulse which leads to the act of misappropriation. The sage characterizes a false scale as an abomination to Yahweh (Prov. 11.1). Again, the prophet Amos is sensitive to the indirect forces at work in oppression when he attacks the wealthy wives of Samaria who exert pressure on their husbands to squeeze the poor (Amos 4.1–3).

In the history of exegesis these commandments have been used as support for a view that private property was inviolable and under God's protection. Calvin even argues that 'what every man possesses has not come by mere chance but by the distribution of God and that to deprive another of his possession is to set aside God's dispensation' (*Institutes*, II, VIII, 45). When this interpretation was secularized and brought into the context of the modern industrial state, the commandments were used by the economic establishment in a way almost directly opposed to their original biblical intent.

Moreover, it is obvious that wholly new concepts of property, private ownership, social classes and state control have emerged which are totally unknown to the world of the Old Testament. Recognition of these factors implies that the biblical commandments must be applied with mature theological reflection and not biblicistically in order to defend entrenched positions on the left or the right. The modern danger of politicizing the commandments in order to bring them in line with a capitalistic or socialist ideology is acute. The biblical commandments strove to protect the social texture of the people of God so that Israel would reflect a way of life commensurate with God's righteous rule. This divine intention can never be identified with any one economic system, yet conversely it continues to strive for concrete realization within all the time-conditioned form of human society. These commandments are primarily formulated to insure the good of one's neighbour within a corporate life. The threat of human exploitation through indirect control of resources, invisible corporations and national self-interest increase both the difficulty and theological relevance of the divine admonitions.

(ix) 'You shall not bear false witness against your neighbour' (v.16).

The original legal background of this commandment is evident. It is directed against one person testifying falsely before a court of elders to the injury of the defendant. Within the setting of the Decalogue the immediate concern is not with truth and lying *per se*, but with lying which destroys a neighbour. The classic example of the false witness within the Old Testament is the story of Naboth's vineyard when Jezebel hired witnesses to lie in order to obtain his death (I Kings 21.1ff.). The fury of Elijah the prophet at the injustice is fully in line with the commandment.

The concern for justice in the courts pervades all sections of the Old Testament. The laws of the Pentateuch continually make mention of this evil (Ex. 23.1, 6–8; Lev. 19.11, 16; Deut. 19.15ff.). Israel's legal tradition sought to check the abuse with heavy sanctions, and with the requirement of multiple witnesses. Similarly, among the prophets a repeated accusation was the bending of justice and the inability of the poor and weak to be vindicated (Amos. 2.7; 5.15; Micah 3.11). Again, Proverbs is filled with admonition against the perversion of justice. Of particular interest is the manner in which the prohibition has been extended in a variety of areas to include slander and tale-bearing (11.9, 11–13). Finally, in the Psalter we have a powerful witness to the suffering and misery with which false witnesses afflict the innocent. Because of his inability to find justice in any human court, the psalmist flees to God for vindication from persistent slander and malice (12.2; 27.2; 64.8).

Because the commandment against false witness had already been extended to cover verbal attacks on a person's honour and reputation, it was natural for the later interpretation to continue in this theological direction. Luther is particularly powerful in his application to one's honour and good name as an indispensable requirement for human dignity. His simple formulation, 'Every report that cannot be adequately proved is false witness', well reflects the Bible's concern for the well-being of the whole person in society.

Bibliography

J. **Calvin**, *The Institutes of the Christian Religion*, ET ed. J. T. McNeill, Philadelphia and London 1959, I, 367–423; B. S. **Childs,** *Exodus*, London and Philadelphia 1979, 385–439; F. **Crüsemann**, *Bewahrung der Freiheit: Das Thema des Dekalogs in sozialgeschichtlicher Perspektive*, Munich 1983; H. **Gese**, 'Der Dekalog als Ganzheit betrachtet', *ZTK* 64, 1967, 121–38; W. **Harrelson**, *The Ten Commandments and Human Rights*, Philadelphia 1980; H.-J. Kraus, 'Die Gebote Gottes', *Systematische Theologie im Kontext biblischer Geschichte*, Neukirchen-Vluyn 1983, 159–83; M. **Luther**, *The Larger Catechism*, ET Philadelphia 1959; E. **Nielsen**, *The Ten Commandments in New Perspective*, ET, SBT II. 7, 1968; H. **Schlüngel-Straumann**, *Der Dekalog – Gottes Gebote*, SBS 67, 1973; J. **Siker**, 'The Theology of the Sabbath in the Old Testament. A Canonical Approach', *StBib* 11, 1981, 5–20; J. J. **Stamm** and M. E. **Andrew**, *The Ten Commandments in Recent Research*, STB II. 2, 1967; P. **Trible**, *Texts of Terror*, Philadelphia 1984; E. E. **Urbach**, *The Sages*, ET Jerusalem 1975, I, 315–79; W. **Zimmerli**, *The Law and the Prophets*, ET Oxford 1965; 'Das Zweite Gebot', *Gottes Offenbarung*, TB 19, 1969, 234–48; *Old Testament Theology in Outline*, ET Atlanta 1978, 109–40.

8

THE ROLE OF THE RITUAL AND PURITY LAWS

(i) *The scope of the subject*

It was a typical attitude of nineteenth-century Protestant biblical study to concentrate the theological discussion of the Old Testament law on an interpretation of the Decalogue, and either to avoid or to deprecate the ritual laws. Certainly Zimmerli has made a decisive point when he protests against such an approach: 'The faith (of the Old Testament) does not live in a state of free spirituality, but in a life that has specific liturgical forms' (*Outlines*, 125).

The subject of this chapter belongs in one sense with the treatment of the cultus in Chapter 14. Yet it seems important to handle the area of purity laws in close proximity to the Decalogue lest a false impression be given. Then again, it is consonant with the canonical approach to Old Testament theology not to represent the cultic material as if it were a closed system, but to describe various aspects in such a way as to remain open to continuing theological reflection on the part of the reader. It is not a serious problem if some of the same material in this chapter is handled later on from a different perspective. Here the focus will be on considering the purity laws along with the Decalogue as an expression of the will of God. The scope of the Old Testament literature encompasses both early and late legal material (Ex. 23.18f.; 34.11–28; Lev. 11; 17–26; Num. 12, 19, 25; Deut. 12ff.) as well as cultic references in the early and late histories, prophets and psalms.

(ii) *Problems of method*

The extreme difficulty of understanding the theological significance of the ritual and purity laws has called forth several typical approaches in the history of interpretation.

(*a*) Very early Christian interpreters sought to discover a moral dimension to these laws by assuming that there was a hidden symbolic foundation. Various forms of this model appeared which continued to find support well into the nineteenth century. For example, one commentator saw in the cud-chewing animals a symbol of meditation on the Word of God and in the cloven-hoof beasts a symbol of a sure and firm step (Keil, II, 122). Less artificial was the interpretation of Kurtz who reduced the symbolism to one element of the *Heilsgeschichte* by having the food laws remind Israel of her separate status (26).

(*b*) Secondly, several rational, historical explanations were offered which were defended by both Jews and Christians. For example, the dietary laws were viewed as a form of primitive hygienic rules. Or the conjecture was made that the prohibition of certain animals (e.g. Ex. 23.19) arose from opposition to Canaanite practice, a view which has recently received some archaeological support.

(*c*) Thirdly, Maimonides' rejection of both the symbolic and rational interpretations and his description of the biblical laws as arbitrary, divine decrees (*Code*, Book 10, cited by Neusner, 7) has been defended by many moderns, often out of sheer frustration.

(*d*) Fourthly, certain modern social anthropologists, who have refined the older approach of W. Robertson Smith, have sought to explain the purity laws within a broad context of comparative religion by viewing them as a holistic symbol system by which to bring into order societal experience by means of the language of the clean and unclean. Neusner's dialogue with Mary Douglas's book *Purity and Danger* is a good example of how seriously the new analysis is being received (Neusner, *Purity*, 28ff., 137ff.).

(*e*) Finally, the most thorough recent attempt to offer a sophisticated theological interpretation of the Old Testament diet laws from a Jewish perspective is Milgrom's essay ('The Biblical Diet Laws'). He argues that *kashrut* is an ethical system devised for the purpose of preventing man from being brutalized by the killing of animals. Moreover, the dietary laws serve to inculcate the root principle of reverence for life through restricted access to animal life, and are the means by which Israel is lead into a high life of morality as 'rungs on the ladder of holiness'.

At this point, rather than to offer a detailed response to these various proposals, my intention is to set forth my own canonical reading which both accepts and rejects features of these previous formulations.

(iii) *Towards a canonical interpretation*

In my judgment, certain broad canonical guidelines can be discerned at the outset.

(*a*) There never was a tension in the Old Testament formulation of the will of God between the so-called ritual and ethical aspects of the divine imperative, that is to say, between the form and the spirit. Attempts to contrast an alleged 'ritual' decalogue (Ex. 34) with an 'ethical' decalogue (Ex. 20) have been unconvincing. Similarly, to set up the priestly forms of the Law in opposition to the prophetic introduces a distinction not found in the canon. Even the more subtle form of denigrating the ritual dimension is still present in Eichrodt when he sees a slow progression away from the objective, priestly concepts to an internalized spiritual understanding. Yet there is no canonical warrant for such a dichotomy.

(*b*) The ritual imperatives of the Old Testament are not only grounded in the Sinai covenant by the biblical writers, but from a modern critical perspective are thoroughly time-conditioned, and reflect the historical and social milieu out of which they arose. The influence of Canaanite form on the agricultural cycle of early Israel is striking. Then again, the similarity to the Ancient Near Eastern vocabulary of the purity laws is frequently apparent. Because there was no attempt within the canonical process to remove these signs of historical particularity, any modern theological reflection is deficient which feels constrained to dehistoricize the setting in the search for eternal ethical principles apart from Israel's concrete historical existence.

(*c*) Not only are the ritual and purity laws treated in the Pentateuchal sections of the Old Testament, but extended interpretations are offered within the other parts of the canon which are not merely to be harmonized or arranged in a developmental sequence, but rather used for theological reflection from the perspective of the whole corpus of scripture.

One of the striking features of the ritual and purity laws, which they share with the Decalogue, is that the underlying motivation for a particular law is seldom offered. Rather, the emphasis falls heavily upon the purpose toward which the law points. Israel, as a covenant people, is separated unto God and her life is to reflect the nature of God which is above all holiness (Lev. 19.1ff.). Proper distinctions are described as 'pleasing to God' and 'acceptable'. Not eating flesh with blood and not practising witchcraft are treated on the same level (Lev. 19.26). Even when occasionally a motivation for a ritual stipulation is offered, as in the well-known instance of Lev. 17.11ff. – 'the life of the flesh is (in) the blood' – the motivation turns out further to clarify its function. The blood makes atonement by reason of the life, but this explanation is far removed from any generalized principle of reverence for life. In a real sense, the social-anthropological view which sees the purity laws as part of a total symbol system comes closer to its canonical function than attempts to provide an explicit ethical motivation for laws which is in excess of the text itself. This observation does not rule out the presence of ethical and rational factors at work in Israel, but these function in the ritual texts of the Old Testament largely on the level of the prehistory.

The one dominant feature is that the laws are presented as being the will of God for Israel, and reflect his divine nature. However, even these formulations tend to be conventional, emphasizing God's holiness, separateness, and purity (Lev. 19.1ff.; Deut. 14.1ff.). The stress again falls on the effect of doing God's will, which is to engender life (Lev. 18.5). To disregard his commands is to incur divine wrath and human destruction. When attacks do come on the cultic laws, they consist in revealing the discrepancy between Israel's life and practice and that of God's, which is a similar criticism of Israel's rejection of the laws of the Decalogue (Hos. 4.1–3).

At the heart of the biblical laws lies a profound sense of human sinfulness as a powerful destructive force which calls forth forms of institutional protection in an effort to check its power. Although the concept of sin in the Old Testament at times seems almost mechanical, when viewed as a whole, sin remains basically an offence against the God of the covenant. Nevertheless, the contrast between Israel and its pagan neighbours in this regard is not an absolute one, and the threat of a magical practice, of not really grasping the goal of the purity laws, continues to persist throughout all of Israel's history. To suggest with Kaufmann that Israel at Sinai broke the back of paganism is, at best, only a half-truth.

As one would expect, Deuteronomy has construed the ritual laws in its own way. Many features are in the closest continuity with the earlier laws. There is no motivation given for the elaborate distinction between clean and unclean animals other than the convention of a holy people (Deut. 14.1ff.). Similarly, the prohibition regarding mixed ploughing and the weaving of mingled stuff of woollen and linen is merely stated. These laws are simply 'good and right in the sight of God' (12.28) and no one is to add or take away from them (12.32).

The link between cultic and social laws which was already present in the earliest legal level (Ex. 20.21–23.22) has been further expanded. Much attention is paid by the Deuteronomic law to the care for the Levite, sojourner, fatherless and widow in the context of cultic stipulation (Deut. 14.29). Because the ritual stipulations were seen as part of covenant law, the Deuteronomic writer could move freely between laws directly affecting God and those chiefly social in nature as portions of the whole (27.9–27).

However, the paraenetic form of the Deuteronomic laws has shifted the emphasis in a fresh direction, especially when compared with the Book of the Covenant or the laws of Leviticus. The writer continues to exhort his hearers to observe the laws, and the purpose of obedience is often expressed in terms of the resultant blessing. A profile is sketched of life filled with joy in the company of a community of faith which eats in the presence of God. Thus, the emphasis in 12.15 of eating 'as much as you desire' (12.15), 'whenever the urge strikes', does not fall on a note of 'reverence for life', which is the grounds advanced by modern vegetarians. The Old Testament, and especially Deuteronomy, shares no element of asceticism whatever, but rather of enjoying the good creation of God in the blessings of the land. There is no hint as yet in Deuteronomy that an abuse of the cult could jeopardize God's full creative activity, but the positive side of a theology of creation is developed beyond that of the other legal corpora.

The subject of ritual and purity laws also appears in several of the Old Testament narratives, although usually in the background of a story which is making another point. In Num. 12.1ff. Miriam is rendered impure with leprosy because of her attack on Moses, and she is excluded from the camp seven days until declared clean.

Jonathan breaks a food prohibition temporarily established by Saul through an oath (I Sam. 14.24), and his guilt is discovered by the use of the Thummim. However, the story serves to illustrate not Saul's piety, but his folly in taking a foolish oath which almost cost him a victory over the Philistines. Finally, there is a certain irony in the narrator's mention of Bathsheba's 'purifying herself from her uncleanness' (II Sam. 11.4) as an introduction to describing a whole new dimension of moral and political evil which the ensuing incident evoked.

In sum, the narratives do not address directly the subject, but indirectly focus attention on other areas of Israel's moral life and thus force the reader of the whole canon to set the cultic and legal stipulations within a larger interpretative context.

A far more explicit theological critique of the purity laws is found in the Psalter and in the prophets. In the nineteenth century the significance of this material was somewhat blunted by the dominant historical interests of the interpreters who often sought to show that cultic law was post-exilic in origin without deep roots in the tradition. Not only has the historical evidence been lacking to sustain an exclusively late dating, but the theological point appears to lie elsewhere. Psalm 50 sets the divine judgment against cultic abuse in the context of God's sovereignty as creator. At the outset the legitimacy of the cult at Sinai is affirmed (v. 5). What is being contrasted is not cultic and non-cultic activity, but all human response in the light of God, the creator and redeemer of Israel:

> Our God comes, he does not keep silence,
> before him is a devouring fire,
> round about him a mighty tempest (v. 3).

The psalmist portrays God in absolute freedom and power, and as not dependent on Israel's sacrifices:

> If I were hungry, I would not tell you;
> for the world and all that is in it is mine (v. 12).

Israel is at fault because of its false understanding of the nature of God: 'Mark this . . . you who forget God' (v. 22), which allows social oppression of members of the covenant to coexist with the maintenance of correct cultic stipulations (vv. 18ff.). Moreover, the point must be strongly made that the positive formulation of a right response to God is made in terms which transcend cultic terminology:

> He who brings thanksgiving as his sacrifice honours me;
> to him who orders his way aright,
> I will show the salvation of God (v.23).

Even more extensive is the canonical guide for interpretation which appears in the massive prophetic criticism of Israel's cult. Again the grounds for the prophetic message emerge as a proclamation of the absolute sovereignty of God and the subordination of all human institutions to the exercise of God's justice. Thus Isaiah (1.10ff.) condemns an excessive cultic activity which combines iniquity and solemn assemblies and calls for Israel to seek justice and to correct oppression (cf. Isa. 58.6ff.). Or again, Amos testifies that God hates feasts and sacrifices which do not effect the increase of justice (5.21ff.; Micah 6.6ff.).

The chief theological point to be made is that the canon has contained within itself a major critique, not just of cultic religion, but of religion in general. The attack is grounded in a vision of God which renders totally inoperative all human response seeking to merit God's favour. The inability to respond to the will of a righteous and holy God serves to relativize all the institutions of the covenant and throw Israel directly upon divine mercy (Hos. 14.1ff.; Jer. 31.12ff.; Isa. 61.1ff.; Ezek. 34.12–15).

It is theologically significant to recognize that within the Old Testament canon these different witnesses are not aligned in a *heilsgeschichtliche* sequence, as if one moved from the cultic to a higher revelation of the prophets. The biblical testimonies are left in theological tension, particularly as historically attention to the ritual and purity laws increased in importance during the post-exilic period (cf. Ezra 9.1ff.) The continuing theological debate between Jews and Christians turns on their very different construals of how this Old Testament tension is to be handled in the light of the developing rabbinical and evangelical traditions.

Bibliography

Mary **Douglas**, *Purity and Danger*, London 1966; W. **Eichrodt**, *Theology of the Old Testament*, ET, I, Philadelphia and London 1962, 98–177; Y.

Kaufmann, *The Religion of Israel,* Chicago 1960, 53–9, 101–21; C. F. **Keil,** *Manual of Biblical Archaeology,* ET, II, Edinburgh 1888; J. H. **Kurtz,** *Sacrificial Worship of the Old Testament,* ET Edinburgh 1863; B. A. **Levine,** *In the Presence of the Lord,* SJLA 5, 1974; J. **Milgrom,** 'The Biblical Diet Laws as an Ethical System', *Interp* 17, 1963, 288–301; reprinted in *Studies in Cultic Theology and Terminology,* SJLA 36, 1983, 104–18; J. **Neusner,** *The Idea of Purity in Ancient Judaism,* SJLA 1, 1973; W. **Paschen,** *Rein und Unrein.* *Untersuchung zur biblischen Wortgeschichte,* Munich 1970; G. **von Rad,** *Old Testament Theology,* ET, I, Edinburgh and New York 1962, 272–89; P. **Ricoeur,** *The Symbolism of Evil,* ET Boston 1967; W. R. **Smith,** *Lectures on the Religion of the Semites,* Edinburgh ²1894.

9

THE RECIPIENTS OF GOD'S REVELATION

God reveals himself to his people, to individuals, and to the nations, all of whom bear testimony in different ways to his divine purpose in history. A major emphasis throughout the Old Testament is that God committed himself to a people who carries his special imprint. But Israel's election does not imply a disinterest in the nations, which also receive signs of God's attention. Moreover, God continues to address individuals from the beginning to the end of the Old Testament, both from the chosen people and from the nations who bear testimony to this word.

From the Old Testament perspective it is important to recognize that these different recipients of the divine revelation are not isolated from one another, but related both to God and to one another. The interrelationship lies at the heart of the biblical testimony. Israel was indeed chosen 'from all the families of the earth' (Amos 3.2), but with the explicit purpose that all the nations of the world would be blessed (Gen. 12.3). Conversely, the nations are to bear testimony that the divine 'law shall go forth out of Zion and the Word of God from Jerusalem' (Isa. 2.3). The nations confess: 'God is with you only, and there is no god beside him' (Isa. 45.14).

Similarly, the relationship between the individual and the group remains a fluid one. From within the chosen people certain individuals, Abraham, Moses, David, were singled out, but always their roles were in closest relationship to the people. Again, Adam was an individual, yet his representative role to all humanity is obvious from his generic name which is 'mankind'. Most frequently the law of God directs its imperatives to the individual: 'You shall not . . .', but invariably the command involves communal behaviour: 'You shall love your neighbour.'

It is now necessary to examine more closely the theological

implications involved in the manner by which God's revelation was
received within the Old Testament.

(i) *Israel as God's chosen people*

For well over fifty years the great importance of the covenant for
the Old Testament has been recognized. The initial credit goes to
Eichrodt who sought to organize his whole theology around the
concept. During the last several decades the full complexity of the
covenant traditions within the Old Testament has appeared and
has consumed much scholarly attention. What are the different
forms of the convenant? What is the prehistory of the term? Was
the covenant understood as conditional or unconditional? By whom
were these traditions carried out and in what socio-political context?

Two strikingly different effects of this scholarly debate can be
seen in regard to Old Testament theology. On the one hand, certain
scholars have projected the traditions of covenant into every aspect
of Israel's life and expanded the term so broadly as to incorporate
virtually everything under the one rubric (Eichrodt, Lohfink,
Hillers, etc.). On the other hand, others have sought greatly to
restrict the term (Kutsch), even characterizing it as a late Deuteronomic formulation with very shallow roots in Israel's historical soil
(Perlitt).

As is often the case in a scholarly debate, both sides within a
dispute have some evidence on which to construct a position. I do
not find it convincing when Perlitt seeks to eliminate every sign of a
pre-Deuteronomic reference to the covenant (e.g. Hos. 8.1). Yet it
is equally clear that the concept of covenant has been greatly
expanded by the Deuteronomist and given a central role which it
did not appear to have at first. The crucial theological issue at
stake is how one interprets this multilayering effect. The canonical
approach lays its emphasis on the many signs within the tradition
that later Israel construed its faith so predominantly in terms of the
Sinai covenant as to blur the exact historical development by
theological interpretation.

Because neither of the contestants deals seriously enough with
the canonical shape of the Old Testament and the specific function
of the covenant within the canonical corpus, it is difficult to adjudi-
cate the argument. Those who stress the inclusiveness of the
covenant usually find their warrant in form-critical, traditio-

historical evidence. Conversely, those who seek greatly to restrict its scope argue largely from redactional-critical evidence. In my judgment, neither side has done justice to the present shape of the literature as scripture, which has registered its own construal by means of subtle patterns of intertextuality.

What can one say about covenant theology in its canonical context? In the first place, the formation of a covenant with this one people is the central theme of the whole Pentateuch and forms a red thread which joins the various parts. The book of Genesis anticipates the covenant with its continued promises to the patriarchs that through a special line a people would emerge in whom God's blessing would rest. The nature of the promise varies (land, posterity), as does also its form (contrast Gen. 15 and 17). However, the climax of the patriarchal promise, which in the final form of the Pentateuch was stretched to cover the long period of the Egyptian captivity, occurred with the exodus from Egypt and with the consummation of the covenant at Sinai. Israel was chosen as God's 'special possession' (Ex. 19.5), and received the divine commitment: 'I will be your God and you will be my people.' The distinctly priestly traditions now found largely in Leviticus and Numbers are firmly anchored to the covenant's description of the people of God as holy and as a pilgrim people who live under marching orders.

Finally, the book of Deuteronomy plays a crucial canonical role in actualizing the covenant for each succeeding generation. The second generation who had not itself participated at Sinai is assured that the covenant applies to them as much as the first. The same imperatives to love God with all one's heart, soul and mind constitute Israel's proper response to God's covenant. The covenant affirms the way of life and assures the blessings of God. The framework of Deuteronomy provides a normative and holistic rendering of the Pentateuchal traditions which has established the major lines of covenant theology. Within these guidelines there remains a variety of different emphases and layers of tradition, but these are not to be played over against each other by isolating them from their canonical context.

The covenant established a relationship between God and his people. Although the language was originally legal, the relationship did not function as a pact or treaty, but was understood as a gracious act of mercy from the initiative of God which was not predicated upon Israel's agreement. Yet the covenant did demand a response and called forth divine judgment if broken. The will of God was spelled out for God's people in clear language which envisioned a communal response of love and justice commensurate with God's covenantal will.

In spite of the surprising infrequency of the technical covenant terminology in the Old Testament prophets, their message is incomprehensible apart from the assumption of a special people of God. For example, the prophet Isaiah, who seldom speaks of the exodus and Sinai, sounds the major theme of the broken relationship right at the outset:

> Sons have I reared and brought up,
> but they have rebelled against me (1.2).

Likewise, Amos confirms Israel's special covenantal relationship with God before drawing the implications from her disobedience:

> You only have I known
> of all the families of the earth;
> Therefore I will punish you
> for all your iniquities (3.2).

One of the most significant aspects of the prophets' message involves the manner in which the continuity of God's dealing with his chosen people is maintained in spite of the execution of divine judgment. Critical Old Testament scholarship has long worried over the sharp polarity between certain prophetic words of absolute and final judgment (Amos 3.12; 8.1) and the picture of a restored and forgiven Israel (9.13–15). Usually the approach of literary criticism has been to sketch a history of development and to consign the message of restoration to a late, post-exilic stage. However, this move clearly runs against the whole tenor of the prophetic message.

The problem of judgment and salvation for the people of God appears in an especially acute form in the book of Isaiah. In the first twelve chapters the prophet speaks of a rejected people (ch. 3) against whom the avenging arm of God is still outstretched in judgment (ch. 5) until the whole tree is utterly destroyed (ch. 6). Yet in these same chapters the prophet pictures a cleansed and sanctified people of God (ch. 4), living in peace and harmony, awaiting the transformation of the kingdom of God (ch. 9) with a return to a paradisal state of the world (ch. 11).

Moreover, it is clear in Isaiah that the hope of a new people is not simply a future wish, but the prophet sees a faithful remnant actually emerging and present in the death pangs of the old. In the signs of the new (Emmanuel = God with us; Shearjashub = a remnant will return), there is the tangible evidence of a restored people of God which is living from the continued mercy of God. In spite of the threatening onslaught of the enemy, a stone of salvation has been laid by God which is unmovable (Isa. 28.16). The true bearers of the new life of God are alive and active, and are not just a hope or ideal of the future.

At times the prophet focuses completely on the description of the obedient and transformed people of God which he sees emerging in God's time. Only from the divine perspective can there be any continuity with an unclean, rejected and disobedient people who are fully incapable of hearing the word of God. Ezekiel in particular portrays the hideous quality of sin and corruption with a terrifying realism (ch. 23), but then he pictures the completely unexpected restoration of the valley of bones into a new people (37.1–5).

For Jeremiah the image of the new people comes in the form of a new covenant when God restores his relation to the house of Israel as he did at Sinai, but this time he actualizes his purpose for them in a new fashion:

> Not like the covenant which I made with their fathers . . . my covenant which they broke . . . but this is the covenant which I will make after these days. I will put my law within them and write it upon their hearts and I will be their God and they shall be my people (31.31ff.).

The sheer miraculous nature of God's reconstituting his people to himself appears finally in the prophecy of Hosea. The prophet envisions a time, when instead of its being said, ' "You are not my people", it shall be said, "Sons of the living God" ' (1.10). Or again, 'I will make for you a covenant on that day – and I will betroth you to me in righteousness and in justice, in steadfast love and mercy' (2.18f.).

It is characteristic of the prophetic picture of a new and obedient people of God that Israel and the nations are often seen sharing in the praise of God. Israel remains the means by which God's whole creation participates in the divine salvation.

(ii) *The individual as recipient*

Within the Old Testament there is no concept of the person in the modern post-Enlightenment sense of a 'rugged individualist'. The individual is always viewed in relation to a larger society and a group. However, it is equally false to conclude that the profile of the individual was blurred into a homogeneous mass. One has only to recall the figures of Abraham, Moses, Deborah to sense the integrity of the individual within the Old Testament. Indeed, few literatures have more impressive individual portraits, even though the Old Testament did not focus on the personality as such.

There are two main directions in which the role of the individual in relation to divine revelation was developed within the Old Testament. On the one hand, the individual is treated as a representative of humanity in general. On the other hand, the individual appears as a member of the people of God, of Israel. Although the two lines are easily distinguishable, there is also a merging and even fusion at times which is of theological importance as, for example, in the figures of Job and Jonah.

(a) The individual as the representative of humanity. Gen. 1.27 speaks of God's creating mankind (*'ādām*) in his own image. Two exegetical points follow immediately. First, *'ādām* is a generic term for humanity in contrast to the Hebrew *'iš*, which is a specific male example of the genus, or *'iššāh*, which is the female instance. Secondly, a fuller explanation follows which is in some way related to the image. He created them male and female, and mankind is given dominion over the rest of the creatures of the earth.

Much scholarly energy has been expended in trying to make specific wherein exactly the image of man lies. What is it that sets human beings apart from the rest of the creation? Often it has been suggested that it lay in human reason, conscience or spirituality. Bonhoeffer, who is followed in part by Barth, suggested that the image is reflected analogically in the relation between male and female, a community between persons in which one addresses the other as 'thou'.

The major exegetical problem is that there is virtually no explanation of the term within the Old Testament. In fact, its theological significance was first developed in the post-Old Testament period by both Jews and Christians, whereas the Old Testament itself offers few hints. Genesis 5.1ff. recounts that Adam's son, Seth, was 'in his own likeness, after his own image'. Whatever the original image was, it does not appear to have been lost in the 'fall'.

Again, Ps. 8 functions as a broad commentary on the creation tradition of Gen. 1. The psalmist places his emphasis on the unique position of man within the created order – 'he lacks little from God (*'elôhîm*)' – but his role derives solely from divine grace – 'what is man that thou art mindful of him?'. Although the image itself does not lie in man's ability to exercise stewardship over all the work of God's creation, the psalmist follows the Genesis tradition in also turning his attention immediately to the divine purpose of the image which relates to his exercise of power. A somewhat similar note is sounded in Gen. 2, when Adam is given the task of naming the animals. He thus assigns them their respective roles within the creative order and functions, as it were, as a co-creator with God himself (von Rad, *Genesis*).

The wisdom books strike a special tone in reference to generic man as recipient of the divine revelation. Ecclesiastes speaks of 'eternity' put in man's mind (3.11), yet man is confined within a restrictive context as a human being which separates him qualitatively from God. He is limited in time and space, and finds his creatureliness a threat to the meaning of his existence. Nevertheless, the author bears witness to the unique possibility of man to whom God has granted life and transitory possession to enjoy God's creation as a gift of God. Indeed, man is not immortal, nor master of his own fate. Countless anomalies remain within the created order. Yet within the boundaries fixed for his life he is granted a measure of joy as a gift of God (5.19). If this sapiential witness is isolated from the rest of the canon, it appears largely negative and deeply pessimistic. However, when set within its canonical context, especially within the setting provided by the book's epilogue (12.11–14), it serves as a sober testimony to human creatureliness which resists all efforts to romanticize, idealize or rationalize human life apart from God.

Job 28 offers another very powerful witness to man's remarkable ingenuity. The sage marvels at his ability to discover hidden places, to dam rivers and to sink shafts in the rocks. Man devises clever techniques and brings out the earth's precious treasures. Yet in spite of his remarkable capacity, he cannot discover on his own the way to wisdom. This remains a divine gift which God bestows on those who fear him.

Perhaps the major witness of the book of Proverbs to this subject lies in seeing that human experience, if understood wisely, instructs the individual into the way of life. By observing correctly the lessons taught by experience one is led into harmony with the divine structures of reality which God has built into his creation. Proverbs does not speak of covenant, people or redemptive history, but of generic man who is given the potential through the gift of wisdom to walk in a way which is favourable to God (8.35), or conversely of forfeiting the promise by being stupid, foolish or wicked. The way of folly is not life, but death itself.

(b) *The individual as representative of Israel.* More central to the Old Testament as a whole is the reference to God's redemptive purpose at work in an individual who serves as a representative of faithful Israel. When viewed from one perspective, the Old Testament is a covenantal history of God's forming a people. Yet the Bible is filled with stories of individuals who in various ways are brought into relation with the larger corporate entity.

The patriarchs serve as classic examples of individuals whose encounter with God affected the character of the whole people. Abraham's faith confirmed the divine promise of an elected people whose members will be as numerous as the stars. Conversely, his lack of faith in exposing Sarah, the bearer of the promised heir, threatened the future of the entire nation (Gen. 20).

Jacob's encounter with God of the Fathers is always represented in Genesis within a strange, dual light. Clearly Jacob is an individual, the second son of his father, Isaac. However, his birth as a twin of Esau is described as a contest between two nations, each struggling for dominion. Not only does he actually bear the name of his people Israel – he wrestles with God – but his stories portray him with a typological dimension in which individual and corporate elements flow together. He manoeuvres the blessing away from the first born, and receives the promise to inherit the land. He succeeds brilliantly by his wits, true to his name of Jacob 'the Supplanter', until he meets God face to face at Peniel (ch. 32), and leaves limping, bearing the mark for every succeeding generation to remember (32.32). Finally, Jacob descends into Egypt as the head of a family, but requests that his bones accompany the deliverance of Israel from Egypt as a people of God.

The Psalter offers another classic example of the role of the individual as representative of faithful Israel. The largest number of Old Testament psalms consists of individual complaints in which an individual pours out his prayers to God under great suffering. These psalms describe every possible affliction of body and soul: attack from enemies, sickness, false charges, imprisonment, isolation, hatred and intimidation. The psalms oscillate between elements of complaint, plea and praise (cf. Pss. 6 and 88).

The suffering Israelite continues to identify with the God of Israel, on whom he depends for his life and welfare. The greatest threat of all is to be cut off from the beloved community and from the worship of God:

> Dost thou work wonders for the dead?
> Can the shades in Sheol rise up to praise thee? (Ps. 88.10).

At times the psalmist confesses that he has experienced the redeeming hand of God (Ps. 6.8ff.). At other times the psalmist ends with the same passionate, unfulfilled plea for God to respond (Ps. 88.1ff.)

It is characteristic of the Psalter that the psalmist often suffers alone, but expresses his experience of God's salvation in the plural. It is as if God's redemptive activity cannot be fully articulated apart from the beloved community. One thinks of that most joyful of all the psalms, Ps. 126, and the sheer, incomprehensible wonder and hilarious joy of deliverance:

> When the Lord restored the fortunes of Zion,
> we were like those who dream.
> Then our mouth was filled with laughter,
> and our tongue with shouts of joy;
> Then they said among the nations,
> 'The Lord has done great things for them'.
> The Lord has done great things for us.
> We are overwhelmed with joy!

Above all, the individual complaint psalm bears witness to the faithful Israelite, who professes to serve God and yet whose life is filled with sorrow and grief. He continues to experience both good and evil and longs for final vindication. The Psalter focuses its major attention on the individual Israelite who lives and suffers with the divine promise of the covenant, and yet who is not sure in his confusion and pleas of innocence what is his place within God's economy. Ultimately the movement of the canonical Psalter is future orientated. Regardless of the moments of experienced salvation, the psalmist is finally forced to look to God's future vindication. The faithful Israelite waits, oscillating between complaint and praise:

I wait for the Lord, my soul waits,
and in his word I hope;
My soul waits for the Lord
more than watchmen for the morning . . .
O Israel, hope in the Lord!
and he will redeem Israel from all his iniquities (130.5–8).

There are two further important biblical witnesses to the role of the individual as recipient of God's revelation which are closely akin to that of the Psalter, but appear in different parts of scripture. In the book of Habakkuk the prophet questions God about the suffering of the righteous and the apparent successes of the oppressors. The prophet is then instructed to live in God's presence and to await the beginning of God's rule in spite of the enemies who tyrannize the faithful. Righteousness is not to be measured by the human ability to comprehend the purpose of God in world history, but instead by a trustful response which is sustained by the divine promise.

The special canonical significance of Habakkuk's witness is that the prophet himself then testifies to the truth of this faith by means of an autobiographical statement. Israel's hope has already become a reality for him and he can bear eloquent witness from his own experience:

I hear and my body trembles,
my lips quiver at the sound;
rottenness enters into my bones,
my steps totter beneath me (3.16).

Yet in spite of this:

I will quietly wait for the day of trouble
to come upon the people who invade us . . .

Yet I will rejoice in the Lord . . .
    God, the Lord, is my strength . . .
    He makes me tread upon my high places (3.16–19).

In sum, the prophet not only preaches a message to Israel, but bears personal witness himself to the reality of salvation which he has experienced and on which he grounds his life. The believer does not just point to the darkness!

A somewhat similar move, relating communal complaint to individual confession, is found in the book of Lamentations, which addresses the misfortunes of Judah as a whole. In the form of a dirge, the writer describes the desecration of the temple, Zion's humiliation, the horrors of famine, and the longing for retribution of the enemy. The effect of rehearsing these traditional themes is to focus on the national sorrow from numerous angles. The influence of the dirge is particularly felt in chs. 1, 2 and 4; it creates an atmosphere of stupified resignation which is reflected in a slightly variant form by the communal complaint of ch. 5.

However, ch. 3 of Lamentations differs from the rest of the book, both in form and content, and plays a decisive hermeneutical function in construing the message as a whole. The chapter begins with an individual complaint which shares all the traditional features of the genre. The writer describes his troubles (vv. 1–18), and seeks aid from God (19–21). In vv. 22–24 he testifies to his own faith in divine mercy by making use of themes from Israel's traditional credal formulations.

Of special importance is the shift of vision which ch. 3 brings to bear on the book. It effects a change from a communal to an individual form, and it moves from the sad events of Jerusalem's ruin in 587 BC to an individual's personal history. The writer has not thereby moved from genuine historical concerns into a timeless area of religion, but rather has incorporated the national history within liturgical language. The pain of this one representative Jew is portrayed in the language of worship, thus transcending any one fixed point in history. An individual Hebrew testifies through his suffering:

The steadfast love of God never ceases,
    his mercies never come to an end,
    My soul says, 'The Lord is my portion.
    Therefore, I will hope in him' (3.22–24).

To summarize, the role of ch. 3 of Lamentations is to render the plight of Israel caused by the destruction of the temple into the language of faith, and by the use of common forms of liturgy to appeal to the whole nation to experience that dimension of faith testified to by one representative individual. The psalmist's confession has now replaced the dirge. The promises of God to his people have not ceased, but they still provide the grounds for hope. Thus, the book of Lamentation serves every future generation of God's suffering people for whom history has become intolerable:

Let us test and examine our ways, and return to the Lord!
Let us lift up our hearts and hands to God in heaven . . .
The Lord will not cast us off for ever,
Though he cause grief, he will have compassion (3.40f., 31f.).

(iii) *The nations as recipients of God's revelation*

Throughout the Old Testament, standing over against the chosen and elect people, are the nations. This sharp distinction between Israel and the nations is built into the very literary structure of the book of Genesis. The writer traces the growth of the family of nations from one source by means of horizontal genealogies (Shem, Ham, Japheth), but indicates that his chief interest lies with the one chosen line which he traces by means of a vertical genealogy (Abraham, Isaac, Jacob).

However, Genesis makes it clear that the election of Israel was a means and not the end of God's purpose for the world. In the important passage of God's promise to Abraham of a posterity (12.1ff.), the fundamental relationship between Israel and the nations is spelled out. 'God said to Abraham: I will make of you a great nation and I will bless your name . . . and by you shall all the families of the earth be blessed' (vv. 2f.). Von Rad has made an astute observation about the position of ch. 12 within Genesis. The election of Israel comes as a climax to the history of sin and alienation which extends from chs. 3–11. The growing expansion of sin from the garden of Eden, to the murder of Abel, to the rebellion of the sons of God (ch. 6), to the flood and tower of Babel, threatened to wrest the world away from the control of God and issue in complete chaos. Then God commanded Abraham, and he obeyed, and Israel became the vehicle by which God's whole creation was to be reconciled to its creator.

To be sure, Israel continually misunderstood the purpose of her election, which called forth the prophetic reiteration of God's original purpose to regain the nations. Repeatedly II Isaiah addresses his oracles to the 'nations', to the 'ends of the earth', and to 'distant peoples', calling them to join in praising the God of the universe. Nor is it accidental that Isaiah paints the picture of the end-time in terms of all the nations converging on a transformed Zion with the intent of going up to the mount of the Lord to learn his ways (2.1ff.; cf. Ps. 147).

Once again, the narrative material offers an important commentary on how to understand God's relation to the nations. Indeed Isaac is chosen over Ishmael, and Hagar is driven out with a shocking ruthlessness (chs. 16 and 21). Although Isaac and not Ishmael is the heir to the promise, God is also deeply concerned with Hagar and hears her cry. Similarly Ishmael is given a promise and granted a way of life in the desert.

Perhaps even more significant are the narratives concerning the role of the foreigners as bearers of the divine revelation. Exodus 18 recounts the story of Jethro, the priest of Midian, who upon hearing of God's deliverance of Israel from Egypt goes out to meet Moses. Jethro rejoices and confesses that Yahweh is 'greater than all the gods'.

The fact that Jethro is a priest from a foreign country who does not belong to the people of Israel is an essential part of the tradition. Nevertheless, he acts throughout the story as a faithful witness to Yahweh. He is not treated as an outsider, nor does he act as one. He offers God praise in the language of Israel's faith and even leads worship as a climax to the event. There is no hint that he has won the right to participate in the cult because of a recent conversion as a proselyte. Rather, he bears witness to the greatness of the God of Israel by praise, confession and sacrifice. What God has done is not limited to his people, but can be perceived and experienced by anyone who is open to the divine wonders in the world.

A host of other stories relates the testimony of foreigners to the greatness of God. They bear witness, sometimes willingly, and sometimes under duress. The traditions in Numbers about Balaam remain in considerable tension. On the one hand, Balaam as a true prophet foresaw the glorious future of Israel under God's blessing.

On the other hand, he instructed the Midianites on how to corrupt Israel, and perished in the ensuing judgment (Num. 31.16). In II Kings 5, Naaman, the Syrian commander, testifies to the power of God in words reminiscent of Jethro. Finally, much of the first half of the book of Daniel is structured about the theme of the proud foreign ruler who is constrained to bear witness to what 'the most High God has wrought'.

In addition, the nations as recipients of God's revelation play a significant role in revealing the sins of Israel, God's chosen people (cf. Ezek. 5.5ff.). In the famous passage of Mal. 1.11 the prophet condemns the dishonouring sacrifices of Israel which deprive God of glory, and he contrasts Israel's sinfulness with the nations:

> For from the rising of the sun to its setting my name is great among the nations, and in every place incense is offered to my name, and a pure offering; for my name is great among the nations, says the Lord of hosts.

Ever since Theodore of Mopsuestia, some interpreters have attempted to understand this passage as affirming that all heathen sacrifices are in fact offered to Yahweh, the one true God. However, this interpretation is inconsistent with the rest of the book of Malachi. The prophet is not putting forth a theory about the nature of true worship, but rather offering a polemic against Israel's irreverence, which is such that the whole Gentile world serves God more faithfully than do his chosen people. In a similar fashion Ezekiel says to Jerusalem: 'Samaria has not committed half your sins; you have committed more abominations than they, and have made your sisters appear righteous . . .' (16.51). Even the heathen are shocked over the things committed by Judah.

One of the most interesting developments of this theme occurs in the book of Jonah. God commanded Jonah to go to Nineveh and denounce its wickedness. However, Jonah refused and, boarding a ship to Tarshish, went in the opposite direction. It is theologically important to observe how the writer of the book portrays the sailors who are pagan in their relation to Jonah. When God hurled a great storm which threatened to destroy their ship, the sailors were terrified. Then in true pagan style the captain demanded that each man call upon his god. Perhaps one of them would come to their aid. But Jonah confesses that he is a Hebrew. He worships the 'creator of the heavens and the earth, who made the sea and dry land', which is a curious note of irony for one who was trying to escape him in a boat to Tarshish! Then Jonah, who is resigned to his fate, requests that the sailors throw him into the sea in order to still the storm, but they are far too merciful to comply. They row hard to bring the ship to land, and even pray to Jonah's God for mercy. Throughout the story the pagan sailors are portrayed with great sympathy as men of character, whereas Jonah, the Hebrew, is the nefarious one.

When God finally delivers Jonah by means of a great fish, the prophet reluctantly goes to the hated city of Nineveh to proclaim to the Assyrians God's word of judgment: 'Yet forty days and Nineveh will be destroyed.' Then, wonder of wonders, the people of Nineveh believe God and repent in sackcloth. It is the pagan king who expresses true knowledge of God's character:

> Who knows, God may repent and turn from his fierce anger so that we perish not.

And it is Jonah, the Hebrew prophet of God, who misunderstands and fears that he would be made a liar by God's show of mercy. Then God instructs Jonah:

> Should not I pity Nineveh, that great city, in which there are more than a hundred and twenty thousand persons who do not know their right hand from their left? (3.11).

There is one final reference to the theme of the nations as recipients of divine revelation. God has revealed his power against all the forces of the world which oppose his kingship. Often in the Old Testament the nations are presented symbolically as the earthly powers organized against the rule of God. Psalm 2 offers a classic example. To those nations who reject God's rule over his creation, he speaks 'in his wrath and terrifies them in his fury'.

Particularly in the prophets and apocalyptic literature the nations are portrayed in a variety of images as attacking Zion, the holy city of God. Joel 3 pictures 'multitudes, multitudes in the valley of decision', and Ezekiel, chs. 38–39, sees Gog and Magog devising an evil scheme to fall on 'that quiet people who dwell securely'. Likewise, Daniel depicts the remnant with its back up against the wall barely holding on before the demonic onslaughts of the Antichrist. Before such sheer arrogance and pride God responds: 'I will show my greatness and my holiness and make myself known in the eyes of many nations. Then they will know that I am Yahweh' (Ezek. 38.23). Significantly, the goal of the divine judgment on both Israel and the nations is the same – that all may know the true character of God and that knowing him they may serve him.

Bibliography

P. **Bird**, 'Gen 1:27b in the Context of the Priestly Account of Creation', *HTR* 74, 1981, 129–59; M. **Buber**, 'The Covenant', *Moses*, ET Oxford 1946, 110–18; R. E. **Clements**, *God's Chosen People*, London and Valley Forge 1968; 'The People of God', *Old Testament Theology. A Fresh Approach*, London and Atlanta 1978, 79–103; J. **Ellul**, 'Naaaman', *The Politics of God and the Politics of Man*, ET Grand Rapids 1972, 23–40; N. **Gottwald**, *The Tribes of Yahweh*, Maryknoll 1979 and London 1980, 88–99; D. R. **Hillers**, *Covenant: The History of a Biblical Idea*, Baltimore 1969; E. **Kutsch**, *Verheissung und Gesetz*, BZAW 131, 1973; N. **Lohfink**, 'Beobachtungen zur Geschichte des Ausdrucks 'am YHWH', *Probleme biblischer Theologie, FS G. von Rad*, ed. H. W. Wolff, Munich 1971, 275–305; R. **Martin-Achard,** *A Light to the Nations*, ET Edinburgh and London 1962; D. J. **McCarthy,** *Treaty and Covenant*, AnBibl 21, 1963, Oxford ²1978; L. **Perlitt**, *Bundestheologie im Alten Testament*, WMANT 36, 1969; S. **Terrien**, *The Elusive Presence*, New York and London 1978, 106–60.

10

AGENTS OF GOD'S RULE: MOSES, JUDGES, KINGS

The Old Testament offers a continual witness to God's grace in providing a succession of leaders and offices by which he exercised and enhanced his rule over his people. For this reason it is a common feature of many recent Old Testament theologies to include a chapter on the 'charismata of leadership' or on the 'offices of the covenant'. The methodological issue involved in treating this subject is posed by Zimmerli in his introduction to the topic:

> Within the framework of a theology of the Old Testament, it is not appropriate to describe the sociological structure of Israelite 'society' and trace its historical development. It is our task instead to depict the way the faith of the Old Testament recognizes and describes Yahweh's work in these individuals or groups (*OT Theology*, 81).

I fully agree with Zimmerli in refusing to confuse a sociological description of Ancient Israel's leadership with the true theological task. However, is his own formulation adequate? In my opinion, Zimmerli cites most of the relevant passages, and offers a useful survey, but he fails to deal successfully with the material as it has been construed by the canonical process. His theological description continues to fluctuate between modern critical evaluation and the witness of the Old Testament itself. In contrast, my concern is at least to attempt a theological reflection of this material which is consonant with its canonical shaping.

(i) *The role of Moses*

Zimmerli begins his discussions of Moses with a description of him as 'a man with an Egyptian name who is charged with the task of leading Israel out of Egypt' (81), and thus illustrates immediately the problem. Nowhere within the Old Testament tradition is Moses thought to bear an Egyptian name. In fact, just the opposite: 'she (his mother) called his name "Mosheh", for she said, because I drew (mšh) him out of the water' (Ex. 2.10). According to the modern etymological derivation, the name indeed means 'son' or 'child' and appears in Egyptian names like Tutmose. However, scientific etymology operates in a different context from that of the biblical tradition, and the two cannot be simply interchanged. Zimmerli next registers the wide variety of portrayals of Moses in the Old Testament according to the usual critical reconstruction of literary sources (cf. Gressmann and Osswald), without ever pursuing the function which the canonical form of the combined corpus assigned to the early traditions.

What, then, can one say about the canonical function of the figure of Moses as agent of the rule of God? It is, of course, obvious that the Old Testament contains a multitude of traditions concerning Moses, some of which stand in striking tension with one another. One only has to recall the story of Moses' circumcision and God's attempt to kill his own recently appointed messenger (Ex. 4.24ff.) to see the inner friction. Similarly, the portrayal of the figure of Moses in the plague cycle differs considerably within the various strata, as Gressmann discerned long ago. Nevertheless, it is equally true that these disparate traditions have been placed in an order and given an overall canonical interpretation. Significantly, early Tanaaite Jewish interpreters of the Old Testament had a clear profile of Moses' role and did not see only a bundle of irreconcilable conflicts.

The most important point to make is that Moses was assigned a unique role within Israel, but one which at the same time encompassed such a rich diversity as to include practically every other office within Israel: deliverer, lawgiver, prophet, priest, psalmist and sage. However, the central focus of Moses' unique place rested on his role as mediator of the covenant. For this reason, the diversity of his roles turned on different aspects of his exercising of this covenantal authority. Moreover, these complex traditions receive their Old Testament cohesion about the *persona* of Moses rather than in an abstract process or stream of tradition.

The report of the theophany at Sinai in Ex. 19 which accompanied the giving of the Law provides an initial aetiology for Moses' central role. The people fled in terror before the sight on the mountain and requested Moses to be their mediator (Ex. 20.18; Deut. 4.14). However, the uniqueness of Moses' role at Sinai is testified to apart from the aetiological tradition in ch. 19. As the theophany increased in intensity, Moses was seen speaking to God and God was answering him in thunder (19.19).

Several other passages reflect on Moses' role at Sinai and from different perspectives. Exodus 33.11 characterizes the special mediatory function with God: 'God used to speak to Moses face to face, as a man speaks to his friend.' Or again, when Moses' unique status was challenged by Miriam and Aaron, 'Has Yahweh indeed only spoken through Moses?', God responded in anger by setting Moses apart from every other prophet. 'He is entrusted with all my house. With him I speak mouth to mouth, clearly and not in dark speech' (Num. 12.1ff.). Similarly, in his obituary in Deut. 34, Moses' uniqueness is emphasized as one whom God knew 'face to face'. Finally, the special role as mediator is reflected in the story of Moses' 'shining face' (Ex. 34.29ff.) – Michaelangelo's horns – imagery which seeks to interpret Moses' continued role of speaking directly with God and communicating his will as a priest to the people.

All these various traditions concerning the unique role of Moses as covenant mediator are placed within a literary framework as a way of providing a clear canonical construal of Moses' chief role. Exodus 24 had spoken of Moses writing down the words of the Lord and having them read in the hearing of the people, but it is the concluding chapters of Deuteronomy which develop this theme into a normative interpretation regarding his office.

Deuteronomy 31 provides a definitive shift from the portrayal of Moses' addressing the people which had dominated the book up to this juncture. Now Moses enters into a series of crucial actions. He ends his sermon, fixes it in written form (31.9), commissions Joshua as his successor, and deposits the Law beside the ark. Moreover, he establishes a routine for the Law to be read at set periods in order that the succeeding generations may hear and do the Law (31.12). This written law is to serve as a witness against any future generations who rebel. Indeed, according to 31.20ff. Moses actually reckons with the certain disobedience of the generation which follows.

The central theological emphasis is that Moses, the mediator of the covenant, transfers his unique role to a written record. He becomes the author of a book which is hereafter called by his name, the Law of Moses (Mal. 4.4). This law carries the full authority of Moses' unique role in Israel's life, but it now functions to address the future generations with the same imperative:

> Lay to heart all the words which I enjoin upon you this day, that you may command them to your children . . . to do all the words of this law (Deut. 32.46).

Of importance to note is that when Joshua assumed the leadership of the nation, he did not acquire the office of Moses, which was unique. Rather, Joshua enjoined the people to obey the Law of Moses. Joshua's role was set in a typological relationship to Moses, and he emulated, as it were, the role of Moses in crossing the sea (Josh. 3), meeting the commander of the army of God (Josh. 5), and raising his staff as a sign against God's enemy (Josh. 8.18).

In addition, the unique role of Moses as covenant mediator of the Law was extended in several directions to provide other significant models for the subsequent leadership of Israel. According to Deut. 18.18 Moses became the prototype of the true and faithful prophet. Whereas other nations sought to acquire divine instruction through soothsayers, augurs and wizards (18.10ff.), Israel learns the will of God through the word of his appointed prophet. God then promises a succession of prophets who will receive God's word and lead Israel in the truth. Still, the prophets who come in succession will not surpass Moses. His role remains unique and unrepeatable. Only a small portion of his spirit can inspire seventy elders to prophesy (Num. 11.24ff.).

Another side of Moses' unique role is his priestly role as intercessor. Leviticus 8 describes in detail Moses' priestly function in the ordination of Aaron's sons and in setting up the service of the tabernacle. Above all, Moses is pictured as interceding for Israel following the sin of the golden calf (Ex. 32). Moses does not hesitate to put his own life on the line: 'If thou wilt forgive their sins – and if not, blot me out of thy book' (32.32). Similarly, Deut. 9.25 describes his prostrating himself before Yahweh in forty days and nights of intercession on Israel's behalf. Increasingly Moses became a type of the innocent suffering servant, bearing the sins of the nation, who stood in Israel's place but could not himself enter the promised land. Later prophetic tradition, in emphasizing the divine verdict to destroy Israel made the point by denying that even Moses' intercession could pacify God's wrath (Jer. 15.1).

(ii) *Judges*

Once again Zimmerli's theological reflection on the role of the judges offers some keen observations and deals with many of the central Old Testament passages. Yet I remain dissatisfied with his methodology, which is again eclectic. He works at times with the canonical form, but then again often tries to base his theology directly upon historical or form-critical reconstructions. The confusion of whether he is writing an Old Testament theology or a history of the growth of the Hebrew literature is never resolved. Nevertheless, Zimmerli's section is highly useful, which can hardly be said of several other modern treatments of the judges, which never arise above being a history-of-religions or sociological analysis.

Zimmerli points out quite convincingly that there are two distinct layers within the book of Judges. He begins with the Deuteronomic framework (2.1ff.) and proceeds to describe the redactor's theology respecting the judges. The Deuteronomist envisions no line of succession, but Yahweh raises up anew each time a hero as deliverer. The people are obedient to the law as long as the ruler lives. Zimmerli goes on to describe the theology of the earlier pre-Deuteronomic level and finds two main elements. First, there is the portrayal in lists of the so-called 'minor judges' who have a legal function (cf. Noth), and secondly, there are old local stories concerned with tribal heroes.

Although I fully agree with Zimmerli that the biblical literature in multi-layered, I would argue that the material of the book of Judges has a very different theological function when read together in its totality. By slicing the book diachronistically and trying to understand theologically each part separately, he fails ever to describe the material according to the manner in which Israel received and construed its traditions within the canonical process.

As is generally agreed, a Deuteronomistic framework begins in Judg. 2.1ff. which offers a theological pattern in the form of a cycle by which to interpret these early traditions. Israel is unfaithful and serves other gods. The Lord in anger delivers them into the hands of their enemies. The people cry to God, who raises a 'judge' to deliver them from the oppressor. However, when the judge dies, they revert to idolatry and the cycle is repeated.

However, it is significant to observe that the book of Judges does not begin with this Deuteronomistic framework. Rather, ch. 1, which precedes, describes the state of the tribes after the death of Joshua. A new period begins which is marked by the loss of a unified leadership, the unsuccessful attempt to conquer the land, and the collapse of the vision of Joshua for the nation. Regardless of the origins of this material – some attribute it to an ancient conquest document – the effect on the book as a whole is highly significant. It offers a theological characterization of the period as one of breakdown. Moreover, the Deuteronomistic interpretation which follows assumes this state of deterioration. The loss of Israel's vision of God, land and people has become the normative state. Only when God sends his deliverers does Israel recover the blessing for a moment, and under one leader serves the God of the covenant.

Within this canonical context Zimmerli's description of the later redactor's theology receives its true theological significance. The judges have no line of succession, but each is raised up from the initiative of God to bring Israel into conformity with his will. The appearance of the judges stems from the sheer mercy of God, who repeatedly intervenes to send shafts of light into a period of great darkness. The focus of the book of Judges is not a theology of repentance, but of divine grace. The book's emphasis is again radically theocentric.

The book's construal also means that the office of the judge was a temporary measure. It functioned 'between the times'. Joshua was dead and 'there was no king in those days' (19.1; 21.25). The repeated formula 'every man did what was right in his own eyes' (21.25; cf. 19.1) also stresses the provisory status of the judge. In the unexpected and yet repeated deliverances through the judges, Israel remembered the great deeds of her past (2.10), and also anticipated the coming of God's chosen ruler whose reign would endure. Each judge brought Israel just for a moment into her 'rest', almost as an eschatological participation of God's rule which was immediately forfeited. Significantly, the coming messianic figure was always portrayed as a righteous king and not as a judge. This office functioned only as a bridge. It was not to be repeated, nor did it have a lasting eschatological function. The office of judge could not be simply extended, but it served as a limited vehicle of God's rule. Gideon makes the theological point explicitly in 8.23: 'I will not rule over you and my sons will not rule over you. It is the Lord who will rule.'

Up to this juncture there has been agreement with Zimmerli and the consensus of critical scholars that the Deuteronomistic redaction formed an interpretative framework about the older material. What was the theological effect of this reinterpretation of the material as a whole? In the first place, the Deuteronomistic framework served to relativize the original historical differences in the early tradition by viewing the history in a typological pattern of disobedience and deliverance. The different local histories became only illustrations and made their theological points in conjunction with the other stories.

Secondly, the historical differences between the original roles of the judges – charismatic, juridical, nazirite – have been largely obliterated. The historical recovery of a so-called 'office of the minor judge' has been assigned no independent theological significance within the canonical book of Judges. The office plays an indirect role in the background of the text, and in providing additional information regarding the legal system of the period does add to the richness of the portrayal.

Thirdly, the Deuteronomistic framework offered a holistic interpretation of the entire period which was subsumed under the rubric of the grace of God, but this theological rubric did not destroy the uniqueness of the individual stories. Within the overarching theological category the earlier stories were given great freedom in retaining their original contours. The separate stories were thus allowed to illustrate a great variety of different theological emphases. For example, the story of Gideon (ch. 7) lays stress on the complete dependence of Gideon upon the divine deliverance by using only three hundred soldiers from an army of thirty-two thousand. Similarly, the story of Abimelech offers a penetrating critique of the false attempt to extend the office of judge to that of a permanent king. Then again, the story of Jephthah, which made use of an ancient aetiological tradition of a fertility rite, illustrates the effect of a foolish vow in turning a great deliverance to dust (11.34ff.).

Finally, as the most powerful creative cycle of stories in Judges, we have those concerning Samson (chs. 13–16). Of particular significance is the manner in which Samson functions theologically within the book and becomes a microcosm for the larger history of the nation. He bears the promise, but finally succumbs to forces arising both from within and without. He personifies the tension between promise and fulfilment, ideal and actuality, freedom and servitude which also constitutes the tragedy of the nation under the judges.

(iii) *Kings*

(a) *The rise of the kingdom.* Any theological discussion of the role of the king in the Old Testament will be strongly influenced by one's handling of the two books of Samuel, in which both the rise of the kingdom under Saul and its full blossoming under David is portrayed. Needless to say, I shall be attempting to present a theological reflection on the Old Testament king which does justice to the peculiar canonical shaping of this biblical literature.

The historical-critical questions respecting the rise of the monarchy have been posed with a special clarity by Wellhausen, who distinguished sharply between two different evaluations of the institution in I Sam. 8–12. On the one hand, he isolated a so-called 'pro-monarchial' source in 9.1–10.16; 11.1–5 in which the anointed leader was viewed as a gracious gift of God offered to an oppressed Hebrew people. On the other hand, he recovered an 'anti-monarchial' source in 8.1–22; 10.17–27; 12.1–25 which regarded the rise of the kingdom as a rejection of God's true reign (cf. 8.7), and saw it as an act of disobedience which emulated Israel's pagan nations.

Once again, Zimmerli's handling of this problem appears to me inadequate in fulfilling the theological task. He registers his agreement with the usual literary-critical analysis, but then contents himself with offering some general comparative background and in tracing a continuity of tradition between the earlier pro-monarchical source and the charismatic leadership of the book of Judges. His observations are useful but hardly decisive.

Von Rad's chapter on the problem is much more satisfactory from a theological perspective (I, 324ff.). He first contrasts the literary style of the two accounts, but then goes on to contest an oversimplification of contrasting a hostile and a friendly account. He remarks:

Both accounts tell of one and the same thing, but from very

different aspects. The older lets the reader understand the event wholly in the context of Jahweh and his plan . . . . The later, which casts up the account of a long experience with kings, views the monarchy as an institution which fell victim to the people's clutches. . . . (I, 326).

Von Rad's treatment is impressive. He does not allow his theological reflections to be dominated by historical-critical reconstructions which arise either from his literary categories or his historical references. However, I feel the need to press beyond von Rad at one crucial point, namely, in regard to the effect of the combination of sources. Certainly he is aware that the final form of the complex – a term which he actually uses – has produced a different entity from its parts. The two different accounts have not simply been juxtaposed within I Samuel, as if the reader had the option to choose which of the two perspectives on the rise of the kingdom he preferred. Still, von Rad has not pursued the issue that the present canonical shape has offered many interpretative indices as to how the material as a whole was to be rendered. The two accounts have been carefully intertwined in spite of some vestiges of friction. Although in a sense the integrity of each account has been retained, a whole composition has been produced from the parts whose meaning transcends both.

What then is the effect of the canonical process? Clearly the anti-monarchical source, which is probably later, has been given the pre-eminence. It now brackets the earlier source at both the beginning and end. The people think that they are resolving an immediate problem by demanding a king, but the dominant note sounded is the prophetic warning of Samuel against the danger of being 'like other nations'.

Nevertheless, the message of the pro-monarchical source remains of great importance, and its emphasis is enhanced by its new editorial function. The establishment of the kingdom, although arising out of unbelief, is not to be regarded as a purely secular act. God is still deeply involved in the rise of the monarchy even when it was not according to his original plan for Israel. When Samuel anoints Saul, the divine blessing is given and the spirit of God brings him the victory.

Chapter 12 functions to summarize the witness of the combined accounts. The fundamental problem of Israel's faith has not been resolved by the changed political status of the nation brought about by the kingdom. Israel, along with its newly appointed king, must still decide existentially for or against God: 'If you still do wickedly, you shall be swept away, both you and your king' (12.25). The canonical shaping wrestled with the difficulty of multiple traditions and rendered a theological construal by relativizing the significance of the political change. Of course, the historical problem of determining the exact forces at work in the change has been left largely unresolved in its canonical form.

(b) *Saul*. The kingdom received its first form under the leadership of Saul. In the earlier traditions of his rise to power he is portrayed much like the charismatic deliverers of Judges. The 'spirit of Yahweh' falls on him and he liberates the besieged city of Jabesh-gilead. As a result, a decision is made to anoint Saul as a permanent ruler. In the later account God instructs Samuel, the prophet, to go along in spite of the bad decision on the part of the people. At least the chosen ruler is to be given a chance.

The effect of combining these various traditions is to emphasize the failure of Saul's rule to establish a legitimate form of kingship. Israel cannot move from judge to king in this manner. Saul's kingship arose in disobedience and served as an example of a false attempt. The true form of God's rule through a chosen vehicle had to await the coming of David. Saul's reign falls completely under David's shadow and he becomes a type of the rejected servant (I Sam. 15.22ff.).

(c) *David*. The account of David's rise to power is given in I Sam. 16–II Sam. 5. Von Rad describes it as a 'murky history' (I, 308f.), a 'tortuous path trodden by this erstwhile warrior' to attain first the kingship over Judah and finally of the whole nation. The canonical process has joined together a variety of different traditions which at times retain considerable tension.

Von Rad develops the thesis that during this period, which he entitles the 'Solomonic Enlightenment', a new understanding of history emerged within Israel. He writes:

Jahweh's control takes in all that happens. It does not let itself be seen intermittently in holy miracles; it is as good as hidden from the natural eye: but it continually permeates all departments of life, public and private, religious and secular alike (I, 316).

I think that von Rad has offered some brilliant observations by which to explain the very different literary form of the Samuel stories when contrasted, say, with Exodus or again with Kings. However, von Rad's interpretation of the theology of these texts cannot, in my opinion, be identified with the construal given by the canonical shaping. In fact, at times the indices run in exactly the opposite direction from that proposed by von Rad.

One sees this move most clearly in von Rad's analysis of the so-called 'succession narrative' (II Sam. 9–20 + 1 Kings 1–2). He follows Rost's original analysis of these chapters which theorizes that the central thread holding together all the major stories of II Samuel was related to the search for David's successor in order to insure the Davidic dynasty. Von Rad finds in Rost's succession narrative a classic example to support his theory of a new understanding of history within Israel. In my opinion, much of what von Rad has discovered lies on the level of the tradition's prehistory. The material as construed in its final form has been given a different interpretation (cf. Gunn).

This evaluation can be most clearly established in regard to the succession narrative. In the present form of the book of Samuel, the sequence of this material has been broken by an appendix to II Samuel in chapters 21–24. Rost and von Rad follow the older literary critics in simply removing these chapters as an unfortunate intrusion into the otherwise brilliantly conceived narrative of the succession. Actually these chapters offer a very definite theological perspective by which the canonical process construed the entire book of Samuel, and especially David's role.

The four separate incidents in ch. 21 shift the focus of David's great victories away from his glorification and form a transition to ch. 22 in which he reviews his career in order to praise God as his redeemer. His thanksgiving hymn picks up many of the same themes as the song of Hannah in I Sam. 2. The same theocentric stress recurs. David lays claim to righteousness which he attributes solely to God. He contrasts then the way of the righteous with the godless, and in the form of a parable (*mashal*) pictures the ideal ruler of Israel as a righteous one. David next confesses that his house conforms to this messianic ideal and he prophesies a glorious future for his dynasty with God's help. His words provide a theological programme for the future of his royal dynasty.

In sum, the final four chapters offer a highly reflective, theological interpretation of David's whole career as adumbrating the messianic hope. These chapters in conjunction with the story of Hannah establish an eschatological, messianic perspective for the whole: God will exalt the poor and debase the proud in his rule of righteousness. Although David's human weaknesses are not suppressed within the tradition, his final role as the ideal, righteous king emerges with great clarity. The effect of this theology of history which is reflected in the canonical process is to establish a bridge between the reading of Samuel and that of Chronicles in respect to the significance of David's kingship.

(d) *The messianic hope.* There is one further aspect of David's kingship which needs to be briefly pursued, namely, its relationship to Israel's messianic hope.

In the prophetic literature David's kingship very shortly became a type of the eschatological rule of God himself. Several pre-exilic prophets rejected the false and arrogant rule of Israel's kings and contrasted their disobedient rule with the eschatological reign of God's true representative. Isaiah portrays a future king with divine attributes on whose shoulders and government will rest:

Wonderful Counsellor, Mighty God, Everlasting Father, Prince of Peace. Of the increase of his government and of peace there will be no end, upon the throne of David and over his kingdom to establish it, and to uphold it with justice and righteousness . . . for ever (9.6–7).

Similarly, Jeremiah castigates the false rulers as 'shepherds who destroy and scatter the sheep'. Then he prophesies a gathering of the remnant by a royal messianic figure:

Behold, the days are coming . . . when I will raise up for David a righteous branch, and he shall reign as king and deal wisely and shall execute justice and righteousness in the land . . . (23.5ff.; cf. Ezek. 34.23).

In contrast to this dominantly prophetic witness to David's kingship, the Psalter takes a somewhat different turn. Several royal psalms use highly extravagant language with striking parallels to the mythopoetic hymns of the Ancient Near East in referring to Israel's ideal king (Pss. 72, 110). Psalm 45 even approaches deification in its attributes toward the king.

Critical scholarship has been divided on how to assess this development. The Scandinavian school has sought to interpret these hymns by means of a hypothesis of a widespread ideology of divine kingship. It has argued that this common mythological ideology regarding kingship was shared by Israel with all its neighbours, and that these hymns are evidence of Israel's deep involvement in the same mythopoetic circle of ideas about kingship. In my opinion, this interpretation is very unlikely. It cannot be reconciled with the dominant prose tradition of the Old Testament, which regarded the king as an earthly, fragile human being, and which remained suspicious of the institution as being originally foreign to the faith of Israel.

Far more convincing is the theory, which both Eichrodt and von Rad have defended, that something occurred within Israel which allowed an appropriation of mythopoetic language for a different end. Because David's rule had become a type of God's reign, an adumbration of the eschatological rule of God, mythopoetic language could be applied to the reigning monarch as the emissary of God's righteous rule. When the Hebrew psalmist spoke in such an ideal fashion, he was confessing his hope in God's rule which would be ushered in one day by God's anointed. Moreover, there are several clear indices in the present editorial positioning of these royal psalms that they were heard in the post-exilic period as eschatological, indeed as messianic hymns. Although the psalms actualize the reign of God liturgically in a different way from the prophets, both testimonies pointed beyond the historical institution of kingship to an eschatological reality.

Bibliography

M. **Buber**, *Moses*, ET Oxford 1946; *Kingship of God*, ET, New York 1967; R. A. **Carlson**, *David, the Chosen King. A Traditio-Historical Approach to the Second Book of Samuel*, Stockholm 1964; A. **Cazelles**, 'Mosheh', *TWAT* V, 28–46; R. E. **Clements**, 'Messianic Prophecy or Messianic History?', *Horizons in Biblical Theology*, I, Pittsburgh 1979, 87–104; J. H. **Eaton**, *Kingship and the Psalms*, SBT II. 32, 1976; W. **Eichrodt**, *Theology of the Old Testament*, ET, I, London and Philadelphia 1961, 472–90; N. **Gottwald**,

The Tribes of Yahweh, Maryknoll 1979 and London 1980; H. **Gressmann**, *Mose und seine Zeit*, Göttingen 1913; D. W. **Gunn**, *The Story of King David. Genre and Interpretation, JSOT Suppl* 6, 1978; M. **Noth**, *Überlieferungsgeschichtliche Studien*, I, Halle 1943, partial ET *The Deuteronomic History*, Sheffield 1981 (contains pp. 1–110); E. **Osswald**, *Das Bild des Mose in der kritischen alttestamentlichen Wissenschaft seit J. Wellhausen*, Berlin 1962; G. **von Rad**, *Old Testament Theology*, ET, I, Edinburgh and New York 1962, 289–96, 306–54; L. **Rost**, *The Succession to the Throne of David* (1926), ET Sheffield 1982; R. **Smend**, *Das Mosebild von Heinrich Ewald bis Martin Noth*, BGBE 3, 1959; J. A. **Soggin**, *Das Königtum in Israel*, BZAW 104, 1967; A. C. **Welch**, *Kings and Prophets of Israel*, London 1952; J. **Wellhausen**, *Einleitung in das Alte Testament von Friedrich Bleek*, Berlin ⁴1878; W. **Zimmerli**, *Old Testament Theology in Outline*, ET Atlanta and London 1978.

11

THE OFFICE AND FUNCTION OF THE PROPHET

(i) *Methodological issues*

The traditional picture of the Old Testament prophet as an agent of God's rule is of a person who has been super-naturally equipped by God to predict the future. This view is reflected in Sirach, rabbinic Judaism, and in Qumran, but it also finds a clear expression in the New Testament within a christological form (cf. Acts 3.24; I Peter 1.10ff.).

In marked contrast, the modern historical-critical interpretation of the prophets has produced a very different profile of an Old Testament prophet. Beginning in the late eighteenth century with Herder and Eichhorn, and culminating in the nineteenth century in the works of Ewald, Kuenen, and Duhm, a strikingly divergent picture has emerged. Moreover, a wide consensus has now been reached on many of the central features of this critical reconstruction:

(*a*) The Old Testament prophets were 'men of insight', although limited by their time-conditioned horizons, who spoke to the people of their day regarding the issues of the day.

(*b*) The present form of the biblical text of the prophets includes a large amount of secondary material – once called 'non-genuine' – which attached itself later to the original saying of the prophet. Often these secondary layers were used to broaden the original limited focus of the prophets by updating the first oracles for another historical period.

(*c*) The prophets stood in a long history of tradition on which they were dependent. The original prophets were primarily proclaimers rather than authors – forthtellers not foretellers – who couched their oracles in traditional, stereotyped speech forms. The preservation of their material derived initially from circles of disciples who treasured and reworked the material through a lengthy period of transmission and redaction.

(d) The phenomenon of Old Testament prophecy is not unique to Israel, but reflects many similarities of like nature from the world of comparative religion in varying degrees of parallelism (cf. Hölscher).

In my opinion, the task of rendering a theology of the Old Testament according to its canonical context is not to accept uncritically either of these two conflicting approaches, whether the traditional or the critical. Rather, it is to see if one can discern the peculiar construal which the canonical process has left in the text as the grounds for a modern theological reflection on the subject. From this stance important insights from both traditional and historical-critical analysis will be gratefully utilized.

(ii) *The theological role of the prophets*

The origins of prophetism in Israel are historically obscure, and also play no significant theological role in the canonical ordering of the tradition. A great variety of vocabulary is simply registered (seer, prophet, visionary) without any clear historical distinctions being preserved. The famous footnote in I Sam. 9.9 – once a prophet was called a seer – is offered merely to aid the reader and does not establish a significant theological or historical development. Moreover, no attempt is made to clarify the different descriptions of the Old Testament prophets within the tradition. The ecstatic behaviour of some (I Sam. 10.10), the dreams and visions of others (Jer. 23.23), and the political role of others (I Kings 1.22ff.) are simply recorded, but the theological evaluation is made in terms of the content of the message.

Although the Old Testament is unconcerned with the historical origins of prophetism, it is deeply interested in the origins of the prophet's own history with God. For this reason, the prophetic call or commission plays such a significant role. Not only are there the well-known and extended reports found in Isa. 6, Jer. 1 and Ezek. 1–2, but many other traces of call narratives are present. Amos 7 speaks of his seizure by God. Or again, the 'servant' in Isa. 49.1ff. describes the beginning of his ministry in a manner akin to a call.

Von Rad has summarized incisively the theological significance of the call:

> So deep is the gulf which separates the prophets from their past that none of their previous social relationships are carried over into the new way of life. 'I was a herdsman, and a dresser of sycamore trees; but Jahweh took me from following the flock and said to me, Go prophesy . . .' (Amos 7.14f.). This was more than simply a new profession: it was a totally new way of life. . . . (II, 58).

A strong sense of divine compulsion lay at the heart of the call. Amos confesses that 'the Lord has spoken; who can but prophesy?' (3.8). Ezekiel speaks of the strong hand of God laid upon him (3.22), and of being completely overwhelmed (3.15). Especially Jeremiah is aware of the lack of a choice:

> Thou didst deceive me, and I let myself be deceived,
> Thou wast too strong for me and didst prevail over me (20.7).

These two elements of sharp discontinuity and divine compulsion do not imply that the prophets were without any cultural moorings. Connections with the cult before and after the call are frequently present. However, the broad sociological factors have been consistently relativized by the biblical tradition itself. From the biblical perspective there is no comprehending the prophets apart from their encounter with God.

When the book of Jeremiah (18.18) characterizes the three offices of prophet, priest and sage, it identifies the prophet as the bearer of the word. It is, therefore, hardly accidental that the proclaiming of the word plays such a predominant role in the call. Isaiah first experiences forgiveness through the touching of his lips with a fiery coal, but his call comes as a verbal commissioning (6.1ff.). Jeremiah objects that he cannot speak and is told: 'Behold, I have put my words in your mouth – whatever I command you, you will speak' (1.6–9). Ezekiel is offered a scroll to eat, which became sweet as honey (3.3; cf. also Isa. 50.4; Amos 3.8). Finally, when Moses was described as the prototype of all subsequent prophets (Deut. 18.18), the promise was offered in terms of a continual speaking by God to Israel through the word. Other nations communicate with their gods through wizards. Not so Israel. God spoke through his word (Isa. 8.19ff.).

In recent years there has been much speculation as to whether the Old Testament concept of the word functioned as a quasi-mythopoetic entity. The defenders of a uniquely biblical Hebrew mentality put much stress on the event-character of the word which created history through its power (cf. Boman). It is possible that the Old Testament concept of the word can be described phenomenologically as akin to certain mythopoetic features found in other ancient religions. However, the Old Testament itself lays its emphasis upon the content of the word and does not explore the psychology or metaphysics of the 'word-event'. Jeremiah speaks of the word which is like fire, a hammer which breaks rocks in pieces (23.29), but this is because its truth stems from God and not the prophet's own imagination.

In spite of the Old Testament's de-emphasis, many modern interpreters are concerned with the psychology involved in the reception of the divine word by the prophets. What was it exactly that the prophets heard or experienced? Is the expression 'thus saith the Lord' to be taken literally or is it a metaphor for an inner conviction? Indeed, several Old Testament texts betray elements which could be interpreted as a psychological dimension of prophetic reception. Amos makes a leap of association from a 'basket of summer fruit' (qayiṣ) to 'the end (qeṣ) has come for my people' (8.1). Similarly, God's word to Jeremiah arose from a connection between a 'rod of almond' (šaqēd) and 'watching over my word' (šōqēd) (1.11f.). However, the implications of this line of thought are never developed within the Old Testament. Rather, the prophetic messenger formula by which they introduce their oracles seems to point in the opposite direction. The role of the messenger was to communicate the exact letter of the message in the form of direct address (Gen. 32.4). Thus, in an analogous fashion the prophet functioned only as a vehicle of a message which he delivered unchanged from its source. In sum, in spite of the fact that there was actually an important filtering of the divine revelation through the different prophetic personalities – compare Hosea with Amos – this psychological dimension was never assigned an autonomous significance by the biblical tradition itself.

In his *Old Testament Theology* von Rad has attempted to come at this problem of the reception of the revelation by the prophet from a different angle. He is concerned to avoid the pitfalls of a psychological interpretation while doing full justice to the freedom of the prophet. Von Rad regards it as theologically important that the prophets were not simply mechanical conduits, but performed an active role in describing and actualizing the divine judgment on Israel.

He begins his discussion by noting that a distinction has often been preserved between the prophetic invective (*Scheltwort*) and the prophetic threat (*Drohwort*). In the former the prophet describes and castigates Israel's specific sins, whereas in the latter he pronounces a general word of judgment as a consequence of the sin. Von Rad notes the great freedom in the use of the invective which reflects the prophet's closeness to the actual, social abuses of his day (Amos 4.1ff.; 6.1ff.) as well as his individual imagination. Conversely, the threat appears as a largely stereotyped oracle of judgment the form of which the tradition had determined.

Von Rad draws some very bold theological implications from his form-critical observations. He writes:

> It is hardly possible to overrate the importance of the prophet's share, for without it the word the prophet receives does not reach its goal and therefore cannot be fulfilled. What makes it such a tremendous responsibility is the fact that the prophet is thus the one who puts the will of Jahweh into effect: Jahweh thereafter commits himself to stand by the decision of his ambassador (II, 73).

I confess to having considerable ambivalence in evaluating von Rad's position. Clearly he has tried to draw some valid theological insights from his form-critical analysis regarding prophetic freedom. Yet is this theological extension of his critical analysis justified?

My first concern in arriving at a judgment is to determine to what extent the canonical process left any indices which would support this direction for theological reflection. This determination could aid in assessing on what level of the biblical text the form-critical distinctions functioned. Did these discrete forms play a role in an early level of the tradition which was later disregarded? Significantly the sharp distinction which von Rad draws between the creative, free invective and the stereotyped threat has been largely lost in the transmission of the later prophets. It is characteristic, for example, of Jeremiah and Ezekiel that the messenger form, when it appears, encompasses both parts of the prophet's speech. God's word is contained just as much in the invective as in the threat. Moreover, even in Amos, which offers the strongest support for von Rad's hypothesis, the form-critical distinctions are not as clear as he would suggest. The collectors and shapers of the tradition have not often preserved intact the original sequence of invective/ threat, but frequently strung together invectives from different settings as well as joining a string of threats in series (cf. chs. 5 and 6).

The issue remains a perplexing one theologically. Although it seems quite evident that the prophets in fact exercised great freedom in their prophetic role as proclaimers of the word of God, there is little evidence to support the thesis that any theological significance was ever assigned by the tradition to this exercise of imagination.

There is another important function of the Old Testament prophet which the canon has clearly recognized, and which has been seriously addressed by critical scholarship only rather recently. This has to do with the prophet's role as intercessor. Amos is pictured in ch. 7 attempting to intercede for Israel's sake before each divine decision of judgment (vv. 2ff.). Again, Jeremiah is described as defending the people until he is commanded by God not to pray for its welfare (15.1ff.). Similarly, Ezekiel is made dumb in order to bring to a halt any intercession on his part for the rejected people (3.25ff.).

To a great extent the enormous passion of Jeremiah's ministry arose from his deep involvement with the very people he was commissioned to judge. Jeremiah is portrayed as a watchman who announces the approach of the destroying hordes, but at the same time he is overwhelmed with the effect of his words:

> O that my head were waters, and my eyes a fountain of tears, that I might weep day and night for the slain of the daughter of my people . . . (9.1).

This deep personal involvement of Jeremiah leads to another significant aspect of the Old Testament prophet which is only rarely revealed in the biblical text. How did the prophet himself as a private person respond to his role as bearer of the word of God? The issue is raised indirectly in the story of Jonah, who refused to deliver a message of judgment against Nineveh and fled in the opposite direction. When forced to carry through his assignment, and when experiencing God's change of heart at the repentance of the Ninevites, Jonah vents his deep rage toward God: 'I knew it all the time

... I knew that you would forgive and not punish ...' (4.2). However, it is also clear that the book's concern is not with Jonah's emotional state; it touches on the larger problem of his being made to appear as a false prophet.

The climax of the Old Testament's witness regarding the inner struggle of the prophet appears in the so-called 'confessions of Jeremiah', which are found in chs. 11, 12, 15, 17 and 20. The prophet is aghast to learn that there is a plot on his life and in his dialogue with God he raises an intense complaint regarding his ministry (11.18ff.). He pictures the desolation and misery of his life and accuses God of having seduced him (15.15ff.; 20.7ff.). The nadir is reached in ch. 20 in which he erupts in a bitter self-imprecation (14ff.).

Scholars have long debated on how to interpret these confessions. Some have thought that they represented momentary periods of depression. Others saw them as the private side of a life which was generally hidden from public view. All seemed agreed that the confessions had little to do with Jeremiah's function as a prophet. Once again, the major credit goes to von Rad for pointing in a new theological direction. In a brilliant article in 1936 he argued – in my judgment, canonically – that the inclusion of the confessions was not a distraction from Jeremiah's public ministry, but represented an important witness precisely in regard to his office as prophet. The struggles of Jeremiah are not to be dismissed as an internal, psychological weakness, but testify to the fundamental theological tension of being a human being called as the vehicle of destruction to one's own people. The trials of Jeremiah which ultimately tore him into pieces bear eloquent and truthful witness to what it is to be a prophet of God in Israel.

(iii) *The prophetic promise*

I began the discussion of the prophet by contrasting the traditional view with the modern historical-critical view. The dominant characteristic of the traditional understanding focused on the prophet's ability to address a word of promise towards the future – indeed a foreteller! However, among modern critical Old Testament scholars the only one who has found the discrepancy between the two approaches to be an important issue has been R. E. Clements. His

Chapter 6, 'The Old Testament as Promise' (*OT Theology*, 131ff.), is a highly creative, illuminating attempt to break new ground. Clements begins with the observations that late post-biblical interpretation (Sirach, New Testament, etc.) focused on two dominant features within the prophets: the unit of the prophetic message ('all the prophets have spoken these things', Act 3.24), and their word of future promise ('they inquired about this salvation', I Peter 1.10). He then observes that precisely these two elements have been consistently called into question by modern research. The prophets are not a unified corpus, and they rarely spoke of future promise, but of judgment to their contemporaries. Clements wishes to argue that this apparent irreconcilable gap between the traditional and the critical is wider than it ought rightly to be. He contends that the New Testament interpretation is not the imposition of a distorted, alien concept, but is rather an extension of a process of the interpretation of the prophets which had already begun within the Old Testament itself. Clements even speaks of a canonical process which led to this later interpretation.

Clements agrees that in general the major pre-exilic prophets (Amos, Hosea, I Isaiah, Micah) spoke predominantly of judgment. They were 'prophets of doom' when addressing the sinful kingdoms of Northern and Southern Israel. He then argues that beginning in the late seventh century, but especially in the exilic and post-exilic periods, the prophets preached a message of hope, indeed not eschatological, but hope for political restoration. Only following the final destruction of Judah was the prophetic message radicalized into a genuinely eschatological one. This message of hope was then read back into all the prophets when the conviction arose that all the prophets were really speaking about the death and rebirth of Israel. History had been subsumed into eschatology. Clements then briefly goes on to suggest that the patterns in which the writings of the prophets were organized confirmed this way of reading all the prophets as a unified message which heralded promise.

I am deeply appreciative of what Clements is attempting and have greatly profited from his observations. Still, there are some important points of disagreement which are significant for the reflection on Old Testament theology. In my opinion, Clements is still committed to a historical referential reading of the Old Testament as the basic model of exegesis. He therefore begins his discussion of the prophets by inquiring what historical situation in the history of Israel would have given meaning to the biblical message of hope. In the pre-exilic period the context for understanding the prophets was the threat of destruction by Assyria. As a consequence the prophets spoke only of judgment. However, because he can accept a prophetic word of promise only when he can find a suitable historical situation within Israel, he seeks one which would give meaning to a message of hope. He finds these conditions in the political resurgence under Josiah in the seventh century, but especially in the new political life afforded to the exilic community under the benign Persian rule of the sixth century.

In my opinion, the hermeneutical assumptions involved in this rendering of the biblical text have adversely affected his interpretation. Rather, I would argue that the relationship between text and historical situation is a more complex and subtle one than is envisioned by a direct, historical referential reading, as if one could easily align the prophetic message of judgment with political threat, and prophetic promise with periods of political prosperity. The prophetic message of the Old Testament is not a commentary on the history of the ancient Near East, but a word concerning the kingship of God which indeed enters into the arena of history. I fully agree with Clements that the biblical text is multi-layered and that later editors construed earlier traditions often from hindsight. However, this shaping of prophetic texts does not stem from a crude attempt to update their message by matching it to new political realities, but derives primarily from a deepened theological understanding of what God intended for Israel. In sum, the theological factor in the shaping of the biblical literature is crucial for understanding the prophets because the text took its form from the hands of a community of faith which sought to render its sacred traditions in such a way as to conform to God's purpose in history with his people.

In my judgment, a careful analysis of the canonical shaping of the prophetic books offers a somewhat different key for understanding why the later biblical interpreters, including the New Testament, envisioned the prophets as a unity and as offering a word of future promise. The book of Amos offers an excellent point of departure to articulate a different hermeneutical model. As is generally agreed, it has been shaped by means of an addition of secondary oracles in ch. 9. Amos' original words of judgment against the sinful kingdom of Israel have been confirmed. The end has come. However, the new layer offers an important divine restriction: 'I will destroy this kingdom from the face of the earth – except I will not utterly destroy it' (9.8). The restriction does not lie in a contrast between the Northern and Southern kingdoms, as if the addition were simply a post-exilic legitimation of Judah's existence. No segment of Israel escapes the judgment, as Amos truly prophesied. Rather, the prophetic restriction has to do with the ultimate purpose of God in the future of Israel. The discourse moves into the arena of eschatology. It turns on the possibility of a new existence after the end has come. The promise concerns the raising up of the shattered booth of David. No human ruler can achieve it. The initiative lies solely with God. The hope is miraculous and rationally incomprehensible. The continuity which the new shares with the old has been established from God's side.

The editing of ch. 9 does not serve to soften Amos' message of total judgment. The destruction is fully confirmed. Rather, the editor effects a decisive theological construal of the book by placing Amos' words within a broader, eschatological framework which transcends the perspective of the prophet Amos himself. From the divine perspective there was hope beyond the destruction announced by Amos. In sum, Amos' words of judgment on the Northern kingdom could not truthfully testify to God's purpose with his people without a fuller witness concerning God's ultimate goal which was promise and salvation. The ending of Amos concerning promise did not arise from some change in Israel's political history because of the Babylonians or Persians, but rather arose from Israel's continued history with God and an increased knowledge of his will for his people.

It is unnecessary to pursue further in detail the peculiar canonical shape of the remaining prophets (cf. my *Introduction to the Old Testament*, 405ff.). Each book has its own canonical shape by which to render the traditions. Yet there are consistent theological patterns, and in all a message of forgiveness and future promise is voiced. When later Old Testament editors and Hellenistic authors, including the New Testament writers, read the prophets both as a unity and as pointing to a future hope, it was because indices of this holistic construal of promise have been built into the canonical structure of the books which they simply pursued.

Still, it is important to understand the nature of the prophet's theological witness. The traditional reading of the prophets which interpreted them as supernatural predictions of contingent historical events rests on an equally superficial understanding of what biblical prophecy is about. To speak of 'prediction' and 'supernatural' has shifted the mode of thought and discourse far away from the true biblical witness. Indeed the prophets spoke of the future, but the future as the arena in which God exercised his kingship in bringing life out of death and forgiveness in spite of rebellion. The Old Testament prophets were not soothsayers, but proclaimers of the will of God who both kills and brings to life. To identify this understanding of prophecy with prediction is to lose its real theological content and to fall into an error just as grievous as that of modern critical rationalism.

Bibliography

R. V. **Bergren**, *The Prophets and the Law*, Cincinnati and New York 1974; J. **Blenkinsopp**, *A History of Prophecy in Israel*, Philadelphia 1983; T. **Boman**, *Hebrew Thought compared with Greek*, ET London and Philadelphia 1960; B. S. **Childs**, 'The Canonical Shape of the Prophetic Literature', *Interp* 32, 1978, 46–68; R. E. **Clements**, *Prophecy and Tradition*, Oxford 1975; 'The Old Testament as Promise', *Old Testament Theology*, London 1978, 131–54; D. J. A. **Clines** and D. M. **Gunn**, 'Form, Occasion and Redaction in Jeremiah 20', *ZAW* 88, 1976, 390–409; H. **Gunkel**, *Die Propheten*, Göttingen 1917; G. **Hölscher**, *Die Profeten*, Leipzig 1914; K. **Koch**, *The Prophets*, ET, 2 vols. London 1982 and Philadelphia 1983; J. **Lindblom**, *Prophecy in Ancient Israel*, Oxford 1962; S. **Mowinckel**, *He That Cometh*, ET Oxford and Nashville 1956; G. **von Rad**, 'Die Konfessionen Jeremias', *EvTh* 3, 1936, 265–70; reprinted, *GSAT* II, Munich 1973, 224–35; *Old Testament Theology*, ET, II, London and New York 1965; C. **Westermann**, *Basic Forms of Prophetic Speech*, ET Nashville and London 1967; R. R. **Wilson**, *Prophecy and Society in Ancient Israel*, Philadelphia 1980; W. **Zimmerli**, *The Law and the Prophets*, ET Oxford 1965 and New York 1967; *Old Testament Theology in Outline*, ET London and Atlanta 1978, 99–107.

12

TRUE AND FALSE PROPHETS

(i) *The search for biblical criteria*

No one can do justice to the theology of the Old Testament prophets without taking seriously the problem of the relationship between true and false prophets. Few would deny that the problem is difficult and thorny. The basic issue turns on the question of truth. How does one determine who is a true and who a false prophet? What are the criteria for distinguishing someone sent from God and someone who falsely claims divine authority? If in the age of Elijah there seemed to be little difficulty separating the prophets of Baal from those of Yahweh (cf. I Kings 18), by the seventh century the problem of true and false prophets had developed into a major crisis. It is precisely because they both shared the same vocabulary, 'Thus saith the Lord', appealing to the same authority, that the problem emerges with such intensity.

In both Deut. 18 and Jer. 28 there are attempts to develop criteria for identifying a false prophet. However, the dangers being addressed in the two classic passages appear to be different in kind (cf. von Rad). Deuteronomy 18 raises the question 'How may we know the word which Yahweh has not spoken?' – even when spoken allegedly in the name of Yahweh. The criterion is then stated: 'If the word does not come to pass or come true, that is a word which Yahweh has not spoken.' Because it is false, there is no need to fear. But why would anyone fear unless the prophet was speaking falsely of divine judgment? In sum, Deuteronomy is seeking to protect the community against false prophets who terrorize the community with threats of coming disaster.

When we come to the confrontation of Jeremiah with Hananiah

in Jer. 28, the issue seems to be just the opposite. Hananiah prophesies a word of salvation and Jeremiah reminds him:

> The prophets who preceded you and me from ancient times
> prophesied war, famine, and pestilence. As for the prophet who
> prophesies peace, when the word of that prophet comes to pass,
> then it will be known that Yahweh has truly sent the prophet
> (v. 8f.)

It would seem evident that Jeremiah is seeking to protect the
community from the false prophet who lulls the people to sleep with
false hopes of peace and security. In sum, one sees from both these
passages that Israel struggled hard without much immediate success
to establish criteria by which to distinguish the true from the false
prophet.

Among modern Old Testament scholars no one has worked more
intensely with the problem than Zimmerli. Particularly in his 1963
article (*FS A. Weiser*), he sought to explore the 'truth-criteria of
Yahweh' in two exilic prophets. Zimmerli finds claims of truth
being made by Yahweh and his prophets in the context of dispu-
tations with the counter-claims of foreign gods. For example, in
Isa. 41 a disputation is set up in the form of a trial. Yahweh lays
down the challenge:

> Set forth your case . . . bring your evidence . . .
> Tell us what is to happen, tell us the former things,
>   what they are . . .
> Do good, or do harm that we may be dismayed or terrified
>   (vv. 21–23).

Similarly, Ezekiel addresses the nations with the recurring formula
'and you will know that I am Yahweh' (25.6, 7, 11; 26.6; 28.26,
etc.). What God has spoken will happen.

Zimmerli makes the point that in the confrontation with the
foreign nations and their cults, never once did the Old Testament
prophet attempt to establish norms of superiority in terms of higher
spirituality, purer morals, or richer cult. Always the argument
turned on the divine presence of Yahweh in history. He then reasons
that apart from the witness evoked by the presence of God, there was
no objective criterion by which a truth-claim could be demonstrated.
The case with criteria for determining the true and false prophet

would be analogous. The truth of God makes itself finally known, but there are no external norms by which its entrance can be tested. In spite of Zimmerli's very helpful insights, large areas relating to the specific issue of true and false prophecies remain unresolved. What are the means of pursuing the problem further?

(ii) *The case of Jeremiah and Hananiah*

I suggest that the best commentary on the problem is offered in the story of Jeremiah's confrontation with Hananiah (Jer. 27f.). For years I thought that I understood the passage. Now I am prepared to disagree with a widespread interpretation, shared by Zimmerli and von Rad, which I would broadly classify as existential (cf. also Buber).

The main lines of this construal are as follows. For years Jeremiah had been prophesying the destruction of the nation by a foreign power, subsequently identified as the Babylonians. He had fought a running battle against prophets of salvation who comforted the people with promises of an impending victory. He denounced their message as false and urged the people not to listen (27.17). Moreover, in order to actualize his message of submission to the Babylonian king, Jeremiah had thongs and a yoke prepared which he put on his neck. Jeremiah's message, both in positive and negative terms, seemed crystal clear.

It seemed clear until Hananiah appeared. This prophet delivered a message of impending deliverance which was just the reverse of Jeremiah's: 'I have broken the yoke of the king of Babylon. Within two years I will bring back to this place all the vessels of Yahweh's house. . .' (vv. 2–3). If ever there was a blatant example of a false prophet, this is it. The reader expects an explosion from Jeremiah, ending in a fiery denunciation (cf. 7.1ff.). But no, astonishingly enough, Jeremiah responds meekly: 'Amen. May Yahweh do so. May he make the words which you have prophesied come true' (v. 6).

Of course, Jeremiah does seem to have some reservations. He reminds Hananiah that usually the earlier prophets spoke of judgment. Because Hananiah's message is one of salvation, Jeremiah is seemingly content to wish him well and reserve final judgment. However, is this not precisely the problem? Jeremiah has some reservations, but no more. After he had been warning Israel of false prophets for years, a prime example appears and Jeremiah suddenly seems very unsure of himself. He even lets Hananiah break the yoke bars: which nullifies his original symbolic act. Then Jeremiah went away – tail between his legs!

However, the story continues. Some time later, the word of Yahweh came to Jeremiah informing him that Hananiah and lied. Then Jeremiah said to him:

> Listen, Hananiah, Yahweh has not sent you, and you have made the people trust in a lie . . . therefore I will remove you from the face of the earth. . . . In that same year. . . Hananiah died! (vv. 15–16).

Now according to the interpretation of Zimmerli and von Rad, which I have characterized as existential, the story has an important point to make on the question of the truth criteria for being a prophet of God. In spite of Jeremiah's having received a message with an apparently clear content by which to test the truth of a prophecy, he could not abstract this message into an unchanging propositional principle. There was no horizontal continuity in prophecy. When Hananiah claimed to speak a fresh word from God, Jeremiah was unable to refute this claim by an inference from the past. Only when God spoke to him again was Jeremiah able to identify Hananiah's prophecy as false. The criterion of truth resides alone in a fresh word from God *hic et nunc*.

This existential interpretation with its somewhat loose connection to early Barthian theology has recently received a massive extension by James A. Sanders ('Hermeneutics'). Sanders has developed the existential interpretation into a full-blown hermeneutic in order to illustrate his understanding of canon. He wants to illustrate that there never were any objective criteria by which to determine the true from the false prophet. The same biblical tradition could be applied by various prophets in different contexts with very divergent results. What determined its truth was largely a question of timing. The prophet was thus engaged above all in the hermeneutical issue which turned on how correctly he applied his received tradition to his new situation. A false prophet was one who practised bad hermeneutics. Because he misjudged the historical situation, he did not correctly understand whether the moment at hand was one under the judgment or the salvation of God.

Sanders argues that there is really only one indirect criterion which can be adduced in evaluating a proper hermeneutical stance. He calls the principle 'monotheistic pluralism', and interprets it as follows: 'Whenever the freedom of God as creator is forgotten or denied in adapting (a) traditional "text" to a given context, there is the threat of falsehood' (38). Because Hananiah had poor timing, he misunderstood the historical moment and threatened the freedom of God. History therefore judged him to be a false prophet.

Behind Sanders' interpretation of canonical hermeneutics lies a strong theological concern. He assumes that the situation of the modern interpreter of the Old Testament stands in close analogy to that of the ancients. We also stand between the biblical text and a historical moment, and we also strive to adapt our tradition into the changing context. The concept is often expressed as moving from 'Israel's story' to 'our story'. By studying the Old Testament and its hermeneutics, we can learn how to apply a correct hermeneutic in our own time.

No one should underestimate the great attraction which such a rendering of the Bible has for the contemporary generation. Especially for those who have grown weary of a sterile, historicist reading of the Bible, this classic move of liberal Protestant theology continues to evoke a widespread and immediate acceptance. Needless to say, I am highly critical of this theological position for a variety of reasons. I do not think that the canon ever functioned in this way in the church prior to the Enlightenment, nor do I believe it to be a correct way of doing biblical theology. The initial assumption of seeing a simple analogy between the prophet's function and ours subverts the essential role of the canon which established theological continuity between the generations by means of the authority of sacred scripture. We are not prophets nor apostles, nor is our task directly analogous.

I would like to return to the Jeremiah passage (chs. 27f.) and attempt a different interpretation. The first step exegetically is to establish the relationship between ch. 27 and 28. There is general agreement that both chapters are part of a larger editorial unit which begins in 23.9 with the superscription 'concerning the prophets', and extends through ch. 29.

Chapter 27 consists of three separate oracles which are clearly divided: 1–11 (to the nations), 12–15 (to Zedekiah), 16–22 (to priests and people). The first oracle is introduced by a series of instructions to Jeremiah which include the making of thongs and a yoke bar. Then the prophet's oracle makes four main points: (a) vv. 5–8, serve Nebuchadnezzar; (b) v. 9, do not listen to your prophets; (c) v. 10, they prophesy a lie; (d) v. 11, if you are disobedient, you will be removed from the land. The significant observation to make is that in the two further oracles which follow in ch. 27, namely to Zedekiah and to the priests and people, the same pattern with parallelled vocabulary occurs: (a) vv. 1, 17, serve Nebuchadnezzar; (b) vv. 14, 16, do not listen to your prophets; (c) vv. 14, 16, they prophesy a lie; (d) vv. 15, 22, if you are disobedient, you or the temple vessels will be carried off into captivity.

We next turn to ch. 28, which records the incident of the confrontation between Jeremiah and Hananiah (vv. 1–11). In v. 12 Jeremiah receives a divine word to address Hananiah. His oracles (vv. 12–16) follow the exact same pattern of ch. 27 with again closely paralleled vocabulary: (a) v. 14, the nations shall serve Nebuchadnezzar; (c) v. 15, Hananiah has spoken a lie; (d) v. 16, I will remove you from the earth. The variation in the pattern, especially respecting the missing (b) element, is clearly related to the preceding historical situation, and the addressing of the judgment oracle to Hananiah personally.

The implications from this literary analysis immediately follow. The word of Jeremiah in ch. 28 conforms closely to the message of ch. 27. The literary continuity between the chapters supports the assumption, as far as the editor was concerned, that the prophet delivered the same message. Jeremiah's confrontation with Hananiah functions to provide a concrete illustration of the one message against false prophets.

Still the difficult problem remains of interpreting the initial encounter between Jeremiah and Hananiah in vv. 5–9 which has been thought to provide the major warrant for the existentialist interpretation. Theoretically it would be possible to argue that these verses reflect a tradition which has a life independent of the later editorial framework into which it has been placed. In that case, the disagreement with Zimmerli and von Rad would turn on what level of the text one is using for theological reflection. They would be dealing with the original historical situation in which Jeremiah is thought to reflect great uncertainty and to seek a fresh existential confirmation. Conversely, I would be treating the later canonical construal which made a different point by editorially shaping the text to conform to the previous chapter.

Although theoretically it is possible to argue for these two exegetical options, in actuality a careful exegesis of this passage rules out the need for these two approaches. Even without an appeal to the effect of the later canonical framework, vv. 5–9 cannot be read in terms of Jeremiah's self-understanding. To interpret the text as reflecting the prophet's personal uncertainty as to his own previous message, and to see no continuity between the past and the present, is to psychologize the text. The issue of ch. 28 is not about Jeremiah's psyche. Rather, the exegetical issue turns on God's will for the nations under the rule of Nebuchadnezzar. The theological focus is fully theocentric. Jeremiah is uncertain regarding God's plan. Verses 5–9 do not make a different point from that of the framework.

Jeremiah is unwilling to deny God the freedom of changing his mind. He does not say to Hananiah: 'God spoke through me of destruction, and therefore he cannot say something different through you.' Instead, he allows for the possibility that God has a different purpose. However, he then sets up a criterion for determining the truth of Hananiah's claim. God has in the past always spoken of judgment. If he now changes his plan, he will demonstrate it in history. If God then reveals the truth of Hananiah's prophecy of imminent salvation by his action, Jeremiah is fully prepared to acquiesce. In sum, the issue at stake is theocentric: what is God's purpose? It is not psychological: how does Jeremiah know whether or not he is right?

This passage has nothing at all to do with Jeremiah's ability to time his prophecy correctly, nor does he differ with Hananiah merely in the practice of hermeneutics. No, the content of Hananiah's message is wrong. He speaks a lie in claiming to be sent from God, since he is not in touch with God's revelation (23.25ff.). The theological issue is the same throughout these chapters, on both the original and redactional levels. The true prophet speaks the word of God, the false prophet only lies (cf. Ezek. 13.1–16). The test of the truth lies in God who makes known his will through revelation. The contrast is not an existential one between a past, horizontal tradition about God and a present, vertical word from God. Rather, the truth of prophecy is determined by God's confirmation in action.

(iii) *The effect of the canonical shaping*

Still the problem of true and false prophets is far from settled. The criteria set up for distinguishing the true from the false prophet appear inadequate in practice. How much help was it for Israel in a given historical crisis to wait until a prophet was proven either true or false in the course of history? J. Crenshaw (*Prophetic Conflict*) goes so far as to argue that the issue was never resolved in Israel. In fact, the inability of the prophets to validate their message created such confusion that post-exilic Judaism found prophecy sorely deficient and turned elsewhere for spiritual direction, namely to apocalypticism and wisdom. I do not share Crenshaw's assessment of the issue. Above all, it does not reckon with the formation of the Old Testament canon.

I would argue that in the editing of the book of Jeremiah, particularly the oracles against the false prophets (ch. 23–29), a canonical interpretation of the problem was offered which functioned both descriptively and prescriptively. I would agree with Crenshaw that there was much confusion beginning in the seventh century caused by the conflicting claims of rival prophets and prophetic groups. At least some of this strife has been preserved in the various incidents recorded in chs. 23–29. In addition, ch. 29 describes Jeremiah's conflict with the prophets in the exile who offered opposing oracles to those of Jeremiah. Finally, the temple speech of ch. 26 and the use of the words of Micah in the ensuing debate further confirm the high degree of conflict and confusion within Israel in this period.

However, the major point to be made is that the present canonical form of the book of Jeremiah has rendered an interpretation of true and false prophecy and thereby provided a new criterion by means of its collected scriptures for distinguishing between the two. Through the canonical process Jeremiah's oracles were collected and treasured in the period following the destruction of Jerusalem, and the original criterion of Jeremiah for prophetic truth was applied. Jeremiah had been vindicated in Israel's history. God's judgment did fall on the nation, as Jeremiah had said. God had demonstrated by his action that Jeremiah was a true prophet. It was from this theological conviction in the exilic and post-exilic period that Jeremiah's words were collected and edited. In their canonical form they served the community of faith as an authori-

tative means for discerning the will of God and as a norm for
distinguishing the true prophet from the false. If there had been
confusion during Jeremiah's lifetime, there need be no longer.
Future generations of Israel do not stand with those who lived
before the fall of Jerusalem, but with those who lived after, and who
now know to distinguish the true from the false. Jeremiah 23–29 set
out a sharp distinction between the true and the false prophet. The
former has stood in the council of Yahweh and overheard what God
willed (23.18). The latter utters visions of his own mind and vain
hopes. One speaks of divine revelation, the other of self-evoked
fantasy.

There is also a distinction in content. The true prophets have a
unified message because God has made his message clear. 'My
servants the prophets' (26.5) have consistently brought a message
of repentance from evil. For twenty-three years Jeremiah had
himself been preaching: 'Turn now everyone . . . from his evil ways'
(25.3). 'If you will not listen . . . to walk in my law. . . I will make
this city a curse' (26.4ff.). Jeremiah 23.22 summarizes the distinction
in the content of the message: 'If they had stood in my council, then
they would have proclaimed my words to my people, and they
would have turned from their evil way.'

In addition, the book of Jeremiah offers a moral test of the prophet
himself:

In the prophets of Samaria
I saw an unsavoury thing:
they prophesied by Baal
and led my people Israel astray.
But in the prophets of Jerusalem
I have seen a horrible thing:
They commit adultery and walk in lies . . .
all of them have become like Sodom to me . . . (23.13f.).

The same point is made in 29.23. In contrast to these false prophets,
the faithful lives of the true prophets are illustrated paradigmatically
by Jeremiah and Uriah, who were killed for speaking the truth
(26.20ff.).

In sum, although historical Israel suffered confusion and uncertainty in the crisis of distinguishing true from false prophecy, the
canonical process of construing Israel's tradition shaped Jeremiah's

oracles with a view to overcoming the confusion and setting up a scriptural norm for distinguishing the true from the false prophet.

(iv) *I Kings 13*

One further passage needs to be discussed in the context of the subject of true and false prophecy, namely the story of the two prophets at Bethel. The narrative is not related in any direct literary fashion to Jeremiah, but within the context of the Old Testament canon affords a striking illustration of another aspect of the problem.

Briefly the content: a prophet from Judah is sent to direct a word of judgment against the altar in Bethel. He also gives a sign which immediately fulfils itself. Jeroboam, the king, first attempts to silence the prophet, then to negotiate with him for reconciliation in an offer of a meal together. He is flatly rejected by the prophet from Judah for whom there is no fellowship allowed with apostates. When the prophet from Judah departs for home, he is pursued by a prophet from Bethel, who, understanding the implication of the oracle of judgment, lies to him and persuades him to return. During the meal together the word of God comes to the prophet of Bethel, now addressing a word of judgment to the prophet from Judah. Because of his disobedience in returning and eating, he will die and not be buried with his fathers. And so it happened. On this return the prophet from Judah was killed by a lion. When the prophet from Bethel heard of it, he took the body and buried it in a grave, confirming that the prophet's original word of judgment against Bethel would stand.

Space is too limited to review the history of the interpretation of this narrative, which has been called by one commentator 'among the strangest in the Old Testament'. However, major credit goes to Karl Barth, who in his exegesis (*Church Dogmatics*, II/2, 399ff.) first opened up the real theological dimension of the biblical text. He observed at the outset the paradigmatic significance of the chapter's being placed at the division of the two kingdoms in order to function almost as a superscription for the remaining history of the divided kingdom. He also correctly noted that the story is not merely about two prophets, but relates to far larger theological issues. The prophet from Judah, in delivering a word of judgment against the altar at Bethel, challenged the legitimacy of the entire cult of the northern kingdom. The offer to negotiate with the prophet at table fellowship was an obvious attempt to soften the divine judgment.

Equally significant is the light which the story throws on the issue of true and false prophecy. The division of the kingdom under Jeroboam in no way called into question the legitimate office of the prophets of the north, nor is this ever claimed by the Judaean prophet. In fact, there would have been no narrative had the prophet from Bethel been identified at the outset as a false prophet. Rather, he spoke the same religious language and delivered his message to return to Bethel as a word from Yahweh. The story highlights accurately the historical problem which arose in Israel. Why then was the prophet from Judah to blame? How could he have known that the prophet of Bethel spoke a lie?

Barth has correctly seen that this whole set of questions lies in the background of the story and plays little role. In fact, because Old Testament scholars are mainly interested in pursuing these historical, sociological and psychological issues – fortunately, there are a few exceptions – they have generally misunderstood the story. What is so remarkable in the narrative is the lack of any moralizing, either to blame or excuse the prophets. The emphasis falls completely on the objective nature of the word of God. The story reaches its climax when the roles of the two prophets are reversed. The true word of God is now proclaimed through the mouth of the false prophet. 'Thus saith the Lord, because you have disobeyed the word of God, and have eaten and drunk in this place, you shall die' (vv. 21f.). The will of God for judgment is not abrogated by the quality of its communicator, whether by a true or false prophet.

In sum, the narrative is presented from such a theocentric perspective that it appears almost incomprehensible to rational reflection. All the ethical issues are simply by-passed. The story has to do with the fulfilment of God's word of judgment which will not tolerate any softening or compromise. In a real sense, the narrative marks the furthest extreme possible from an existentialist interpretation of prophecy. Timing and hermeneutics have nothing to do with the true and the false. The distinction is unrelated to the ethical sensitivity of an alert prophet, but measured completely by the effect of the word of God.

Of course, it would be an error to attempt to abstract an entire doctrine of prophecy from this one narrative. Rather, the theological task of Old Testament theology is to relate its message to the larger canonical context, and both to gain a grasp of the full range of witnesses and to discern the inner dynamics of prophecy.

Bibliography

K. **Barth**, *Church Dogmatics*, ET, II/2, Edinburgh 1957, 393–409; M. **Buber**, 'False Prophets', *Biblical Humanism*, ET London 1968, 166–71; J. L. **Crenshaw**, *Prophetic Conflict*, BZAW 124, 1971; S. J. **DeVries**, *Prophet against Prophet*, Grand Rapids 1978; W. **Grosse**, 'Lying Prophet and Disobedient Man of God in I Kings 13: Role Analysis as an Instrument of Theological Interpretation of an Old Testament Narrative', *Semeia* 15, 1979, 97–135; F. L. **Hossfeld** and I. **Meyer**, *Prophet gegen Prophet*, BibB 9, 1973; A. **Jepsen**, 'Gottesmann und Prophet. Anmerkungen zum Kapitel I Könige 13', *Probleme biblischer Theologie, FS G. von Rad*, Munich 1971, 171–82; I. **Meyer**, *Jeremia und die falschen Propheten*, OBeO 13, 1977; T. W. **Overholt**, *The Threat of Falsehood*, SBT II.16, 1970; E. **Osswald**, *Falsche Prophetie im Alten Testament*, Tübingen 1962; G. **Quell**, *Wahre und falsche Prophetie*, Gütersloh 1952; G. **von Rad**, 'Die falschen Propheten', *ZAW* 51, 1933, 109–20; reprinted *GSAT* II, Munich 1973, 212–23; J. A. **Sanders**, 'Hermeneutics in True and False Prophecy', *Canon and Authority*, ed. G. W. Coats and B. O. Long, Philadelphia 1977, 21–41; W. **Zimmerli**, 'Der Wahrheitserweis Jahwes nach der Botschaft der beiden Exilspropheten', *Tradition und Situation, FS A. Weiser*, ed. E. Würthwein and O. Kaiser, Göttingen 1963, 133–51.

13

THE THEOLOGICAL ROLE OF PRIESTHOOD

Few Old Testament problems are as complex as that of the priest-hood. There is much continuing scholarly debate, but few lines of broad consensus have been established. I shall try to avoid excessive detail, and seek rather to illustrate the problem of reflecting theologically on the subject.

(i) *The nature of the critical problem*

There is no more powerful way of focusing on the problem than to confront Wellhausen's brilliant chapter on 'Priests and Levites' (*Prolegomena*, 121ff.), which poses the critical issues with extraordinary sharpness. According to Wellhausen, the Old Testament portrayal of the priests and Levites in its canonical – that is, its traditional – form is completely incomprehensible. In order to make any sense of the biblical text, it is necessary to reconstruct the record according to its genuine historical development, which has been badly misconstrued.

What, then, is the difficulty of understanding the office of priest-hood in the Old Testament? According to the present biblical order the cult was established by Moses at Sinai. Exodus 28 describes the selection of Aaron and his sons, and their consecration to an eternal priesthood (Lev. 8–10). Essential to the Mosaic cult is the sharp distinction between priests and Levites. The priest in the line of Aaron performed the essential cultic rites, whereas the Levites were viewed as minor cultic personnel in charge of the external maintenance of the tabernacle. The book of Numbers continues the same distinctions for Israel on the march.

The first major friction arises in the book of Deuteronomy because no distinction appears between priests and Levites; rather, the term

'Levitical priest' is now used. Moreover, every Levite can function as a priest, although various priestly duties are recognized. According to Wellhausen, the problems grow even more intense when one reaches the early historical books. In Judges and Samuel all signs of a professional clergy of Aaronites disappear. Eli, the chief priest, is from the tribe of Ephraim, and there is only a loose description of the role of Levites (Judg. 19).

Then again, there are enormous tensions surrounding David's cultic role. The portrayal of Israel's cult in Samuel/Kings diverges greatly from that of Chronicles, which again carefully separates priests and Levites. Although the reader gets the impression that something very important happened with Josiah's reform (II Kings 23), only hints are given of the significance of the removal of the non-Jerusalemite priests from the high places. Finally, Ezek. 44 offers a legitimation for Zadok's predominant role, but the effect is to defend a distinction which Ezekiel regards as new, though it has already been assumed as normative in the books of Leviticus and Numbers.

Wellhausen next offers his brilliant theory by which to explain the confusion. The basic problem of interpretation arises from a false analysis of the biblical literature. The Priestly material of Ex. 25–40, Leviticus and Numbers is not Mosaic in age, but rather post-exilic. Similarly, the book of Deuteronomy is not Mosaic, but stems from the period of the late monarchy. Moreover, in addition to this erroneous dating, the traditional interpretation failed to see that the key to the historical development of the priesthood was to be found in the centralization under Josiah in 621 BC, which effected a fundamental change in the character of the priesthood.

However, lest anyone is tempted to dismiss Wellhausen's position as extreme and no longer to be taken seriously, its similarity to von Rad's formulation is to be noted:

> . . . the rigid demarcation of the priests from the Levites which we find everywhere in P, and without which its whole theological sacral picture is incomprehensible, was set in motion by an event which only took place in the late monarchical period, namely Josiah's centralization of the cult (I, 249).

Wellhausen next sets out to reconstruct the true history of the development of Israel's priesthood in his three classic stages. Early Israel had no professional classes, which explains why judges and kings sacrificed freely. The second stage occurred with the reform of Josiah, who centralized Israel's worship by disenfranchizing the non-Jerusalemite priesthood. The policy, which was politically motivated by the Aaronite priesthood of Jerusalem, succeeded in subordinating the rival priestly clans, namely, the Levites, to the line of Zadok. Both Ezek. 44 and the conflict stories in the Pentateuch, such as Num. 16, reflect this struggle for hegemony. The final stage which is found in the post-exilic Priestly code and in Chronicles, occurred when the one line of the priestly line of Zadok established its complete control of the priesthood and the Levites were demoted to hierodules.

How should one react to Wellhausen's massive challenge to the traditional position? Soon after the first shock from his critical assessment of the priesthood, a flood of articles and books appeared which sought to buttress the traditional view (cf. e.g. Curtiss). Significantly, these conservative responses shared the same historically referential reading of the Old Testament as the critical, but they differed in trying to identify the canonical presentation with the actual historical development of the Israelite priesthood. By and large, the conservative rejoinders were deemed unsuccessful by the scholarly guild. However, more significant was the hermeneutical effect of the ensuing debate. The conservatives wanted to reconstruct a less radical picture than Wellhausen's, but in the end they based their exegesis on a reconstruction of Israelite history which also differed from the biblical presentation.

During the last hundred years since Wellhausen posited his brilliant reconstruction there have been many efforts to modify and correct it. Certainly one of the most impressive of the recent attempts has been that of Frank M. Cross. He has argued in detail that all the various tensions which were pointed out by Wellhausen can be resolved by positing an ancient and prolonged struggle between two priestly houses. On the one hand, there was the Mushite (Mosaic) priesthood which flourished at the sanctuaries of Dan and Shiloh along with local shrines in the Negeb. On the other hand, there was the opposing Aaronite priesthood centred in Bethel and in Jerusalem. Cross opposes Wellhausen's reconstruction at several crucial places, but especially he is successful in showing the ancient roots of the priesthood extending far back into the pre-monarchial period. However, the major point to be made is that hermeneutically Cross's historical reconstruction is equally as radical as Wellhausen's in rejecting the traditional view and in hypothesizing a true historical development which only a modern critical historian could recover. Cross fully agrees with Wellhausen that the present form of the canon is hopelessly confused and must be thoroughly reworked in order to be properly interpreted.

In the light of the great discrepancies between the traditional view of the priesthood and the various critical reconstructions, one is at first tempted to argue that there is no theological relationship between the actual, historical development of the priesthood and the biblical portrayal. These are two separate realms which function fully independently of each other. One can accept either Wellhausen's or Cross's historical reconstruction and then proceed to describe a theological interpretation based on the Old Testament canon as a separate enterprise without any historical referent.

However, in my opinion, there are major theological and hermeneutical difficulties with such an approach. If Wellhausen or Cross were right that the present form of the Old Testament priesthood reflects a completely artificial construct, and that the real forces determining the priestly institution were internal political struggles for power, then one could no longer meaningfully speak of a canonical shape. It would be virtually meaningless to focus on the religious use of authoritative traditions in order to form a theological witness if the forces at work were really of a radically different sort. I do not wish to oversimplify the canonical process. No human action is without ambiguity and no religious force is entirely isolated from so-called secular influences. However, it runs directly in the face of a canonical understanding to assume that the present form of the text is merely a cover for the real political forces which lie behind it, or to posit that the later theological use transformed the tradition into something different in kind from the original secular function. To use a crude analogy: one cannot take Richard Nixon's Whitehouse tapes and transform them into literature akin to Augustine's Confessions!

To summarize up to this point, although I have been highly critical of a historical referential reading of the Old Testament in the preceding chapters, the reverse construal is just as unsatisfactory, namely to lay claim to a completely non-historical reading of the Bible. To identify the canonical approach with structuralism, as J. Barton suggests (cf. ch. 1), is very far from the truth. The main hermeneutical point to stress is that the canon makes its theological witness in numerous ways in relation to historical referentiality. At times it forms a very loose connection, whereas at other times a genuinely historical component belongs to the heart of the witness. It is fully inadequate to restrict the nature of the Old Testament's theological witness either by demanding absolute historical coherence or by positing in principle no relationship whatever. The attention to the text's canonical shape arises precisely from the concern to discern how the biblical material was construed in faith within the world of common human experience.

Fortunately, some recent research on Old Testament priesthood by modern scholars has opened up other options, so that one does not simply have to choose between Wellhausen and a pre-critical traditional reading. A good illustration is the monograph of Gunneweg, *Leviten und Priester*. Space is too limited to offer a detailed review of his criticisms of Wellhausen's reconstruction. However, he makes the rather convincing case that the distinction between priests and Levites is not just a post-exilic construct to legitimate an ideology, but reflects ancient, pre-exilic tradition which was subsequently refined and schematized. Or again, he argues that Deuteronomy's apparent identification of priest and Levite is placed in a very different light when seen as a programmatic claim of the writer for the purity of worship in which the Levitical zeal for the law subsumed the entire institution under a religious ideal. Finally, Gunneweg does much to relativize the close linkage of Josiah's reform with the downgrading of the Levites, and he outlines a very different historical process from that of Wellhausen.

I do not wish to be misunderstood. I am not saying that one can now accept Gunneweg's reconstruction instead of Wellhausen's or Cross's and build an Old Testament theology on top of it. I am still opposed to any direct historical referential reading as a substitute for the canonical witness. Nevertheless, I am concerned to show that a reconstruction which is totally alien to the canonical construal can have a negative effect in preventing a theological understanding by robbing the text of its freedom.

(ii) *Towards a canonical construal of the priesthood*

The theological task is to try to sketch a theological understanding of the office of priesthood which does justice to the peculiar shape of the literature. According to the clear witness of the Pentateuch, the worship of Israel was established by God at Sinai and formed an integral part of the divine will along with the giving of the Law. The goal of the exodus from Egypt was to establish a holy nation, a kingdom of priests (Ex. 19.6). Moses is viewed as the founder of the priestly order who was faithful when tested (Ex. 33.7–11; Lev. 8.1ff.; Deut. 33.8). The role of the priest was not merely to sacrifice, but to instruct the people in the ways of God. In Ex. 24 Moses ascended Mt Sinai to receive directions regarding the building of the tabernacle and the institution of the priesthood. Ex. 28 speaks of the preparation of Aaron's consecration which was then executed in Lev. 8–10. Leviticus summarizes the great task of the priesthood: 'You are to distinguish between the holy and the common, and between the unclean and the clean, and you are to teach the people of Israel all the statutes which Yahweh has spoken to them by Moses' (Lev. 10.10–11; cf. Ezek. 44.23). Moreover, a clear distinction was made between priests and Levites, the latter being appointed to minister over the tabernacle and the furnishings (Num. 1.47ff.).

However, the Levites are integrally connected with another basic witness in the Pentateuch. In Ex. 32 Aaron the priest led the people astray into idolatry. The threat of false worship was present even at Sinai. Both Ex. 32 and Deut. 10 derive the special role of the Levites from their zeal for Yahweh. Deuteronomy 10 elaborates on their distinction of being separated with a special inheritance: 'The Lord set apart the tribe of Levi to carry the ark of the covenant . . . to stand before the Lord to minister to him and to bless his name. . .' (v. 8). Similarly, Deut. 33.8f. stresses their role as guardians and keepers of the covenant. Throughout the rest of Deuteronomy they are always mentioned along with the poor and the landless of Israel, who must be invited to Israel's festivals in order rightly to share in the joy of God's blessing (12.19ff.; 18.6ff.)

Other prime examples of the threat to Israel's proper worship are represented in the Pentateuch by the narrative of Nadab and Abihu, the sons of Aaron, who offered 'unholy fire' (Lev. 10.1–3), and by the revolt of Korah, who was a Levite (Num. 16.1ff.), but who rebelled against Moses in an effort to gain priestly privilege for himself. It is very likely that both Ex. 32 and Num. 16 reflect some earlier stages within the tradition, and show evident signs of struggles within the priesthood between competing clans. However, the canonical process had largely blurred these original contours in order to make the stories now function as representatives of false claims of priesthood. Conversely, the special role of the Levites as zealous adherents of the faith has been anchored literally to one particular historical moment in the Mosaic period according to which the office was defined.

Then again, the period of the judges has been interpreted canonically as one of decline and disobedience. The results of lawlessness are illustrated by reference to the abuses of the cult, particularly in the story of Micah's idols and the role of the wandering Levite (Judg. 17.1ff.). The loss of the ark to the Philistines (I Sam. 4.1ff.) is also construed to the same effect. This period which Wellhausen interpreted as reflecting historically the early stages within Israel without an organized priesthood is used canonically to illustrate a retrogression from the ideal of Moses. Similarly, the priesthood of Eli and his wicked sons (I Sam. 2.22ff.) receive the divine judgment. Significantly, this theological use of the material has left enough tensions within the various stories to demonstrate that one cannot simply identify the canonical construal with the historical development of the cult within Israel, as traditionalists have often attempted.

Again, the historical development of the priesthood under David and Solomon remains quite obscure. That there was a political struggle is clear from the story of Abiathar's involvement in the succession story and his replacement by Zadok (I Kings 2.26). The canonical construal interprets the establishment of Zadok typologically as a representative of a righteous priesthood and Abiathar's rejection as the fulfilment of the prophetic word against Eli. Nowhere is there a hint that Zadok stemmed from a Canaanite priestly clan of pre-Davidic Jerusalem, as has occasionally been suggested.

The picture in Chronicles of the Levites is again idealized to represent the struggle for a purified, zealous priesthood against various forms of corruption. Recent critical research on the book of Chronicles has rightly rejected the extreme theories of de Wette and Wellhausen which spoke largely in terms of fabrication. Rather, the Chronicler has systematized and expanded the role of the Levites to represent a programme which conforms theologically to the laws of Leviticus and Numbers.

Within the canonical context of II Kings the Josianic reform has been assigned a much more modest role than that afforded it by critical scholarship. In both Kings and Chronicles it has been set in continuity with the earlier reform of Hezekiah as a restoration of the legitimate and purified worship of God found in Deuteronomy. It is not construed as a political innovation. However, II Kings 23.9 does record that the priests of the high places did not come to Jerusalem to minister, but remained in their villages. Significantly, the canonical construal which did not tie this demoting of the local priests with the Levites, as suggested by Wellhausen and many others, has been vigorously defended as historically accurate by Gunneweg. It is also clear that the biblical account has passed over the many serious social and political effects of the purification of worship through centralization which critical historians have often been able to discern.

Ezekiel 44 is another highly significant passage in evaluating the role of the priesthood, but again it is difficult to recover the exact historical circumstances surrounding the controversy. The singling out of Zadok is set against the vague historical background of the pre-exilic Levites who went after idols, led Israel astray, and therefore must bear their punishment. The canonical interpretation is consistent in seeing the history as a corruption of the revealed will of God for the priesthood and not as an innovation. The close parallels between Ezekiel and the priestly writings of Leviticus serve canonically to support the interpretation that God's purpose was one of the restoration of pure worship.

In general, the same pattern of a return to the original Mosaic ideal is continued in the books of Ezra and Nehemiah. Of course, there is recognition of the changing historical situation which the exile produced. Thus Ezra discovers that not enough Levites had returned from Babylon to support the needed ecclesiastical staff (Ezra 8.20). However, basically the new arrangements of the priests and Levites for the service of God in Jerusalem were made to conform to what 'is written in the book of Moses' (Ezra 6.18). The same contrast between the faithful and disobedient priest is voiced throughout the books of Ezra and Nehemiah (Ezra 10.5; Neh. 11.10).

(iii) *Summary of the theology of priesthood*

Let me attempt briefly to summarize the theological implications of the canonical construal of the priesthood within the Old Testament.

(a) The Old Testament offers a theological interpretation of the priesthood which derives from its own particular use of the tradition within the canonical process. The actual historical development of the priesthood is not afforded canonical status, but left in the background of the text as prehistory. Rather, the post-exilic form of the Israelite priesthood has been made normative. The canonical shape reflects a variety of moves by which to render its witness, such as schematizing, idealizing and typologizing the tradition. For this reason an interpretation which is directly dependent on a historically referential reading is theologically inadequate. It reorders the text diachronically and in so doing misses the Old Testament's unique message. Conversely, an interpretation which cuts all connections with Israel's peculiar history is unable to do justice to the canon's interpretation, which has incorporated crucial elements of the history into its testimony.

(b) The role of the priest is viewed primarily as the guardian of the will of God to separate the clean and the unclean, the pure and the sacred. A faithful priesthood was constitutive of an obedient, worshipping people of God from the beginning and was grounded in the theophany at Sinai. Especially the role of the Levites emphasized the unity of the will of God for the proper forms of worship, the distortion of which remains a constant threat.

(c) The canonical construal saw fit to blur and omit many of the historical features of the priestly institutions. Its main stress lay on contrasting the ideal, obedient forms of the priesthood with the recurring inroads of corruption (golden calf, Korah, Baal-Peor, Bethel). In my judgment, the challenge of Old Testament exegesis is not to rest content with refocusing the biblical text in order to reconstruct its prehistory. Rather, its theological responsibility lies in following with precision the direction which is given by the shaping of the biblical text itself, and to relate one's modern theological reflection to the unique dynamic which arises from the Bible's intertextuality.

Bibliography

A. **Cody**, *A History of Old Testament Priesthood*, AnBib 35, 1969; F. M. **Cross**, *Canaanite Myth and Hebrew Epic*, Cambridge, Mass. and London 1973, 195–215; S. I. **Curtiss**, *The Levitical Priests*, Edinburgh 1877; M.

Greenberg, 'A New Approach to the History of the Israelite Priesthood', JAOS 70, 1950, 41–7; A. H. J. **Gunneweg**, *Leviten und Priester*, FRLANT 89, 1965; M. **Haran**, *Temple and Temple-Service in Ancient Israel*, Oxford 1978; H. J. **Kraus**, *Worship in Israel. A Cultic History of the Old Testament*, ET Oxford 1966; K. **Möhlenbrink**, 'Die levitischen Überlieferungen des Alten Testaments', *ZAW* 52, 1934, 184–231; T. **Polk**, 'The Levites in the Davidic-Solomonic Empire', *StBib* IX, 1979, 3–22; G. **von Rad**, *Old Testament Theology*, ET, I, Edinburgh and New York 1962, 232–79; R. B. **Robinson**, 'The Levites in the Pre-Monarchic Period', *StBib* VII, 1978, 3–24; J. **Wellhausen**, *Prolegomena to the History of Israel*, ET Edinburgh 1885, 121–51; W. **Zimmerli**, *Old Testament Theology in Outline*, ET London and Atlanta 1978, 93–9.

14

BENEFITS OF THE COVENANT:
THE CULTUS

The gift of the covenant also involved the establishment of institutions by which to regulate Israel's common life before God together with the agents of its administration. One of the major institutions which was closely tied to the inauguration of the covenant of Sinai was that of the cultus. The term includes all those fixed conventions of worship, observed by both the individual and the group, by which the benefits of divine favour in everyday life could be realized. The cultus provided a form of communal living, which sought to conform to the will of the God of the covenant by correctly distinguishing between the areas of the sacred and the profane.

(i) *Methodological issues*

(*a*) An initial problem for interpreters arises from the peculiar nature of the biblical witness. The cultic material is concentrated in a very few sections of the Old Testament (e.g. Ex. 24ff.; Lev.; Ezek. 40–48), but far less direct attention is found in the remaining portions of the canon. Even the Psalter reflects only one aspect of cultic life with little direct concern for the institutional settings in which its hymns and prayers function. As a result, the problem of relating the cultic life of Israel to the fragmentary source material is a persistent one.

(*b*) The literary problem is closely tied to the historical problem. Wellhausen's reconstruction of the development of the cult in Israel sought to resolve the literary issue by positing a late post-exilic date for the Priestly source which contained the bulk of the cultic laws. Although his theory has been greatly modified during the last hundred years, and many scholars would now insist that much of the Priestly material is actually pre-exilic, nevertheless the issue of a development within Israel's cult cannot be denied (cf. Rendtorff). The difficult methodological issue turns on deciding how to treat the growth within the institution from a theological perspective. To suggest with Haran (*Temple*, 5ff.) that the Priestly material was codified early in the pre-exilic period by a small, almost esoteric group, and that only in the post-exilic period did it enter into public life, does not greatly help either from a historical or theological point of view.

(*c*) Then again, the hermeneutical problem in correctly handling the cultic material is complex. On what level is the biblical text to be interpreted? De Vaux's attempt to reconstruct the historical forms of Israel's cult is useful for some questions (*Ancient Israel*, 271ff.), but he nowhere addresses the major theological issues at stake. Clearly the biblical text does not simply describe cultic institutions. The book of Leviticus has construed the material, both by selection and perspective, so that its witness is only indirectly related to the historical practices. The hard question arises in deciding how to approach such an interpreted text. The striking differences in modern hermeneutical methodology are seen, for example, when comparing von Rad's theology of the growth of Priestly tradition with Milgrom's description of a closed, unified cultic system.

(*d*) Finally, the need for any modern theological reflection to render the material in a coherent fashion cannot be avoided by claims of purely objective analysis. Yet the nature of the construal must be constantly tested by the biblical text itself. Apologetic elements are to be eschewed which are found both in traditional Christian denigration of the cult as mechanical and in various Jewish defences of its purely ethical rootage. The widespread attempt to gain a theological advantage by contrasting the Old Testament's cult with pagan religion (e.g. Eichrodt, Kaufmann, etc.) has some justification because of the obviously shared elements. However, the approach has diminishing returns and is inadequate as a major form of theological interpretation.

(ii) *The canonical shape of Leviticus*

There are some important features in the book of Leviticus which offer broad guidelines for its interpretation. First, Leviticus presents only a small selection of material from Israel's cult which is construed from different perspectives. Chapters 1–5 appear to focus on various offerings from the perspective of the layman, whereas chs. 6–7 function as a kind of priest's manual. The material is often arranged from a topical perspective (e.g. 'offerings which please Yahweh'), and one gets a very fragmented view of the entire ritual (cf. Ex. 29.38ff. in contrast). Usually little attention is paid to the mechanical features of the cult, or to the various occasions in which the different rites are operative.

Secondly, the biblical text is virtually silent on the theory behind sacrifice and atonement. Although much scholarly energy has been expended in an effort to describe the basic concept on which sacrifice was grounded (communion, gift, expiation), the biblical text does not address this issue directly. It remains a moot question whether one such clear understanding was ever assumed, or whether a variety of different eclectic interpretations were at work among different participants. Lev. 17.11 does indeed touch upon the issue: 'For the life of the flesh is (in) the blood . . . for it is the blood that makes atonement, by reason of the life.' However, all the competing theories have also found some support from the same text. In sum, the biblical weight falls on the function of sacrifice rather than on a theory of its meaning.

Thirdly, the book of Leviticus has been given a definite historical setting as instructions to Moses in the context of the Sinai covenant. Even elements of the narrative are continued from the previous book (Lev. 8–9 join Ex. 29). The final chapters look forward to the imminent entrance into the promised land and connect smoothly with the book of Numbers. However, this literary setting plays a minor role within the book itself, which is organized largely according to topics and association. The canonical setting functions largely as an overarching theological construct in which one historical moment has become the medium to measure all the subsequent history of proper worship. Indeed all the later developments of legal tradition within Israel's history are usually also subsumed under the rubric of Mosaic law. The many and various historical rationales which once lay behind the original rites have been either blurred or removed and now function according to conventional terminology as being pleasing to God or separating the clean from the unclean.

Finally, the material of Leviticus is rendered in a highly objectivized fashion. Von Rad (I, 246f.) has pointed to the function of the declaratory formula (e.g. Lev. 13.8, 17, 39), from which one can infer that the style of Leviticus stands in continuity with ancient priestly ritual practice. Little attention is paid in Leviticus to the subjective responses of the participants. In my opinion, Milgrom's attempt to psychologize the guilt offering (*'āšām*) as the guilty feeling of the conscience which evokes an attitude of repentance badly misconstrues the highly objective stance of the Priestly writer (*Cult and Conscience*, 7ff.).

There is another feature in the formal rendering of the book of Leviticus which has not been adequately treated up to now, but which has some important theological implications. The material in Leviticus has not been merely organized in a roughly topical fashion, but it has been characteristically rendered by the repetition of key phrases. Moreover, a phrase is used within a discrete literary unit, and as a cluster is not repeated elsewhere in the book with rare exceptions. Compare the following examples:

Lev. 1–3   'a pleasing odour to Yahweh', 1.9, 13, 17; 2.2, 9, 12; 3.5, 16 (cf. 4.31; 23.13; 26.31).

4–5:   'the priest shall make atonement . . . they shall be forgiven', 4.20, 26, 31, 36; 5.6, 10, 16, 18.

6–7:   'this is the law of. . .', 6.9, 14, 25; 7.1, 11, 37.

8–10:   'as Yahweh commanded (Moses)', 8.4, 9, 13, 17, 21, 29, 36; 9.6, 10, 21; 10.15.

11–15:   'they are unclean', 11.8, 28, 31, 36, 38, 43.
'she shall be unclean', 12.2, 5, 7, 8.
'pronounce him clean (or unclean)', 13.3, 8, 14, 17, 23, 27, 30.
'he shall be clean', 14.7, 9, 20, 53.
'it shall be unclean', 15.4, 6, 9, 18, 19, 20, 24, 25, etc.

16:   'he shall make atonement', 16.6, 10, 11, 16, 17, 18, 24, 32, 33, 34.

17:   'he shall be cut off', 17.9, 10, 14.

18–22:   'I am Yahweh', 18.2, 4, 5, 6, 21, 30; 19.2, 3, 4, 10, 12, etc.; 20.7, 8, 24, 26; 21.12; 22.2, 3, 8, 30, 33.
'I will set my face against', 20.3, 5, 6.
'I am Yahweh who sanctify you (them)', 21.8, 15, 23; 22.9, 16, 32.

23:     'do no laborious work', 23.7, 8, 21, 23, 28, 31, 35,
        36.
        'it is a statute for ever', 23.14, 21, 41; 24.3.
26:     'my soul abhors', 26.11, 15, 30, 43, 44.
27:     'holy to Yahweh', 27.(9, 10), 14, 21, 23, 28, 30, 32,
        33.

From the perspective of the growth of the Priestly tradition into a fixed literary composition, the repetition of certain key phrases within a unit of material is hardly surprising. It simply reinforces the impression that much of the material functioned separately in the early stages of the book's formation, and these signs of independent life have been retained within the final form of the book. Chapters 6–7, which appear to be a type of priestly manual, are logically arranged under the rubric 'This is the law of. . .'. Similarly, material concerned with the priest's function of determining the status of purity or impurity is dominated by declarative formulae (chs. 11–15).

The theological significance, however, derives from the effect on the synchronic level of this technique of repetition upon the reading of the book. The literary form aids in establishing both the semantic level on which the text now functions as well as the manner in which it seeks to actualize its message. As has already been stated, the book of Leviticus does not contain a systematic tractate on the cultus, nor does it contain a closed sacrificial system. The text's relationship to the *realia* of the cult is at best fragmentary and illustrative. Taken as a whole, Leviticus is not a priest's manual. Conversely, there is no attempt to communicate its message by means of homiletical exposition. The contrast in this regard with Deuteronomy is striking; in Deuteronomy, even in the legal section (chs. 12ff.) there is a constant homiletical appeal to the hearer.

Nevertheless, the highly formalized effect of such massive amounts of repetition serves to involve the reader in a manner equally effectively as the homily. It is not by chance that the blessing and cursing ritual makes the same use of repetition (Deut. 27.11ff.). The book of Leviticus has not only construed its material by a selection from the tradition, but by ordering it in this manner has assigned it a particular function. In spite of its historical variety, it still functions to create a unified impression of divine imperatives. Its role is not to present a closed cultic system which can be applied casuistically, but to illustrate aspects of the cult in such a way as to engender obedience to the covenant. Leviticus' manner of theological construal is already one step removed from the actual historical activity of Israel's cultic worship.

There is an additional literary feature of the book of Leviticus which strongly affects its reading. Chapter 26 functions as the conclusion and summary of the book by offering a series of blessings and curses. The form is conventional and appears elsewhere in the Old Testament (Deut. 27f.), and in ancient Near Eastern treaties. However, the style of ch. 26 is unique to Leviticus, and for the first time makes a direct appeal to the reader for obedience. The content of the chapter, in contrast to Deuteronomy, has a strong cultic flavour and picks up many of the earlier phrases in the book, such as 'I will not smell your pleasing odours' (v. 31), 'my soul will abhor you' (vv. 11, 30), and 'I am Yahweh' (vv. 2, 45).

However, in spite of this level of continuity, ch. 26 stands in a striking tension to the rest of the book for two reasons. First, the nature of the sin described is of such a quality as to call into question the continuing validity of the covenant. Israel's disobedience evokes a judgment which is bent on destroying the nation. Up to this point in the book a cultic activity has been described which functioned to order life into the spheres of the clean and the unclean. A means has been established as the great benefit of the covenant by which sins of inadvertancy could be atoned for in the sight of God. Even wilful sins were purged on the Day of Atonement. Now ch. 26 uncovers a totally new dimension of sin and judgment:

> I will destroy your high places, and cut down your incense altars ... I will lay your cities waste, and will make your sanctuaries desolate ... and I will scatter you among the nations ... and you shall perish among the nations, and the land of your enemies shall eat you up (vv. 30–38).

The language of judgment in ch. 26 makes use of all the terminology found in the prophets. It transcends the cultic issues of clean and unclean and focuses on that of life and death in the presence of the covenant God. Moreover, when forgiveness is held out to the disobedient people, it is in terms of the mercy alone of God who remembers his promise to restore the repentant. The language is again more closely akin to the theology of the prophets than to the

Priestly theology of atonement which has engaged the book of Leviticus up to this point.

Secondly, ch. 26 evokes a tension with the rest of Leviticus because its language of judgment quite clearly reflects the historical experience of the destruction of Jerusalem and the Babylonian exile. From a canonical perspective the theological significance of this observation turns on determining the effect of including this dimension of historical reality within the formulation of the blessings and curses. To formulate the problem form-critically, what is the role of this *vaticinium ex eventu* in ch.26? Certainly the chapter does not function to introduce eschatology into the picture according to the manner of prophetic judgments, nor are the historical experiences of exile structured into a pattern of *Heilsgeschichte*. The same cultic distinction between the status of acceptance and rejection, between clean and unclean, is maintained but now projected into a different dimension of intensity and broadened by a new angle of vision.

The effect of ch. 26 is to set up a theological tension which is part of the construal of the cult in Leviticus. The tension is not between the ideal and the actual, nor is it a legal contrast between obedience and disobedience. Rather, in the realistic terminology of the cult a tension is maintained between acceptance and rejection, between a life sacred to God and one which is abhorrent. However, the nature of the theological issue is such that the cultic language in itself and the mechanisms contained in its institutions for atonement are inadequate to do justice to the reality of disobedience and rejection which even calls Israel's life into question.

(iii) *The sacred dimension of reality*

It has been a long-standing practice of Old Testament theologies to organize the material according to the rubrics of comparative religion: sacred times, sacred space, sacred objects, sacred personnel (cf. Eichrodt). The approach has the advantage of recognizing elements both of continuity and discontinuity with other religious practices, especially those of the Ancient Near East. The danger involved in the use of these categories is of missing the peculiar theological dynamic of the Old Testament which does not structure its material in this way. My approach will be to make use of the categories in order to provide a useful perspective on the material, but also to supplement the approach with other angles of vision in an effort to hear more closely the witness of the full canon.

(a) *Sacred times: the festivals.* The Pentateuch contains several detailed calendars which seek to regulate the sacred seasons of Israel's festivals (Ex. 23; Lev. 23; Deut.16). In addition, other festivals which often performed a special function are described (Sabbath, Passover, Day of Atonement, Purim), and often secondarily incorporated within the seasonal cycle. It has long been recognized that Israel's calendar was at first synchronized with the agricultural cycle, a feature which it inherited and never fully removed. The effect was to encompass religious worship within the basic routines of societal life and not to allow any separation between the concrete realities of life – day and night, summer and winter, sowing and reaping – and religious faith. However, it is also evident that Israel's faith strongly affected the interpretation of the role of the festivals, and some of this transformation is reflected in the differing emphases in the classic Hebrew calendars.

The major theological alteration in understanding the festivals was the subordination of the natural cycle to a historical one. Israel celebrated the Passover and Feast of Unleavened Bread as a remembrance of her deliverance. Only in later Jewish interpretation has the Feast of Weeks been tied to the giving of the Law at Sinai. In contrast to the role of the myth in the Babylonian New Year Festival which sought to re-activate the order of the world in ritual representation against the elemental powers of chaos, the Hebrew festivals used their rituals to preserve solidarity with the past and to participate through memory in the great redemptive events which constituted the people of God (Ex. 12.11). Observance of the Sabbath celebrated both the creation of the world and the deliverance from Egypt (Ex. 20.11; Deut. 5.15). The element of thanksgiving and joyfulness characterized the harvest festivals (Deut. 16.11), repentance and solemnity the Day of Atonement (Lev. 16.31). Significantly, whenever Israel sought to reform the corruption which had entered its religion, the restoration of the proper function of the festivals played an important role (II Kings 23.21; Neh. 13.19ff.; II Chron. 30.2).

In the celebration of the Jubilee year, one can discern elements of theological idealization which set it apart from the concrete, earthbound quality of the ordinary festivals. Scholars debate to what extent the Jubilee was ever celebrated historically (cf. Jer. 34.8, 14, 17; Ezek. 46.17, etc.), but the year remained in the calendar as an expression of Israel's faith that the just distribution of the land was an essential part of the covenant. Following the destruction of the temple in AD 70, Judaism increasingly built into its cultic calendar an eschatological hope: 'next year Jerusalem'.

(b) *Sacred space: tabernacle and temple.* The patriarchal stories are filled with references to sanctuaries whose sacred quality preceded the Hebrews entrance into Canaan (Gen. 12.6; 28.16–22, etc.). However, following the covenant at Sinai, the form of the tabernacle became the established means of protecting God's sacred space. Although from a historical perspective the influence of the Solomonic temple strongly coloured the Priestly description of the desert tabernacle, the tradition envisioned the tabernacle as normative for the worship and service of God, and saw the temple as its extension under the new conditions of David's kingdom, but requiring a special divine legitimation (II Sam. 7.1ff.). The Priestly tradition of the book of Exodus makes clear that the portable tabernacle served as a continuation of God's presence which had been revealed in the theophany at Sinai, and accompanied Israel through the wilderness, symbolized by the cloud and fire (Ex. 40.38).

The same tension found in Ex. 20 between God's dwelling on Sinai and his coming to the sacred mountain continues in the traditions of the tabernacle. The early terminology associated with the tent (*'ōhel mô'ēd*) is always that of God's visiting the tabernacle to make known his will (Ex. 33.7ff.; 34.29ff.). Conversely, the language associated with the tradition of the ark, both in earlier and later forms, is of God's dwelling above the ark. When these earlier traditions were united in the Priestly theology of the *miškān* (tabernacle), both elements were retained.

The tabernacle and temple were constructed to symbolize the various gradations of holiness within God's sacred preeinct, which were further represented by the different quality of appurtenances. There was an outer court, and an inner court, and a 'holy of holies' which was visited only by the high priest at a designated time. The tabernacle stood in the centre of the camp, and provided the means on which all ordinary life was orientated. It represented in concrete form the heart of Priestly theology that God was holy and no human being could approach unprepared into his presence.

One has to turn to the Psalter to gain an impression of what the temple meant to the community of faith. The psalms reverberate with the sheer joy of approaching into the presence of God who dwells on Zion (Ps. 29). God's presence in the temple provides the visible sign of the divine rule of the world, and the source of all of Israel's trust and confidence:

There is a river whose streams make glad the city of God,
The holy habitation of the Most High,
God is in the midst of her, she shall not be moved (Ps. 46; 4f.).

When Exodus and Leviticus are read apart from the Psalter, one fails to recognize the dual aspects of an inner and outer dimension of divine space.

Of course, the Old Testament Priestly tradition deals in several ways with the inevitable tension between God's transcendence and immanence. God dwells in the temple, the house of God, yet he is not contained in a human structure. The prayer of Solomon expresses succinctly the paradox:

Behold, heaven and the highest heaven cannot contain thee;
how much less this house which I have built (I Kings 8.27).

It was recognized as a gesture of divine condescension that God let 'his name dwell there' (v. 29). Within Priestly theology the glory of God, his outward visible form, was further developed as a means of maintaining the tension. Other metaphors such as his 'face' or 'messenger' served a similar function in the earlier traditions.

It is highly significant that the inherent threat to the nature of God which was present in the institutions of sacred space played such an important role in the Old Testament. The editor of the book of Exodus has arranged the Priestly traditions regarding the construction of the tabernacle (Ex. 25–31; 35–40) in such a way as to have them disrupted by the episode of the golden calf (Ex. 32–34). Even while Moses was on the mountain receiving the instructions from God on the building of the sacred tabernacle, Israel had instituted a false worship. There is also clear evidence in the books of Samuel of considerable resistance to the building of the temple, which was finally overcome (II Sam. 7.4ff.).

The sharpest attack on the dangers of the Priestly institutions of sacred space comes from the side of the prophets. Amos' confrontation with Amaziah, the priest of Bethel (7.10ff.), offers a classic example of institutional religion which was zealous of the king's sanctuary – not God's – and interpreted any criticism as political treason. Equally as powerful is Jeremiah's well-known temple speech (chs. 7 and 26), which brought a thunderous judgment against a superstitious reverence for the protection of God's temple. The prophet has only bitter sarcasm for a people who 'steal, murder, commit adultery . . . then come and stand before me in this house . . . and say "We are delivered" ' (7.8ff.). Or again, Ezekiel can interpret the departure of God's 'glory' from the temple as the result of the evil deeds of his people (8.5ff.). There is one final witness to discuss. Although Ezek. 20 offers one of the most devastating litanies of Israel's sinful history within the entire Old Testament, the chapter comes to a climax with an oracle concerning the new exodus from Babylon. The goal of this return lies in the establishment of a pure cult when God will again accept Israel's sacrifices and manifest his holiness to his people before the nations. Again, in the eschatological vision of Ezekiel the restoration of a new temple occupies nine chapters. Its exact dimensions are once again set forth with all the accoutrements of the original temple. Again minute attention is paid to the guarding of God's holiness (44.23) and the purity of proper worship. This portrayal belies any theological construal which would see the institution of the temple only as a primitive accommodation to Priestly tradition which has been superseded by the ethical ideals of the prophets.

Moreover, the true function of the temple emerges with great clarity in Ezekiel's vision, which was often beclouded by the events surrounding Solomon's building. From the new temple there issues the water of life and a restoration of God's original intention for the creation in the imagery of a return of paradise, a holy people, and a pure worship (47.6ff.). The centre of this new vision focuses on the presence of God whose city bears the name 'The Lord is there' (48.35).

(c) *Sacred objects*. The same general theological lines emerge regarding sacred objects. Much attention is devoted to the altar and the other objects within the tabernacle as commensurate with the proper worship of God (Ex. 30.1ff.). Already the Book of the Covenant (Ex. 20.21ff.) regulated the building of altars of earth, and certain taboos are still enjoined whose exact motivation has long since been lost (20.25). A major refrain in the book of Deuteronomy was that Israel could not worship wherever and however it pleased, but only at the altar where 'God let his name dwell'. Moreover, it remained a deep conviction throughout the Old Testament that false objects of worship were conducive to idolatry. Gideon made an ephod which later led him and his family astray (Judg. 8.27). Similarly, the molten image of Micah also became a form of idolatry (Judg. 17.1ff.). Even the sacred ark became a fetish and fell into the hand of the Philistines rather than procuring the expected victory (I Sam. 4.5ff.).

In spite of the constant threat of misuse, the Old Testament never moved in the direction of dispensing with sacred objects for a purely spiritual expression of faith. Perhaps Jeremiah comes closest to such a position when he prophesies that the ark of the covenant will not be remembered or missed (3.16), but his oracle is in the context of an object which had become a hindrance to recognizing the true presence of God. The most sustained attack on sacred objects as the foolish expression of false religion is that of Second Isaiah, who mocks the substitution of man's own creative ingenuity for the true presence of God who rules the world (44.9ff.). However, in Ezekiel's portrait of the new temple the proper role of sacred objects is still maintained as a needed symbol for the faithful response to God. There are 'holy things' which dare not be desecrated (Ezek. 44.8). Likewise the psalmist could find no more horrifying signs of being abandoned by God than to see the destruction by the enemy of the sacred things of the sanctuary (Ps. 74.4ff.).

(d) *Sacred personnel.* The pure worship of God required proper tradents of the tradition who had been trained in the knowledge and practice of the Law. In addition, the priests must represent a sacred genealogical line and conform to special requirements of marriage in order to maintain the purity of descent. Even Moses was replaced by the office of the Aaronic priesthood, and excluded from the tent of meeting (Ex. 40.35). The priest wore special clothes, and had no inheritance as the other tribes in order to symbolize complete dependency upon God. The priest performed a sacred task, but as an acknowledged sinful human being who had first to offer atonement for his own sins (Lev. 9.7). No sin was more grievous than improper service. The consecration of Aaron and his sons as sacred ministers of God (Lev. 8–9) is set in stark contrast with the cultic sins of Nadab and Abihu who offered 'unholy fire before the Lord . . . and they died' (Lev. 10.1ff.). In spite of the threat inherent in the office of the priesthood to corrupt the worship of God (cf. Ex. 32.1ff.; Ezra 9.1ff.), the Old Testament never contrasted adversely the established priesthood with a charismatic office. Rather, both priest and prophet had a legitimate role, but neither was immune to abuse. The fact that in the historical development of Israel's religion the priesthood grew in importance while the prophetic office in itself declined provides no basis for a theological judgment. Certainly the canonical construals anchored the priesthood at the centre of the Sinai covenant from the beginning, and continued to support the complete continuity of the office through the restoration of worship under Ezra and Nehemiah (Ezra 2.59ff.; 3.10; 6.10; Neh. 8.9ff.)

(iv) *The cult as blessing*

No Old Testament passage better summarizes the benefits of the cult than does the Aaronic blessing of Num. 6.24–26:

> The Lord bless you and keep you:
> The Lord make his face to shine upon you
>   and be gracious to you,
> The Lord lift up his countenance upon you,
>   and give you peace.

The blessing of God entails a life of wholeness in which the inner and outer dimensions of life cohere. For the Old Testament the material and the spiritual blessings were two sides of one coin. God gave protection from the attack of both external and internal enemies. In trust and confidence one could eat from his table even in the presence of enemies (Ps. 23.5). The favour of God – when his face shone – was a source of peace and well-being. Job describes his life which had once been under God's blessing:

> When God watched over me;
> when his lamp shone upon my head
> and by his light I walked through darkness . . .
> when the friendship of God was upon my tent (29.2–4).

Such a picture of wholeness was only possible in the context of corporate worship. To consider it a form of 'self-salvation' or 'works righteousness' is utterly to misconstrue its significance. Rather, as an act of grace God had established for Israel a life of worship which resulted in divine blessing. The cult was the conduit through which God lavished his benefits.

(v) *Sacrifice and atonement*

The function of sacrifice as a means of atonement plays a central role in Leviticus. Yet the subject is difficult and remains highly controversial for a variety of reasons.

(*a*) The priestly system reached its present form only after a long history of development, and it is difficult to know, even if one were to admit that the P material is often ancient, how it relates to sacrificial practice which is reflected in other parts of the Old Testament. Rendtorff's study (*Opfer*) demonstrated clearly some of the important changes which took place, such as the loss of an independent life by the 'peace offering' (*šelāmîm*) when it was joined to the 'sacrifice' (*zebah*). Even more significant was the increasing role of the 'sin offering' (*hattā't*) in the post-exilic period to become the chief expiatory rite.

(*b*) The problem of understanding the nature and significance of the various sacrifices within the Priestly tradition has long been recognized. Leviticus presents the material from differing perspectives and in fragmentary form. G. B. Gray (*Sacrifice*) moved in the right direction when he sought to focus on usage rather than etymology. In recent years some illuminating studies have been published by Levine and Milgrom. Especially the latter has sought to work out the exact distinctions between the sacrifices and to determine their function within the priestly system, but no consensus has yet been reached in the field.

(*c*) The nature of atonement in Leviticus involves a variety of difficult problems, philological, historical and theological. Not only is there difficulty in interpreting the meaning of atonement within priestly theology, but in addition, the relationship between prophetic and priestly tradition on the subject remains unsettled.

We now turn to the subject itself. Certainly the most serious modern treatment of atonement in the Old Testament is that of H. Gese ('The Atonement'), which has recently received a full elaboration by his student, B. Janowski (*Sühne*). Gese argues that the basic meaning of the verb to atone (*kipper*) is restoring a right relationship with God which has been disrupted through sin by means of a substitution of life. He cites examples from the pre-exilic period such as Ex. 32.30ff.; II Sam. 21.1–4; Deut. 21.1–9 to prove that atonement involves the total surrender of one's life. According to Gese, the significant contribution of priestly theology under the influence of prophetic theology was in ritualizing this concept of atonement within the sphere of sacrifice. Although in the pre-exilic period there was no sign of expiatory sacrifice, in the post-exilic period expiation became the dominant feature of the entire sacrificial system. Atonement was effected by the slaying of a specially designated animal whose shed blood was bearer of the substituted life instead of the offerer, and his identification was symbolized by the laying on of hands.

In my judgment, Gese has made a strong case for his interpretation of sacrifice and atonement in priestly theology. However, I feel that Gese's reconstruction of the historical development of sacrifice is too hypothetical largely because of the lack of clear evidence. I doubt very much that the element of expiation in priestly theology is simply post-exilic and that the discontinuity between the earlier and later stages can be so sharply drawn. Even more important, Gese has structured his theological interpretation according to his developmental scheme, and disregarded the present function which the canon has assigned the priestly system. In sum, sacrifice and atonement have a different theological dynamic when viewed from the perspective of the whole canon from the historical reconstruction which Gese has sketched.

A very different understanding of the subject is offered by J. Milgrom in numerous articles and monographs. At the outset he is very concerned to assign the Priestly source to the pre-exilic age and to establish as much continuity as possible between earlier and later stages of Israel's practice. Milgrom interprets the basic meaning of the verb *kipper* to be 'to rub off' or 'to purge'. He reconstructs what he calls the 'missing priestly doctrine of theodicy' which envisions sin as a miasma attaching to the sanctuary and accumulating to a point where God can no longer abide it. To avert God's abandoning his sanctuary, Israel purges the sin by the *ḥaṭṭā't* blood which functions as a ritual detergent (*Studies*, 77).

Milgrom envisions the priestly system as a closed theological one, the mechanism of which can be recovered by the close study of the Bible and rabbinic tradition (*Studies*, 85ff.). According to Leviticus,

only sins of advertency or omission can be atoned for by an *'āšām*
offering. Milgrom argues that when accompanied by repentance –
'āšām is 'to feel guilty' – the offering transforms the deliberate sin
into the lesser category of inadvertent sin which can then be purged
by sacrifice (*Studies*, 65).

Milgrom's essays are to be commended for their close attention
in terms of both philology and theology, to the details of the Priestly
material, which many scholars have frequently dismissed as tedious
or unintelligible. Nevertheless, Milgrom's approach represents the
exact opposite extreme to Gese's historical reconstruction. He views
the Priestly material largely on one flat dimension as a seamless
garment and then introduces a type of casuistic argument to support
his theological construals. As a result, tensions are harmonized and
lacunae within the tradition are filled in with later rabbinic exegesis
(cf. his application of the theory of the 'merits of the Fathers', *EJ*
10, 1971, 142f.).

It is my hope that a canonical approach will provide a way
through the Scylla and Charybdis of Gese and Milgrom. First, I
think that there was an important historical development in the
concepts of sacrifice and atonement within Israel, but that the lines
of reconstruction are often blurred beyond recovery. However, the
canonical process has not fused the witnesses of the historical
narratives and the prophetic oracles into one monolithic system,
but left them as separate and discrete witnesses. Only within the
priestly tradition has the canonical process had a different effect.
Not only has the Priestly material been integrally attached to the
Sinai covenant, but the earlier and later elements have been united.
Therefore to claim that expiation played a role only in the post-
exilic period is certainly to run in the face of the present canonical
construal.

I am much inclined to agree with A. B. Davidson's interpretation
(*Theology*, 307ff.) of seeing two very different understandings of
sacrifice and atonement in the Old Testament, namely, the priestly
and the prophetic, which remained largely in unresolved tension
and only occasionally interacted. On the one hand, the priestly
institution provided a means of atoning for sins committed within
the covenant. It was not a superstitious form of *ex opere operato*, but a
profoundly theological interpretation of atonement as a gracious
means of access into the presence of God which sin had disrupted.
On the other hand, the prophets were dealing with sins of high-

handed rebellion which could no longer be encompassed within the framework of the covenant, but undermined its very existence. For such a dimension of evil there was no atonement possible through institutional means, but only total judgment and annulment of the covenant. However, the prophets and the psalmists discovered through their experience that God remained faithful to his promise in spite of everything, and in a humanly incomprehensible fashion sought to restore his people to himself (cf. Ps. 40 and 51). No one metaphor emerged for God's redemptive intervention – new covenant, new people, new temple, new branch – nor were the witnesses ever joined into one unified theological formulation, at least not within the Old Testament.

In sum, from the perspective of Old Testament theology it is important that the peculiar diversity of witness to God's atonement be maintained and not refocused either by a historical reconstruction or a systematic rationalization. Because these divergent and often fragmentary witnesses do at times come together in surprising fashion, especially in Ezekiel and the Psalter, the continuing theological task depends on pursuing as closely as possible the special profile which emerges from viewing the entire canon.

(vi) *The psalms and the cult*

From a theological perspective the psalms perform a unique role in bridging the testimonies of both priest and prophet to the forgiveness of God. The psalms arose within a cultic setting and everywhere reflect the accoutrements of the sanctuary. Yet slight attention is paid to the mechanics of priestly ritual, or to the specific occasions in which the psalms function. Some writers have sought to describe the contribution of the psalms as being the 'inner' side to the 'outer' liturgy, but this distinction runs the risk of introducing confusion. The psalms are not simply expansions of subjective feelings of pious Israelites, but are constructed from liturgical conventions and reflect a highly objective dimension of communal worship.

Nevertheless, within the formal structure of traditional hymnody, the reader is introduced into the most intense religious wrestling with God. In the majority of the psalms the sense of sin and disruption is foremost. The psalmist has once experienced in worship the presence of God and the joy of his communion. God is the source of all life and in his forgiveness is blessing and wholeness.

The psalmist in his suffering struggles to overcome the dreadful sense of separation from God which deprives him of blessing and has turned his life into a form of death. In no sense is he alienated from the cult; in fact, just the opposite. He avails himself of all the means of sacrifice and thank-offering to gain entrance into God's presence. It is even possible that the sudden shift of mood in some psalms (e.g. 6.8ff.) is a response to a form of priestly absolution.

However, most characteristic of the Psalter are those moments when the psalmist appears to transcend the prescribed religious means and confesses to have confronted God himself directly:

> Sacrifice and offering thou dost not desire;
> but thou hast given me an open ear.
> Burnt offering and sin offering
> thou hast not required.
> Then I said: Lo, I come . . .
> I delight to do thy will, O my God;
> thy law is within my heart (Ps. 40.6–8).

Similarly, in Ps. 73 the psalmist confesses his bitterness over the prosperity of the wicked while he suffers:

> . . . until I went into the sanctuary of God;
>   then I perceived their end . . .
> Whom have I in heaven but thee?
> And there is nothing upon earth
>   that I desire besides thee . . . (vv. 17, 25).

In sum, for the psalmist the mercy of God which forgives and restores is not a theological possibility, but a reality which he has experienced and on which he grounds his whole existence.

(vii) *The prophets and the cult*

At the end of the nineteenth century and well into the early twentieth, there was a widespread tendency in Old Testament studies to make a sharp contrast between priestly and prophetic theology, indeed to set them in a harsh antithesis. Many assumed that the prophets were anti-cultic in principle, and many of the biases of free-church Christianity were transferred to the Old Testament as characteristic of prophetic charisma. However, beginning with such books as A. C. Welch's *Prophets and Priests*, a far more balanced picture has emerged. The prophets were not free-floating individualists, but usually belonged to a prophetic guild. Many of their well-known attacks on sacrifice and ritual (Amos 4.4f.; Isa. 1.10ff.; Micah 6.6ff.; Jer. 7.1ff.) appear now to be *ad hoc* formulations within an invective and directed to certain abuses, but were not ideologically based on an anti-cultic principle.

Yet recently the other extreme has been defended by Milgrom (*Studies*, 273), who, in my judgment, takes the sharp edge off the prophetic invectives against the cult. He argues that Jeremiah in such passages as 7.21–23 only attacked the free-will offerings and 'had nothing whatever to say concerning the fixed temple sacrifices such as the *tāmîd*'. The first problem with this interpretation is that Milgrom assumes that the priestly system of P was fully operative at the time of the prophets so that he renders Jeremiah's inclusive terminology for the cult (*'ôlāh* and *zebaḥ*) in the restrictive sense of the Priestly Code's free-will offerings. The second problem is that the whole thrust of Jeremiah's temple speech shatters completely the limitations placed on his attack by Milgrom.

In sum, the integrity of the prophetic witness must not be either threatened by projecting an anti-cultic stance or flattened by subsuming it under the rubrics of priestly theology. How these two biblical witnesses relate remains a difficult yet important theological problem whose very tension bears testimony to one significant aspect of the role of the cult within the life of Israel.

Bibliography

R. E. **Clements**, *God and Temple*, Oxford 1965; A. B. **Davidson**, *Theology of the Old Testament*, Edinburgh 1904; W. **Eichrodt**, *Theology of the Old Testament*, ET, I, London and Philadelphia 1961, 98–177; G. **Fohrer**, 'Kritik an Tempel, Kultus und Kultusausübung in nachexilischer Zeit', reprinted in *Studien zu alttestamentlichen Texten und Themen* (1966–1972), BZAW 55, 1981, 81–95; H. **Gese**, 'The Atonement', in *Essays on Biblical Theology*, ET Minneapolis 1981, 93–116; G. B. **Gray**, *Sacrifice in the Old Testament*, Oxford and New York 1925; M. **Haran**, *Temple and Temple-Service in Ancient Israel*, Oxford 1978; H.-J. **Hermisson**, *Sprache und Ritus im altisraelitischen Kult*, WMANT 19, 1965; B. **Janowski**, *Sühne als Heilsgeschehen: Studien zur Sühnetheologie der Priesterschrift und zur Wurzel KPR in Alten Orient und im Alten Testament*, WMANT 55, 1982; Y. **Kaufmann**, *The Religion of Israel*, ET Chicago 1960; H.-J. **Kraus**, *Worship in Israel. A Cultic History of the Old*

Testament, ET Oxford 1966; B. A. **Levine**, *In the Presence of the Lord*, SJLA 5, 1974; J. **Milgrom**, 'Day of Atonement', *EJ* 5, 1384–87; 'Kipper', **EJ** 10, 1039–44; *Cult and Conscience*, SJLA 18, 1976; *Studies in Cultic Theology and Terminology*, SJLA 36, 1983; S. **Mowinckel**, *The Psalms in Israel's Worship*, ET, I–II, Oxford 1962; G. **von Rad**, *Old Testament Theology*, ET, I, Edinburgh and New York 1962, 232–79; A. F. **Rainey**, 'The Order of Sacrifice in Old Testament Ritual Texts', *Biblica* 51, 1970, 485–98; R. **Rendtorff**, 'Der Kultus im Alten Israel', *GSAT*, ThB 57, 1975, 89–109; *Die Gesetze in der Priesterschrift*, Göttingen ²1963; *Studien zur Geschichte des Opfers im Alten Israel*, WMANT 24, 1967; J. J. **Stamm**, *Erlösen und Vergeben im Alten Testament*, Berne 1940; S. **Terrien**, *The Elusive Presence*, New York and London 1978, 161–226; A. C. **Welch**, *Prophet and Priest in Old Israel*, Oxford 1953; C. **Westermann**, *Blessing in the Bible and the Life of the Church*, ET Philadelphia 1978.

15

STRUCTURES OF THE COMMON LIFE

(i) *The modern debate*

The previous chapter attempted to deal with the relation between covenant theology and those institutions integrally connected with it. Various forms of the cult served primarily as the media for the benefits which stemmed from Israel's special relationship to God. However, many institutions and conventional practices were essential to Israel's life which were only indirectly related to the covenant, and did not derive from direct divine imperative even according to the Old Testament tradition itself. Rather, numerous institutions were inherited, adopted or assumed. Traditionally the Old Testament discipline has tended to treat this subject as an historical, archaeological enterprise which in recent years has been expanded and strengthened by newer sociological research. R. de Vaux's valuable study (*Ancient Israel*) remains a classic attempt to bring the concrete forms of Israel's major institutions into sharp focus.

In addition, the theological dimension of the subject has also been recognized, at least in part. One of the lasting contributions of Eichrodt's *Theology* in distinction, say, from von Rad's, was his consistent attention to Israel's institutional life in relation to its general background in comparative religion. However, the hermeneutical and theological problems involved are many and complex. At the end of the nineteenth century the development of Israel's religion was thought to be capable of being easily charted according to an evolutionary pattern from a primitive stage of natural religion to a higher form of ethical monotheism. In spite of Eichrodt's powerful criticism of such schemata, he too tended to describe Israel's true religion as a movement from external trappings to internalized faith and from impersonalized forces to personal piety. Others have sought to separate sharply the content of Israel's faith from the forms of Ancient Near Eastern religion which is inherited (G. E. Wright), or to limit the influence of common culture to external and peripheral matters (Fohrer).

A new phase in this debate has been initiated in recent years by N. Gottwald's provocative book, *The Tribes of Yahweh*. He dismisses as 'idealistic' all attempts which separate Israel's religion from social phenomena, and he proposes a sociological method by which to interpret the effect of Israel's rootage within a social system on the secondary ideological articulation of its faith. In a previous chapter I have offered a broad theological criticism of the assumptions involved in his 'cultural-materialist' theory of interpretation. In this chapter my concern is to look more closely at the details of his sociological analysis of Israel in the pre-monarchial period (1250–1025 BC), which has to do largely with an interpretation of institutions.

Gottwald argues that Israel developed institutions which reflected an egalitarian view of reality. This stance set Israel apart from the hierarchical function of Egyptian and Canaanite cults, which were politically centralized and economically stratified. Each of these differing expressions was enforced by a form of socio-political organization. In conscious opposition to Hyksos and Canaanite 'feudalism' with its social classes, exploitation of the poor and monopoly of political power, Israel developed an anti-imperialist, anti-feudal society which brought together segments of underclass populace into a social order with the aim of liberating its people by means of the radical decentralization of power, by equal access to basic resources, and by the restriction of class privilege. Gottwald is insistent on defending the cultural-materialist priority of social relations over religious formulation. The genius of Yahwism derived from its system of social equality which the religion sought to legitimate and empower.

In the light of this description of Israel's institutions, it appears somewhat ironical for Gottwald to characterize earlier attempts in interpretation as 'advocatory literature' (668)! It is difficult to imagine a more politicized interpretation of early Israel than that offered by Gottwald. He projects a form of historical idealization which not only makes use of a limited selection of evidence, but also interprets it anachronistically by bringing to bear a whole battery of modern philosophical categories. The clear elements of continuity between the institutional life of Israel and its neighbours during the pre-monarchial period is replaced by the sharpest polarity between a proposed egalitarianism and a class-oriented, feudal society. However, the point must be made that, strictly from the historical evidence, Israel's society in the pre-monarchical period reflected different social classes, which included slaves and non-citizens. Political and economic power in the villages resided in the hands of a few. The *paterfamilias* possessed the power of life and death over his family, and women's rights within both the family and society in general were sharply curtailed. Captives in battle were either massacred or reduced to slavery. There was no distinction between civil and religious law and blasphemy was punishable by death.

Of course, there were differences between Israel and her neighbours, and the Old Testament shows many signs of change and development within the society. The difficulty lies in determining the nature of the differences and in establishing the direction of growth. From a historical perspective it seems far more likely that we should think in terms of Israel adapting common cultural institutions which were constantly modified and reinterpreted in different degrees throughout her history than posit a radically new classless society.

According to Israel's own tradition the major force for change came from Israel's faith, which not only sought to bring institutions in line with divine sanctions, but offered major critical opposition in the name of God to social and political abuses. Gottwald's application of his sociological method, far from bringing a new dimension of concreteness to bear on the religion of Israel, has transformed Israel's history into an abstract idealization of modern social values without genuinely historical moorings. In sum, the problem lies not with the sociological method as such, which remains a valuable modern tool of critical inquiry, but in its heavy-handed and tendentious application.

(ii) *A theological interpretation of Israel's institutions*

The task of interpreting the theological significance of Israel's institutions is not simply to be equated with the historical enterprise of reconstructing the social dimensions of an ancient people. Rather, its task is to understand from the form by which Israel rendered its tradition how its various institutions functioned in relation to its theological confessions. To see that a dialectical relationship obtains between interpretations which are from within the tradition and a modern critical analysis which is outside the tradition requires a subtlety which resists dogmatism from both the left and right of the theological spectrum.

It will shortly become evident that a major characteristic of the approach in the canon to Israel's institutions lies in the fact that few generalizations are offered in direct connection with the larger issues. Rather, a highly complex variety of institutional relationships appear which are integrally related to Israel's faith, but which often function on different levels of the biblical text. It is essential that a theological interpretation is not won at the cost of abstracting into an artificial principle elements which function sometimes in the foreground of a narrative, but at others in the distant background.

(a) *Civil institutions.* The Old Testament had no concept of the state either in the ancient Greek sense or according to modern theory. There was also no clear separation between the civil and religious spheres of life. The term 'Israel' designated the covenant people, and in the tradition it was derived from the family of Jacob in a highly schematized form. The shift from a family organization to a national entity occurs in the transition from the book of Genesis to Exodus, but this move is a literary rather than sociological one. The ancient tribal divisions retain their integrity long after the settlement, but have been structured in such a symbolic manner in Numbers as to reflect little direct historical information on the original political organization.

Ever since the seminal work of Alt and Noth, great energy has been expended in an effort to understand the nature of Israel's social structure in the period after the settlement and before the rise of the monarchy. The Alt/Noth theory of a twelve-tribe league which was patterned after the Greek amphictyony was a highly attractive hypothesis which seemed for a time to do justice to a cohesive force within the loose tribal confederation formed around a central sanctuary. However, increasingly its initial simplicity has been eroded by new historical research, and a genuine historical lacuna is again appearing. From within the tradition the period has been highly schematized within a theological pattern of decay and restoration, the latter move occurring by means of divinely appointed heroes. Each 'judge' is presented as a single ruler of all Israel for a fixed period, much like a king's reign. Nevertheless, the earlier levels of the tradition have been frequently retained, and these paint a very different historical picture. It was an age of social and political disorder as the forces of cohesion slowly dissolved before the centrifugal influences of the settlement. The stories of divine deliverance are all set against the background of disorganization and impotence (cf. Judg. 6.11ff.). The story of Abimelech's usurpation of power calls forth in Jotham's fable one of the most powerful polemics against kingship in the Old Testament in a remarkably non-theological form (Judg. 9.7ff.). Gottwald's idealization of this period runs against both historical evidence and the theological perspective of the canon which views it as a dark period preceding the rise of the kingdom.

Much more concrete historical information, of both an inner and extra-biblical sort, is needed for understanding the civil institutions of the monarchy. One of the striking characteristics of the literature is the variety of perspectives on the kingship which is still retained (cf. ch. 10). Although it is possible even from within the tradition to reconstruct a number of new political forces such as the Philistine invasion which evoked a crisis within Israel's political federation, the tradition itself places little theological significance on the radically new form of government which shortly emerged. Samuel's speech (1 Sam. 8.5ff.) reflects the traditional fear of kingship as a license for social abuse, but in the end serves to relativize the significance of the institutional changes by continuing to focus on a theological test of loyalty to God. One gets only very indirect hints regarding the actual form of Saul's kingship, which increasingly is viewed as a foil for David's reign (I Sam. 15.28).

There is sufficient historical evidence to point to a massive reorganization of Israel's political and economic structure under David, but the evidence largely functions in the background of the narratives. David's kingship is increasingly rendered as a type of the future messianic rule of God, although his personal history is recorded with considerable historical realism. Even the power struggle to secure a successor to David is finally construed from the theological perspective of maintaining the promise to David of an eternal rule. Conversely, Solomon's rule is largely viewed negatively, not because of his introduction of foreign administrative structures of government *per se*, but in so far as his openness to innovation led to an erosion of Israel's faith. The royal abuses under Solomon which culminated in the political schism under Jeroboam are recounted by the tradition in such a manner as indirectly to censure the harshness, oppression and folly of the Solomonic rule (I Kings 11–12).

It is from the prophetic writings that one receives the clearest theological appraisal of the monarchical institutions. Amos is devastating in his criticism of social injustices arising from greed and luxury which result in oppression of the poor and disregard for the ancient covenantal rights (2.6ff.; 4.1ff.). The royal office has even been legitimated by the cult which construes all criticism as disloyalty (7.10ff.). Hosea attacks the manipulation of political power which has lost all understanding of the kingship as a representative form of divine rule:

They make kings, but not through me.
They set up princes, but without my knowledge (8.4).

Isaiah is bitter toward the elders and princes who exploit the poor and increase the size of their property by means of an economic system which deprives the small farmer of his land (5.8ff.).

Within recent years there has been a major effort to revise the picture of the prophet as an individual standing outside the political establishment and voicing his independent social criticism. Clearly the prophets were also part of a social context; they often functioned in guilds and shared traditions and conventions with their culture. Yet the attempt, usually under the guise of sociological analysis, to see them as bound by institutional ties, and conforming to the social pressures of support groups, completely reverses the role which the Old Testament tradition has assigned to them, and renders their theological witness largely mute. Certainly it was a misconstrual when biblical scholars once projected a theological contrast between the spirit-filled charismatic prophet and the institutionally orientated king and priest. Nevertheless, the prophets' continual opposition to the social abuses of the state in the name of God cannot successfully be translated into merely an issue of conflicting party loyalties.

A very different kind of theological reflection on Israel's civic institutions is found in the Hebrew wisdom literature, especially in the book of Proverbs. There is no question here of violent protest, as social conventions and practices are generally taken for granted.

Frequently conformity to the *status quo* of society's customs is recommended as prudent behaviour fitting to a wise man (Prov. 25.6). Nevertheless, there are consistent concerns for the protection of the poor and sharp disapproval of wickedness and violence which is consonant with the prophetic witness. Moreover, it is clearly acknowledged that behind the king's power there lies a divine power which rules and overrules all human decisions. In sum, the style of social criticism in unique to the wisdom circles, but the content shares much with the other portions of the canon.

(*b*) *Class structures.* Israel's earliest societal form was not organized according to class distinctions, but in families and tribes. Of course, within the tribes there were orders of privileged status (Lev. 4.22ff.). Built into the conventions of the Hebrew language were forms of address which distinguished between superiors and inferiors (cf. Lande). However, in the period after the settlement there are some clear signs of growing class distinctions. The 'Book of the Covenant' regulates the treatment of slaves (21.7ff., 20ff.). The presence of slaves stemmed largely from the impoverishment of families which resulted in the selling of children (21.7). According to Hebrew law, slavery was for a limited period for Hebrews, but slaves were considered a form of property (21.21). However, it is also evident that the earliest Hebrew laws differ strikingly from the highly class-oriented legal structure of the Babylonians, which afforded the upper classes inordinate privilege.

The establishment of the kingdom and the erosion of the older tribal society greatly increased class distinctions within Israel. The king's officials formed a definite caste, and a variety of technical expressions for government administrators begin to appear in the records, some of which reflect the concern to imitate the Egyptian court (e.g. 'recorder', 'men of rank'). The formation of a professional army added to the stratification. By and large, the growing social distinctions stemmed from economic differences which emerged with the social transformation under the kingdom. There were wage-earners, craftsmen, merchants, but the 'people of the land' who made up the bulk of the population were increasingly identified with the poor. The resident alien (*gēr*) fell in the same category and the law sought to provide some marginal protection.

The most significant point to make theologically is that the Old Testament does not direct any attention to the question of class *per se.* There is no hint that a classless society was seen as an ideal. When Gottwald talks about an egalitarian society, he is reading into the Old Testament a post-Enlightenment ideology, largely in its nineteenth-century formulation. Nowhere is it directly argued in the Old Testament that all human beings are equal before God, much less that they should also be equal in human society. Rather, the biblical emphasis falls elsewhere. The concern is consistently to humanize society from the side of Israel's faith. Slaves were not to work on the sabbath in order that all Israel could worship God. Slaves were not to be brutalized, and had some definite rights (Ex. 21.7ff.). 'You shall remember that you were a slave in Egypt . . .' (Deut. 5.15). The earliest laws seek to protect the poor and are explicitly buttressed with religious sanctions (Ex. 23.25–27). When the prophets launch a polemical tirade against a particular class, such as the rich wives of Samaria (Amos 4.1ff.), or the wealthy merchants and rulers (Micah 3.1ff.), the attack invariably turns on the oppression and injustices to the poor and defenceless of the society.

Of course, it is a serious misunderstanding of the Old Testament to suggest that its writers were only concerned with religious ideas or moral intentions. Israel's faith was hammered out in all areas of concrete human society, and her faith remained inseparable from practice. However, it is equally misleading to politicize the Old Testament by proposing that Israel's faith was only a secondary derivation of social practice.

(*c*) *Legal institutions.* Few institutions within Israel played such an important role as those concerning the exercise of law. At every stage of Israel's history there was explicit concern with legal matters, and at no time was Israel's faith abstracted from the concrete practice of law. Although the Old Testament is filled with long sections of laws, there are very few descriptions of the structures of the actual legal institutions or indications of how they functioned in detail. Only by culling bits and pieces, largely taken from the narratives, can one partially reconstruct the forms and history of the legal institutions (cf. L. Köhler's classic essay, 'Justice in the Gate').

Several important narratives testify to the family law of early Israel (Gen. 31 and 38). The head of the family had authority even to pass the death sentence. Laban's authority as *paterfamilias* hovers in the background of the Jacob narratives as a constant threat (31.29). The exercise of 'blood vengeance' long remained a vestige from early clan law. The story of Ruth offers some of the clearest evidence of how local law operated in a small Hebrew village during the pre-monarchical period. The elders assembled at the gate and after hearing the evidence rendered a decision. For the period of the judges the evidence is too slight to determine with certainty the precise legal structures (cf. Whitelam), but that some legal forces were operative beyond that of clan law seems highly likely. In addition, the role of ancient sacral law from the earliest period on is undisputed (Josh. 7; I Sam. 14).

The establishment of the monarchy brought major changes in the legal system with new powers accruing to the king. Saul's reign marked a period of transition, but several stories reflect legal proceedings (I Sam. 14.34–46; 22.6–19), and cases were judged which were considered challenges to royal authority. Similarly, with David, several narratives illustrate the exercise of his legal authority (I Sam. 30.9–10; II Sam. 1.11–16; 3.6–39). Often narrative material simply assumes a previous legal action on the part of the king such as David's control over Saul's estate (II Sam. 9.1ff.). Solomon's legal authority is largely idealized by the writer's concern to portray him as the 'just king' (1 Kings 3.16ff.). In a similar way, the wisdom sayings depict the ideal king whose judgments are inspired by God (Prov. 16.10ff.). Much debate has turned on how to interpret the legal procedures which played such an important role in the trial of Naboth (I Kings 21). The controversy turns on whether Jezebel was invoking a particular form of Canaanite law in demanding the sale of Naboth's family property, or whether such a transaction was in accordance with current legal practice in Israel. Because the interest of the biblical presentation falls completely on the flagrant abuse of false witnesses in perversion of justice, the narrative omits the details by which to decide. Finally, of great historical interest is the description of Jehoshaphat's reform of the Law (II Chron. 19), which enters into considerable detail when treating the forms of the legal procedure. The continuing scholarly debate turns on deciding the balance between historical verisimilitude and theological construal.

To summarize, once again the main theological implications to be drawn concern the characteristic effort of the Old Testament to derive the law of Israel from God alone as an expression of the one divine will. Israel's kings are not assigned a role in promulgating the law (Deut. 17.18–20). Jehoshaphat's admonition to his newly appointed judges reflects the consistent theological perspective of the whole Old Testament: 'Consider what you do, for you judge not only for man but for the Lord; he is with you in giving judgment' (II Chron. 19.6). That the rise of the monarchy greatly increased the potential for abuse of the Law by the king is a major cause for the continuous friction between prophet and king. It remained the great eschatological hope associated with the Messiah that his reign would be marked by the exercise of justice and equity for the poor and meek of the world (Isa. 11.3–4).

(d) *Military institutions.* The whole Old Testament is filled with stories of wars and conflict. In the patriarchal period the members of an extended family formed a military group for fighting battles (Gen. 14.13ff.). During the early settlement period the male citizens of a clan formed the bulk of the army. With the rise of the monarchy the use of mercenaries played a significant role. David himself served as a Philistine mercenary, and later formed the core of his army with paid professional soldiers (II Sam. 15.19ff.). His military experience did much to break the control of the Philistines, who had exploited their military prowess with a more advanced technology (I Sam. 13.19–22) and highly trained professional units. The introduction of chariots and a standing army under Solomon, a force which continued throughout the monarchy, not only affected the military structure, but had wider implications for the society in general. It accelerated the social stratification, required heavy taxation for its support, and increased the influx of foreign influence.

The most difficult critical problem relates to the institution of holy war. Von Rad developed the theory that holy war was a defensive function of the tribal league and he sought to reconstruct its cultic setting. He also envisioned its subsequent role under Josiah as a religious model which was repristinated for a new historical situation. A very different model for reconstructing the holy war traditions in Israel has been developed by F. M. Cross and P. D. Miller, who see in the institution a line of continuity with ancient Canaanite mythology in which Yahweh played the central role as divine warrior. Of course the difficulty of determining with certainty the origin and profile of the institution of holy war arises from the lack of sufficient evidence. The biblical narratives either assume a knowledge of the tradition or push the *realia* so much into the background as to be of little help for the modern historian.

Once again it is evident that the dominant interests of the biblical writers lay on the theological level. Yet nowhere within the Old Testament can a development be discerned which envisions pacifism as the ultimate divine purpose for Israel. Rather, a very different theological dynamic develops. The image of God as the divine warrior extends throughout the Old Testament and even receives new life in the later prophetic and apocalyptic writings. The cultic forms on Israel's holy war assured that God fought for his people in bringing victory. The radical contribution of the prophets lay, not in denying God's warlike activity – he still waged war against his enemies – but in projecting Israel as God's new enemy. Not only does he summon the Assyrians to do his destructive work (Isa. 10.15ff.) and whistle for the 'enemy from the north' (Isa. 5.26ff.; Jer. 5.15ff.), he is also pictured personally involved in wreaking havoc on his wicked people (Isa. 2.12ff.). Because Israel fails to trust in God for protection, but relies on Egyptian chariots (Isa. 31.1ff.), Israel will fall in battle.

It is in this context that the image of salvation as peace begins to emerge (Isa. 30.15). Peace is not simply the absence of war, but a derivative of God's reconciliation and restoration of his creation. The prophetic hope is expressed in terms of peace among the nations who together learn the ways of God (Isa. 2.1–4). The new Jerusalem will be without walls because God now protects a righteous people (Zech. 2.4f.). However, even in the end-time, the imagery of battle and armies is continued in the Old Testament because resistance to the rule of God persists, now raised to a cosmological dimension, until finally God shall usher in his kingdom (Dan. 12.1ff.). Yet for Israel who awaits the end the imperative to deal with the prisoner and captive in mercy is firmly rooted in God's righteousness (II Chron. 28.8–15).

(*e*) *Family institutions.* Finally, the centrality of the family in Hebrew society is attested to by the numerous institutions associated with it. Social customs regulated life in all its important spheres: birth, puberty, marriage, children, property, inheritance, old age and death.

Early Hebrew society was patriarchal in its organization, with the family head exercising absolute power over its members much after the fashion of early Bedouin cultures. That other factors beside strictly legal ones entered into the execution of family law is made abundantly clear from numerous narratives, e.g. in the case of Sarah's intense dislike of Hagar which forced Abraham to expel the rival slave woman (Gen. 21.8ff.). The enormous influence on family life exerted by the concept of the extended family is also everywhere evident. Much of the initial friction between Saul and Jonathan focused on David's disruptive role in attracting Jonathan outside the family sphere (cf. Pedersen, I,278–84). The intensive concern for the maintenance of the family found expression in the importance attributed to sons. Israel shared with her neighbours all the various forms of legal fiction to insure a line of legitimate descent (Gen. 16.1–2). The joys of children are frequently extolled by the psalmist (113.9; 127.3–5), and Job portrays the presence of children as part of his former blessed state (29.5).

Marriage in Israel was largely monogamous, but polygamy was sanctioned especially in the case of the first wife's sterility. There is no explicit law forbidding more than one wife, although increasingly monogamy became the rule, and polygamy and divorce were severely criticized (I Kings 11.1–5; Mal. 2.14–17). The woman retained a subordinate position in the family and could be divorced by the husband (Deut. 24.1). However, there were a number of laws which did offer a limited protection (Deut. 22.13ff.). She could inherit property only under exceptional circumstances (Num. 36.1ff.), and any vow could be rendered invalid by her father or husband (Num. 30.1ff.). This depressing picture is tempered somewhat by the portrayal of the ideal wife in the wisdom literature, which describes a role with considerable responsibility and creative potential (Prov. 31.10ff.).

The death of a member of the family was observed by a fixed pattern of mourning and burial conventions which was little different from Israel's neighbours. The idiom to describe the death of a patriarch reflects a sense of family solidarity even in death: 'he died in a good old age . . . and was gathered to his people' (Gen. 25.8). One of the important roles of the family was in offering consolation which sought to heal the break in the social fabric (Gen. 24.67).

Once again the theological implications from a study of the family institutions supports an interpretation that Israel's faith not only was formed in relation to the common social structures of the period, but also resulted in an effort to reshape aspects of her communal life to conform more closely to her faith. The relationship remains a subtle one. Nowhere does the Old Testament address the issue in principle nor propose a social programme radically to alter its institutional life. Change occurred gradually and often resulted from a consequence of many factors, both religious and political, such as the gradual cessation of the practice of blood vengeance. The biblical writers struggled to see the hand of God at work in their lives, and bore witness to its presence in all the concrete aspects of social life. To suggest that Israel's institutions developed a 'liberated' society different in kind from its neighbours is a vast oversimplification. Yet to recognize powerful forces at work which stemmed from a profoundly religious conviction is fully supported by critical historical analysis.

Bibliography

A. **Alt**, *Essays on Old Testament History and Religion*, ET Oxford and Garden City, NY 1966; F. M. **Cross**, *Canaanite Myth and Hebrew Epic*, Cambridge, Mass. and London 1973; W. **Eichrodt**, *Theology of the Old Testament*, ET, II, London and Philadelphia 1967, 231ff.; G. **Fohrer**, 'Zur Einwirkung der gesellschaftlichen Struktur Israels auf seine Religion', (1971) reprinted in *Studien zu alttestamentlichen Texten und Themen (1966–1972)*, BZAW 155, 1981, 17–131; N. K. **Gottwald**, *The Tribes of Yahweh*, Maryknoll 1979 and London 1980; T. **Jacobsen**, 'Primitive Democracy in Ancient Mesopotamia', *JNES* 2, 1943, 159ff.; L. **Köhler**, 'Justice in the Gate', ET *Hebrew Man*, London 1956, 149–75; I. **Lande**, *Formelhafte Wendungen der Umgangssprache im Alten Testament*, Leiden 1948; A. D. H. **Mayes**, *Israel in the Period of the Judges*, SBT II. 29, 1974; J. L. **McKenzie**, 'The Elders in the Old Testament', *Analecta Biblica* 10, 1959, 388–406; G. **Mendenhall**, *The Tenth Generation*, Baltimore 1973; P. D. **Miller**, *The Divine Warrior in Early Israel*, Cambridge, Mass. and London 1973; M. **Noth**, *Das System der Zwölf Stämme* (1930), reprinted Darmstadt 1966; J. **Pedersen**, *Israel*, ET, I–II, Copenhagen and London 1926; G. **von Rad**, *Der Heilige Krieg im Alten Israel*, AbTANT 20, 1951; L. **Rost**, *Die Vorstufen von Kirche und Synagoge im Alten Testament*, BWANT 76, 1938; P. **Trible**, 'Depatriarchalizing in Biblical Interpretation', *JAAR* 41, 1973, 30–48; R. **de Vaux**, *Ancient Israel. Its Life and Institutions*, ET New York and London 1961; K. W. **Whitelam**, *The Just King: Monarchial Authority in Ancient Israel*, *JSOT Suppl* 12, 1979; G. E. **Wright**, *The Old Testament against its Environment*, SBT I. 2, 1950; Y. **Yadin**, *The Art of Warfare in Biblical Lands and in the Light of Archaeology*, ET, I–II, New York 1963.

16

MALE AND FEMALE AS A THEOLOGICAL PROBLEM

In the previous chapters an attempt was made to reflect on the theological significance of the particular forms of Israel's social institutions. Because of the mass of material, the treatment had to be sketched in broad lines. It seems, therefore, appropriate to approach one specific area of reality in more detail in an attempt to gain a fuller theological understanding.

The subject of male and female in the Old Testament offers an ideal area of exploration. It is closely related to the issues of family institutions already discussed, but it is not to be simply identified with that of husband and wife. Then again, it is treated at great length in several classic passages which call for a more detailed exegesis than the former chapter would allow. Finally, the subject has emerged as a major issue of contemporary debate, and well illustrates the extent to which reader response – of course, according to the analogy of faith and not natural human capacity – affects the theological understanding of the Bible.

(i) *Male and female in Genesis 1–3*

The first passage to be considered is Gen. 1.26f.:

> Then God said, 'Let us make man (*'ādām*) in our image, after our likeness, and let them have dominion over the fish of the sea, and over the birds of the air. . . .' So God created man in his own image, in the image of God he created them; male and female he created them.

The passage is formulated in the peculiar style and vocabulary of the Priestly writer (1.1–2.4a). In a sequence of seven days the creation of the heavens and the earth is described. The creation of the animals and creeping things occurs on the sixth day, but in addition the creation of 'ādām. Moreover, this latter act (1.26f.) is depicted in a different style from the previous acts of creation. It does not occur by a verbal command – 'God said let there be . . . and it was' – but first God expresses his intention in the context of a heavenly court ('us', v. 26). Only after this reflection does the creation of man take place. The word 'ādām is the generic Hebrew term for human being which consists of both male and female species. This genus is assigned a special role within the creation – 'let them have dominion' – but above all is given a special relation to God. 'Ādām is the bearer of the 'image of God'. The exegetical difficulty of determining exactly what is meant with this phrase has already been discussed (ch. 9). Nevertheless, the threefold repetition of the verb 'create' ties closely together the special act of creation with its form of human sexual duality: God *created* man in his own image, in the image of God he *created* them, male and female he *created* them. No differentiation is made between male and female in terms of temporal priority or function. Their creation occurs simultaneously and only together is their creative role described. Surely this is a witness of absolute equality.

When one turns to the next chapter (2.4b–25), the shift to the different style, vocabulary and perspective of the Yahwist is immediately evident. The divergent order between the chapters in the sequence of the creation has long been noticed. The initial exegetical issue turns on determining the relation of the creation of the human being (hā'ādām) in 2.7, who is a creature formed from the dirt, to the subsequent creation of a 'helper' ('ēzer) in 2.18.

Traditional exegesis interpreted v. 7 as describing the creation of man, the male, and v. 18ff. the creation of the woman, the female. Accordingly, most traditional Christian theological reflection on the relation of the sexes in the Church Fathers, Schoolmen and Reformers found a warrant in this ordering of the creation for the dependence or subordination of the woman to the man.

Within recent years this traditional interpretation has been subjected to a lengthy criticism and re-interpretation, especially by P. Trible. Trible argues that the denotation of 'ādām in 1.17 as a sexually undifferentiated species of earth creature continues throughout ch. 2. Until the differentiation of male and female in 2.21–23 'ādām is basically androgynous, that is, one creature incorporating two sexes. Later Trible dropped the term androgynous because it assumes the phenomenon of sexuality, and resorted to speaking only of an original 'earth creature'. From this one earth creature ('ādām) was formed a male ('îš) and a female ('iššāh). The sexual identity of each depends on the other and derives from the one flesh of the 'ādām. Although they are distinct creatures, they do not exist in opposition to each other, but in unity. According to Trible, also in ch. 2 there is no priority of the male, nor any dependent relation of the female. The woman's creation is simultaneous, not sequential.

What can one say about this interpretation of the Genesis accounts? In my opinion, there are several reasons which speak against it:

(a) First, from a literary perspective one questions whether the relationship of 'ādām in 1.26f. to the creation of the male and female in ch. 2 is that proposed by Trible. Chapter 2 has a very different narrative movement from ch. 1. Accordingly, a deep sleep falls on the 'ādām. A rib is taken from the sleeping 'ādām and formed into a woman ('iššāh). Then the woman is brought to the 'ādām who exclaims: 'she shall be called woman ('iššāh) because she was taken from man ('îš)'. There is no indication that 'ādām was split into an 'îš and a 'iššāh, but rather the 'iššāh is derived from the 'îš. There is no sign of a simultaneous creation of sexuality. The description of the woman being formed from a portion of the man is given in a way which is not parallel to the creation of 'ādām in ch. 1.

(b) Secondly, the exegetical arguments of Trible cannot be sustained linguistically. She argues that the earth creature ('ādām) was differentiated in 2.18ff. into an 'îš and an 'iššāh (male and female human beings). However, the term 'ādām is not used differently before and after the formation of the woman. Indeed, after her appearance 'îš and 'iššāh are paralleled with 'ādām and 'iššāh (vv. 23 and 25).

(c) Thirdly, the Masoretic tradition points the term man before the creation of the woman as a proper name, Adam, in 2.20: 'The man gave names to all the beasts, but for Adam there was not found a helper.' The Septuagint renders both occurrences of the noun in the verse as a proper name. In other words, according to both the Hebrew and Greek traditions the oscillation within the term is between 'ādām as generic man, and Adam as one example of the species. It is not between a sexually undifferentiated earth creature and two examples of a sexually differentiated species. In ch. 2 *'ādām* who is representative man is instantiated in Adam.

What then are the theological implications to be drawn from this exegesis? If in ch. 1 the creation of male and female as generic man was simultaneous in time, identical in form, and unified in significance, a very different witness is sounded in ch. 2. The creation of woman followed that of the male example of the species, Adam. There are no notes of inferiority, but the relationship is not that of similarity, nor of independence. Rather, the woman is assigned a function as helper which is not identical with the role of the one being helped. To speak of the creation of the woman as an afterthought is certainly to do an injustice to the sense of the chapter, but the stress clearly falls on her support of Adam. The creation of the woman, which is sequential in time, forms a climax to the creation which resounds with joy at the close of the chapter. In sum, the relationship between male and female in chs. 2–3 is different from that in ch. 1. According to the witness of ch. 2 a distinction between their roles in the creative order is not a sign of the so-called 'fall' (ch. 3), but derived from the intentionality of the creator.

Of course, another major theme of Genesis has to be sounded immediately. A crucial point in the story which follows in ch. 3 lies in depicting the origin of the distortion and dislocation of God's original creative purpose. One of the elements in the distortion of the creation was the subjugation of the woman to the man which is expressed aetiologically in 3.16 as part of the divine judgment:

> I will multiply your pain in childbearing . . .
> your desire shall be for your husband,
> and he shall rule over you.

This judgment on the woman parallels that of the man for whose sake the ground is cursed. Neither condition belonged to the original intention of God's good creation.

If ch. 1 and chs. 2–3 of Genesis make such different witnesses, how are they to be related theologically? The answer is not obvious, but requires strenuous theological reflection. However, the close interrelationship of these chapters within the book of Genesis confirms the legitimacy of the question. It is a totally inadequate response simply to suggest that two different historical authors offered variant views on the subject, and thus to close off the larger theological question. Certainly an Old Testament theology which works seriously with the biblical text as scripture of the church requires a different quality of response.

I would argue that the relation of male and female is a very subtle one in the Bible. Looked at from one perspective the witness is to equality, even identity, in a unified role within the kingdom of God. However, when viewed from another biblical perspective, there are different roles and varying functions assigned to men and women, in the realms of both creation and redemption. Therefore, in order to recover and maintain the richness of the entire Old Testament witness, the interpreter has to fight theologically on two fronts against two prevalent dangers. On the one hand, the danger from the theological right is to read into the Old Testament the traditional ideology of a male dominated society which would transfer the *mores* of a fallen society to the kingdom of God. To them the answer is No. 'Male and female created he them.' Together in their unity they constitute true humanity. On the other hand, the danger from the theological left is to equate the biblical witness with a modern egalitarian ideology which would simply identify the sexes in every respect with the same roles, goals, and capacities. To them the answer is likewise No. 'It is not good that the man should be alone. I will make for him a helper . . . therefore, a man leaves his father and mother and cleaves to his wife. . .' God chose to create two different forms of humanity for different functions within his creation.

Admittedly the theological task of doing justice to the full content of the subject has only begun with this reflection on Genesis. The crucial issue of understanding and interpreting the nature of the various functions of male and female requires all the knowledge and wisdom of the entire theological enterprise, including the New Testament, systematic theology, ethics and church history. Nevertheless, attention to the diversity of the Old Testament witness does provide an initial critical norm within which to pursue theological reflection.

(ii) *Male and female in the Song of Songs*

There is an additional Old Testament witness to the subject of male and female found in the Song of Songs to be considered. Traditionally there has been much debate on how to interpret this book. One school of Jewish interpreters sought to construe the Song as a midrash on Gen. 2 which expanded on conjugal life in the Garden of Eden. However, in spite of elements of shared content, the Song is not midrashic in genre. It does not interpret a text, but rather relates directly to the human experience of love. Or again, the attempt to render the Song allegorically as a portrayal of God's love to Israel or to the church is without textual warrant. Finally, it is not a prophetic oracle which envisions a future return to paradisal bliss.

The Song of Songs consists of a series of love poems which celebrate the joys of physical love between a man and a woman. There is no clear structure to the book, nor is there a dramatic plot with a unified movement. Rather, the experience of sexual love between two people is treated from a great variety of different perspectives. The two voices of the male and the female lovers pour out their feelings of longing for and satisfaction in mutual surrender. Usually the woman takes the lead in seeking out her companion in complete and unrestrained freedom of passion.

It is theologically significant to note the manner in which the canon has construed these love poems. By assigning them to the category of wisdom the canonical editors do not alter the quality of the Song as poems of human love, but retain the phenomenon in the world of human experience. Wisdom, not human love, is divine. Yet love between a man and woman is of inestimable value, a power stronger than death which cannot be quenched (8.6ff.).

The major theological question turns on establishing the proper context for interpreting this picture of human love which is viewed from a perspective of innocence completely untouched by the entrance of sin. The lack of any integral connection with the Genesis chapters prevents it from being understood as the lost paradise of the primaeval past. Another intriguing suggestion is offered by Karl Barth, who characterized the love in the Song as 'eschatological' (III/1,314). He contrasts the function of Genesis, which is to portray the commencement of covenant love, with the Song of Songs, which describes its future goal. However, in my judgment, there is no canonical warrant within the Old Testament for aligning these two witnesses in such a *heilsgeschichtliche* sequence.

Rather, I would argue that the Song of Songs as wisdom bears witness to a present reality of erotic love in the world of human experience. It celebrates a moment of human ecstasy evoked through a unique relationship between a man and a woman which transcends the stains of historical reality. It reveals the joyous mutuality of strength and joy in uninhibited surrender. Only on the very edges does it allow the darkness of a potential shadow to obscure the exuberant pleasure between the couple. The witness of the Song to the present reality of human love prevents this experience from being assigned either to the distant past or the expected future.

Yet within the context of the entire Old Testament canon the mysterious joy of human love which continues to erupt as an unquenchable flame is balanced by the threat of that same human love to destroy and to twist its beauty. 'Then the eyes of both were opened, and they knew that they were naked . . . and they hid themselves from the presence of God.' The Old Testament bears witness to the reality of human love as a gift of the creator for human benefit, but one which carries with it both the promise of enriching joy as well as the threat of egoistic destruction.

The recent attempt of some theologians to find a biblical opening, if not warrant, for the practice of homosexuality stands in striking disharmony with the Old Testament's understanding of the relation of male and female. The theological issue goes far beyond the citing of occasional texts which condemn the practice (Lev. 20.13). Nor is the heart of the issue touched by the historicist's claim that Israel was obsessed with the propagation of children to assure the nation's survival. Rather, it turns on the divine structuring of human life in the form of male and female with the potential of greatest joy or deepest grief. The Old Testament continually witnesses to the distortion of God's intention for humanity in heterosexual aberrations (Judg. 20; II Sam. 13). Similarly the Old Testament views homosexuality as a distortion of creation which falls into the shadows outside the blessing.

In sum, the truly remarkable quality of the theological witness of the Old Testament to the issue of male and female becomes immediately apparent when one recalls the social realities of ancient Israel. In a society which shared numerous traditional features with its ancient Near Eastern neighbours, which often exploited women in numerous ways, there emerged a biblical testimony to an understanding of human society which far transcended all the concrete historical forms of social practice. Does it seem irrational to claim with generations of Jews and Christians that this biblical testimony concerning mankind stems from a new vision of God and of his intention for creation?

Bibliography

K. **Barth,** *Church Dogmatics*, ET, III/4, Edinburgh 1961, 116–240; P. **Bird,** 'Gen. 1:27b in the Context of the Priestly Account of Creation', *HTR* 74, 1981, 129–59; B. S. **Childs,** 'Proverbs, chapter 7, and a Biblical Approach to Sex', *Biblical Theology in Crisis*, Philadelphia 1970, 184–202; W. **Eichrodt,** 'Homosexualität – Andersartigkeit oder Perversion?', *Reformatio* XII, 1963, 67–82; V. **Eller,** *The Language of Canaan and the Grammar of Feminism*, Grand Rapids 1982; H. **Gollwitzer,** *Song of Love: A Biblical Understanding of Sex*, ET Philadelphia 1979; P. **Jewett,** *Man as Male and Female*, Grand Rapids 1975; O. **Loretz,** *Die Gottesebenbildlichkeit des Menschen*, Munich 1967; P. **Trible,** 'Depatriarchalizing in Biblical Interpretation', *JAAR* 41, 1971, 30–48; 'A Love Story Gone Awry', *God and the Rhetoric of Sexuality*, Philadelphia 1978, 72–143; R. **de Vaux**, *Ancient Israel. Its Life and Institutions*, ET New York and London 1961, 19–61; H. W. **Wolff,** *Anthropology of the Old Testament*, ET Philadelphia and London 1974, 166–76; W. **Zimmerli,** *The Old Testament and the World*, ET London and Atlanta 1976.

17

THE THEOLOGICAL DIMENSION OF BEING HUMAN

(i) *Introduction*

Although I have continually stressed the dominantly theocentric perspective of the Old Testament, it is a false implication to suggest that the Hebrew Bible has little interest in anthropology. The subject of man has already been discussed in his role as a vehicle of revelation, as the bearer of the divine image, and as a creature of sexual differentiation. Yet the Old Testament's approach to the subject is multi-faceted and requires analysis from many different angles in order to capture its richness. Another basic aspect is the theological role of man as a human being. However, the hard question turns on how best to construe the Old Testament in order to do justice to the material from this perspective. No issue has generated greater methodological confusion. A brief review of some of the traditional options illustrates the difficulty:

(*a*) The Christian church took over from Graeco-Roman antiquity the genre of the biography of the holy man (Cox, *Biography*), and soon sought to interpret the Old Testament characters as heroes with ideal traits and virtues. This moralistic reading of the Old Testament was doomed to failure and resulted in fanciful allegory so as to avoid the obvious difficulties.

(*b*) Later, under the influence of Romanticism, the biographical interest was once again revived, but with an eye to recovering the genuinely earthy quality of human life, both good and bad, and to tracing the development of character and personality. But again, the approach did not provide access into the biblical material, which remained singularly disinterested in character development and inner motivation.

(*c*) Then, beginning in the later part of the nineteenth century and extending up to the present time, there have been frequent attempts to employ various forms of social science in an effort to gain a more objective measurement of man in the Old Testament. At times scholars have sought to find the key in a peculiar form of pre-logical or Hebrew mentality (Pedersen, I, 99ff.), or to recover a psychological point of entrance (H. W. Robinson). However, in most recent times the emphasis has fallen on techniques or comparative anthropology and sociology affecting group behaviour (Rogerson). Although it would be false to reject all such studies as futile, since some have been quite useful, the more difficult question lies in determining to what extent the new tools have provided adequate theological understanding of the material.

(d) Finally, in an effort to remain close to the biblical text, a precise philological study of the specific anthropological terminology of the Hebrew Bible has been attempted – flesh, body, soul, spirit, etc. – with a view to interpreting the significance of being human. Although scholars like Köhler and Wolff have been successful in sharpening the profile of ancient man, the approach has difficulty in penetrating beyond external observations which in the end do not prove to be the vehicle by which the Old Testament's theological witness has been made. Von Rad's sensitive recognition of this fact caused him to abandon this type of word-study as a fruitful avenue into the Old Testament's multi-layered anthropological reflections. Even such a highly beloured subject as the image of God did not provide the key for understanding the theological dimension of being human.

(ii) *Canonical indices within the tradition*

The first and most obvious feature to observe is that large portions of the Old Testament consist of stories about human beings who in innumerable ways lived their lives in the presence of God. At times men and women had direct encounters with God (Moses). At other times the relationship was of an indirect (Joseph) or distant kind (Nehemiah). Yet the point to be stressed is that the medium for the theological witness did not take the form of a theological tractate. Even the legal stipulations have been set within a narrative context. Equally important, the stories are rarely given a directly didactic interpretation.

Sometimes the narratives are of ordinary persons whose experiences were judged to be theological paradigms and were retained as an integral part of Israel's sacred history. Then again, some of the stories have been rendered with such a literary density as to transcend by far the experience of one individual person. Clearly typological features accrued to the great figures of the Hebrew tradition, not in terms of idealization, but rather as vehicles of Israel's accumulated experience of life under God, both in terms of obedience and disobedience. The major point to be emphasized is that the narrative with its potential for polyvalence is a major vehicle for probing the Old Testament's understanding of being human.

Then again, it is of particular theological significance that the canonical shaping of the sacred tradition developed in terms of *persona* who became the nucleus around which the tradition received its focus: Moses for the Law, David for psalmody, Solomon for wisdom. Certainly an important canonical index for rendering the tradition was lost when the form-critical method was unable to do justice to the biographical form in which the tradition was transmitted and fell back to a sociological *Sitz* as the only recoverable setting (cf. Noth, *Pentateuchal Traditions*, 156–75). Even the need to reconstruct biblical tradents who are equipped with semi-personal features such as the 'Yahwist' of the 'Deuteronomist' testifies to the problem of correctly interpreting the canonical form of the biblical *persona*. Although H. Gunkel was able to illuminate conventional forces at work in the pre-historical stages of Israel's Psalter, he disregarded the new function assigned to the *persona* in the psalms titles as a way of focusing the tradition on a historical representative of universal human suffering (Childs, 'Psalm Titles').

Finally, it is significant to recognize that genuinely historical and biographical features of the prophets have been joined with a variety of other theological concerns to create a special form of human witness to God's word for Israel. Indeed, the prophetic *persona* of Isaiah differs markedly from that of Jeremiah, and the stages by which traditions were constructed about an individual prophet are quite unique. However, both have in common the rendering of God's word through a human vehicle, in a given historical situation, and towards the goal of Israel's redemption.

In sum, the form in which Israel's sacred traditions were rendered in the canonical process provides a basic hermeneutical guide for a modern theological reflection on the Old Testament's witness to what it means to be human.

(iii) *Theological reflections on Old Testament anthropology*

It is preferable to speak of dimensions of the text rather than topics because the lines of the material flow together and the same text can function in different ways depending on the angle of vision. Nevertheless, there are some consistent features of the Old Testament's understanding of what it involves to being human which, in a variety of different formulations, continue to reverberate throughout the Hebrew canon.

The basic tension in man's existence has already been described in the first chapters of Genesis: created male and female, to have dominion over the work of God's creation (1.27), and yet formed from the dirt (2.7). Man is a fragile creature, fully dependent on the breath of God for life. The entire Old Testament is aware of his frail and precarious nature. Man is not a semi-divine creature striving to realize some ideal by which to fulfil a destiny, but rather a short-lived mortal, born in a family, given a community, and greatly restricted in time and place. Because Israel's sacred stories are about real people tied to all the limitations of being human, the Old Testament had no place for myths about superhuman heroes. Even Samson was 'demythologized' to perform his function as a badly flawed human being.

It has long been noticed that according to the Old Testament man does not *have* a soul, but *is* a soul (Gen. 2.7). That is to say, he is a complete entity and not a composite of parts from body, soul and spirit. Yet it is also true that the Old Testament views man from different holistic perspectives. He can be described in terms of his will, or his emotions, or his physical prowess. It is also indicative that man has a spirit much like God, but it cannot be detached from his body. Indeed, all parts of the body – heart, liver, kidneys – function in a metaphorical-like manner to describe realistically different aspects of total life as a human being. Moreover, his ability to remember, to recall the past, joins the individual indissolubly with the nation (Ps. 77.11ff.).

The stories of the Pentateuch simply take it for granted that man has a limited period of life. There is a rhythm in nature from youth, to full strength, to inevitable decline. In death man returns to the dust from which he came. Yet the writer of Ecclesiastes reflects a sense of sadness, even futility, as he observes the slow disintegration of human strength in old age (12.1–8). However, even more important than the shortness of life is man's vulnerability to threats on every side. Although most of the Old Testament stories have to do with various forms of affliction, suffering in itself is not seen as inevitable, but as an ever-present contingency. The psalmist does not proceed from some overarching concept of fate, but simply describes the variety of ills which assault mankind, and from which there is no human recourse: sickness, enemies, slander, fear, exile and death.

Equally a constitutive part of human existence is his openness to God which sets him apart from all other creatures. Although man cannot transcend his own time-conditioned humanity, he has been given a sense of the divine. Ecclesiastes speaks of God's having planted eternity into his being (3.11). The psalmist often exhibits an unquenchable longing for God which is a desire far greater than thirst (42.1). Yet this sense of the presence of God does not always work for man's comfort, but can function as a terror from which he seeks to flee (Ps. 139.7ff.). The Old Testament does not locate this knowledge of God as a human capacity such as conscience – man has no eternal spark of the divine within him – rather, it recognizes the continuous activity of God in drawing man to himself.

A consistent feature of Old Testament narrative is its describing the entrance of God in human life. There is no fixed pattern, but still in innumerable ways God makes himself known. The young Samuel cannot at first distinguish the voice of God from that of Eli (I Sam 3.2ff.). Jacob is unaware of God's presence until he perceives him in a dream (Gen. 28.10ff.). David must be reminded of God's former mercies by Nathan before he recognizes the full nature of the offence. The superscription of Ps. 51 serves to actualize the extent of David's response by joining the psalm to this historical context. Moreover, even arrogant rulers are forced finally to acknowledge God's rule (Dan. 4.1ff.). In very different ways the psalmist, prophet and sage describe the strange, unexpected moments of God's intervention in the human heart. The presence of God can evoke fear or the highest joy, but it cannot be escaped. Only the fool thinks he can (Ps. 14.1).

Although the Old Testament has not developed a fully-fledged doctrine of sin such as one finds in Paul and in rabbinic Judaism, there is everywhere recognition of disruption, alienation and falsehood within human society, and above all in relation to God. Usually this side of human nature is brought out in the realistic narrative accounts of brutality (Lamech), deceit (Jacob), anger (Samson) and hatred (Absalom). Yet such action is not simply taken for granted, but condemned in different ways as an offence to God. For example, Abimelech is described as a ruthless tyrant who is intoxicated with power until he is destroyed by his own evil (Judg 9.1ff.). Often the Old Testament narratives reflect the subtle interchange between the powers of good and evil. Saul is pictured as being slowly consumed by his madness, but still experiencing moments of genuine repentance which leave open a way of possible escape from his ˙ self-inflicted destruction almost until the end (I Sam. 24.16ff.).

Another essential feature of the Old Testament lies in its setting the description of human existence within various societal relationships. Man in the Old Testament is always part of a group. He is a son, brother or father; a daughter, sister or wife. Even Job, who lays so much emphasis upon his individual integrity as a human being who is being bullied by God (9.13ff.), depicts his ideal state before his trials completely in terms of fullness and peace within his household (Job. 29.1ff.). Moreover, the paradoxical nature of human behaviour emerges most clearly in man's relationship to his fellows. David had the capacity for great friendship (I Sam. 18.1ff.), and he was able to evoke from others tremendous loyalty (I Chron. 11.15ff.). Yet he could be utterly ruthless (II Sam. 3.14f.), and exploit others such as Michal for his own political ambition. The Old Testament registers the ambiguity of human relations in a particularly penetrating fashion in the stories of Absalom's revolt. The real motivations behind the defences of Ziba and Mephibosheth are left unresolved in a strange twilight of half-truths (II Sam. 19.16ff.). Similarly, the sayings of the sages consistently sound a fully realistic appraisal of human ambivolence, and praise true friendship and loyalty as of great value (Prov. 17.17; 27.6, etc.).

One of the greatest contributions of the Hebrew prophets was in reinforcing the basic affirmation of the Mosaic law by insisting that loyalty to God must be demonstrated by righteous behaviour toward one's fellows. In the Old Testament, religion and ethics are not identical, but neither can they be separated. The prophets are bitter in their attack on any piety which would obscure human responsibility for one's neighbour under the pretext of a primary loyalty to God (Isa. 58.1ff.). Because the prophets fully shared the realistic appraisal of human sinfulness, they continued to couch their demands for justice in legal terminology by which societal relationships were regulated rather than in appeals to modes of ethical intentionality (Isa. 1.16f.).

The various parts of the Old Testament bear eloquent witness to human nature as both rational and emotional. Many of the biblical narratives reflect an individual's uncanny ability logically to plan and order his existence. Joseph showed his skill not only in reorganizing the Egyptian wheat supply (Gen. 41.46ff.), but in devising an ingenious plan to test his brothers (42.6ff.). Naomi also showed a calculated cleverness in arranging for Ruth's eventual marriage of Boas (Ruth 3.1ff.). Finally, the sage marvels at man's rational powers in devising means for mining the earth's riches (Job 28.3ff.). Yet human reason is viewed in a neutral fashion within the Old Testament as a human potential for both good and evil. Above all, it is God who rules and overrules human plans, especially those conceived in arrogance (Isa. 14.24–27).

A particular characteristic of the Hebrew Psalter is the portrayal of the widest possible range of human emotions in the worship of God. The Hebrew did not suffer in silence, nor was stoic resignation ever an ideal. Rather, both in joy and sorrow the psalmist poured out his emotions to God in thanksgiving and complaint. Because of the Old Testament's holistic understanding of human nature, the lines separating physical and spiritual afflictions were often indistinguishable and the energetic complaints of the suffering psalmist oscillates between internal and external troubles. It was not, therefore, by accident that Israel's worship involved the worshipper's total being and was celebrated with dancing, procession and loud music, or conversely, with fasting, dirges and rending of garments.

There is one final aspect to consider respecting the Old Testament's understanding of being human. Elsewhere it has been observed the extent to which the element of hope and promise provided an important force in shaping the canonical tradition (ch. 20). The same note of promise and a new beginning is frequently reflected in the narrative material. Abraham buys a piece of the promised land in order to bury his wife, and so bears testimony to his belief in the promise of a future inheritance (Gen. 23.1ff.). Joseph dies in Egypt, but commands his bones to be carried home when Israel returns (Gen. 50.25). Jeremiah purchases a plot of land in Anathoth as a sign that one day the destroyed land would be restored (Jer. 32.1ff.).

Moreover, this element of new beginning reflects itself throughout the Old Testament in stories of individual reconciliation, forgiveness and healing. One of the effects which the elaborate Joseph cycle achieves is to emphasize the growth in Joseph's maturity. He seeks to test whether his brothers have changed in regard to the innocent younger brother, only to reveal by his reconciliation the extent to which he has been altered in disposition. 'You meant it for evil, but God meant it for good' (Gen. 50.20). The Old Testament is far too realistic to project radical shifts in human nature: 'Can the leopard change its spots?' (Jer. 13.23). Yet because of its profound faith in a God who wills good for his people, it bears witness to healing, restoration, and a new beginning even in the life of the rejected and outcast of society (Hos. 2.21ff.). 'Behold . . . new things I now declare' (Isa. 42.9).

Bibliography

K. **Baltzer**, *Die Biographie der Propheten*, Neukirchen-Vluyn 1975; K. **Barth**, *Church Dogmatics*, ET, III/2, Edinburgh 1960, 3ff.; B. S. **Childs**, 'Psalm Titles and Midrashic Exegesis', *JSS* 16, 1971, 137–50; P. **Cox**, *Biography in Late Antiquity. A Quest for the Holy Man*, Berkeley 1983; F. **Delitzsch**, *A System of Biblical Psychology*, ET Edinburgh 1867; W. **Eichrodt**, *Man in the OT*, SBT I. 4, 1951; J. **Goody**, *The Domestication of the Savage Mind*, Cambridge 1977; A. R. **Johnson,** *The Vitality of the Individual in the Thought of Ancient Israel*, Cardiff 1949; L. **Köhler**, *Hebrew Man*, ET London 1956; J. L. **Mays**, "What is Man . . .?" Reflections on Psalm 8', *From Faith to Faith, Essays in Honor of Donald G. Miller*, ed. D. Y. Hadidian, Pittsburgh 1979, 203–18; A. **Momigliano**, *The Development of Greek Biography*, ET Cambridge, Mass. 1971; M. **Noth**, *A History of Pentateuchal Traditions*, ET Englewood, NJ 1972; J. **Pedersen**, *Ancient Israel: Its Life and Institutions*, I–II, London 1926; H. W. **Robinson**, 'Hebrew Psychology', *The People and the Book*, ed. A. S. Peake, Oxford 1925, 353–82; 'The Hebrew Conception of Corporate Personality', *Werden und Wesen des Alten Testaments*, BZAW 66, 1936, 49–62; J. W. **Rogerson**, *Anthropology and the Old Testament*, Oxford 1978; H. W. **Wolff**, *Anthropology of the Old Testament*, ET London and Philadelphia 1978; W. **Zimmerli**, *The Old Testament and the World*, ET Atlanta and London 1976.

18

THE SHAPE OF THE OBEDIENT LIFE

Up to this point the emphasis of these theological reflections on the Old Testament has fallen largely on the great acts of God in revealing himself to Israel. He made himself known in his creation and preservation of the world, in acts of deliverance and covenant, and in the gift of land and leadership. However, equally important in the Old Testament is that the initiative of God called forth a response on Israel's part. Attention now turns to this response.

(i) *A review of some theological approaches*

The Old Testament is filled with constant testimony that Israel did respond in hymns and prayers, in complaints and groans, in songs of joy and cries of despair. Traditionally it has been an important part of any Old Testament theology to pursue the various aspects of this side of Israel's faith. For example, Eichrodt has dealt with the subject in the final section of his theology under the rubric 'God and Man'. As always, there is an impressive thoroughness to his discussion. He begins by analysing the relationship between the individual and the community which in a sense reflects the effects of a late nineteenth-century debate. The chief problem of Old Testament ethics was considered to be Israel's effort to break out of a form of collectivism in which the individual had no integrity apart from the group until the period of Jeremiah and Ezekiel. Eichrodt offers incisive criticism to modify considerably this older picture in order to defend the legitimacy of treating the individual theologically throughout the Old Testament. He concludes that this polarity between community and individual was not correctly described in the older works. Although there was a development in Israel's understanding of the place of the individual following the destruction of the nation's political structure, a certain integrity of the individual was always present within Israel from the start. This same issue was revived in the 1930s in a somewhat different form with the appearance in English of J. Pedersen's *Israel*. Pedersen did not pose the relationship as one of historical development, but rather as a form of peculiar primitive mentality which fused the one and the many. Eichrodt occasionally mentioned Pedersen in his footnotes, but did not have a serious debate with him. This form of the discussion was further extended by H. Wheeler Robinson under the rubric of 'corporate personality', and by A. R. Johnson in *The One and the Many* (1942). A similar approach was frequently exploited theologically within the biblical theology movement of the 1950s. It has left its impact on modern theology in the current discussions on the solidarity of the human race, and in the debates on ecology and nature as an extension of the human family.

Eichrodt went on to discuss in considerable detail the peculiar Old Testament vocabulary by which human relationship with God is expressed: fear of God, faith in God, love for God, etc. (II, 268ff.). Such research is often helpful in gaining an insight into how Israel articulated its response to God. At times one can discern a change in the formulae used and can trace some development within the various concepts. For example, Eichrodt sets up a movement from an earlier stage in which the concept of fear of God slowly gave way to a more intimate sense of love as mutual belonging (II, 290ff.).

Since Eichrodt's work in the 1930s it has become increasingly clear that there is also a problematic side to this kind of word study. One sees the danger of misinterpretation especially in Kittel's *Theological Dictionary*, which is a learned extension of this method of research. The most obvious problem is of isolating words from their contexts; by placing them in a developmental pattern one finds an easy correlation between literary and theological growth. The confusion which obtains between the word, the formula, and the concept is also acute, as James Barr has clearly shown (*Semantics*, 206ff.). Specifically in terms of Eichrodt's proposal, one can seriously doubt whether there is a genuine development from the concept of the fear of God to the love of God. These terms have a different function within Israel's faith which do not stand in a sequential relationship. The once widely used book in the English-speaking world of Norman Snaith, *The Distinctive Ideas of the Old Testament*, suffers from the same inadequate approach to Israel's theology through isolated words.

Finally, Eichrodt develops his interpretation of Old Testament ethics under the rubric 'The Effect of Piety on Conduct (Old Testament Morality)' (II, 316ff.). He discusses the norms of moral conduct, particularly in the light of the standards of popular morality which Israel inherited from its ancient Near Eastern environment. In addition, he treats the relation between natural and religious goods, and the motivation behind moral conduct. Traditionally, no section within the discipline of Old Testament theology has been as vulnerable to the criticism of imposing unsuitable philosophical categories on the biblical material as the section on ethics. Eichrodt's treatment is no exception, and in the eyes of many of his critics his categories of an ethical system seem unusually dependent on a post-Kantian perspective.

Von Rad's criticism of Eichrodt is directed to another crucial methodological problem (I, 355f.). Eichrodt develops his theological understanding of Old Testament anthropology by drawing on all the literary, historical and comparative material available to construct a picture of Hebrew man. Von Rad questions whether what emerges is anything but a variant of a common ancient Near Eastern legacy without any of the special features of Israel's relationship with God. In regard to this criticism a canonical approach to Old Testament theology would share many of von Rad's 'kerygmatic' reservations toward Eichrodt's strictly phenomenological approach. However, to what extent von Rad's own positive formulation is satisfactory – he only uses statements of how Israel saw herself before God (I, 355f.) – requires further elaboration.

Under the rubric 'Israel before Yahweh' (I, 355ff.), von Rad offers some of his most brilliant reflections. There is a closeness to the biblical text which, in my opinion, stands in contrast to Eichrodt's tendency to construct overarching abstractions. Von Rad is particularly helpful in this section because he does not treat the tradition diachronically to the same extent as in his study of the Hexateuch, but tries to discern the inner structure of Israel's response from different angles.

My purpose in reviewing the theological approach of Eichrodt and von Rad is to acknowledge important areas of legitimate theological reflection which I shall not be pursuing, at least in this form. It is included also to confirm the initial position taken by this Old Testament theology that the subject matter does not constitute a closed system to be historically described, but rather different dimensions of Israel's faith are offered which lend themselves to a variety of theological construals by modern interpreters.

(ii) Canonical guidelines to Israel's response

How does Israel's response to the activity of God on her behalf function theologically in the context of the canon? This manner of posing the question serves initially to shift the focus of the investigation away from traditional approaches. Even von Rad sets up a dichotomy between the acts of Yahweh, which he finds in the Hexateuch and histories, and Israel's answer, which he finds largely in the Psalter and wisdom literature. An even more extreme form of this dichotomy is represented by G. E. Wright's position which stresses the 'objective' side to such an extent that he can find no real place for wisdom at all (*God Who Acts*). The formation of an authoritative canon would suggest that all the scripture reflects both the action of God and the response of Israel, and that the goal of the shaping process was directed to the continuous response of the people of God to what God had done and would do with them. Nevertheless, it is significant to recognize that the shaping of the material through a lengthy process has assigned a variety of different roles to the biblical material, some of which emphasize the divine activity, whereas others stress the human response to this initiative.

(*a*) *The Psalter.* A clear hermeneutical guideline has been offered to the canonical function of the Psalter by the role assigned to Ps. 1 as an introduction to the corpus. The editorial positioning of this original Torah psalm has provided the psalm with a new interpretative function. As an introduction it designates those prayers which follow as the medium through which Israel now responds to the divine word. Because Israel continues to hear God's word through the voice of the psalmist's response, these prayers now function as the divine word itself. Israel's prayers are not simply spontaneous musings or uncontrolled aspirations, but an answer to God's prior speaking which continues to address Israel in the Torah. The redactional position of Ps. 1 testifies that a hermeneutical shift has taken place and that the prayers of Israel which are directed to God have themselves become identified with God's fresh word to his people. The prayers are indeed the response of Israel, but offered in a continuous conversation with God through the use of this tradition.

This somewhat formal side of the shaping of the Psalter has been supported by the content of the prayers themselves. Again it has been von Rad, in an insight confirmed by Zimmerli, who has seen the central importance of the Psalter's understanding of righteousness (*ṣᵉdāqāh*). Von Rad points out that the fundamental relationship between God and man has been misunderstood because of the confusion surrounding this biblical term. According to the tradition of the Western world derived from Roman law, an individual's proper conduct was judged over against an absolute ethical norm. To be righteous was to be measured by a standard which stemmed from a fixed rule of justice. However, in regard to the Old Testament no one could satisfactorily determine what the absolute norm was. The mistake lay in positing an ideal standard as a form of a legal abstraction, whereas righteousness in the Old Testament was understood in terms of specific relationships between covenant partners. A righteous person was one who measured up to the responsibilities which the relationship had laid upon him.

When the Old Testament spoke of the righteousness of God, it was primarily a reference to the saving acts of Yahweh by which God had established a covenantal relationship with Israel. Yahweh's righteousness was not a fixed norm, but rather acts which bestowed salvation. His intervention into Israel's life established a social bond between him and his people which was defined by the quality of his saving acts.

The term righteousness also characterizes the nature of human conduct. A person is righteous who has fulfilled the claims (*mišpāṭîm*) which derived from the covenantal relationship. Zimmerli ('Zwillingspsalmen') has pointed out the inter-relatedness of the divine and human activity from two parallel psalms (Pss. 111 and 112). The extent to which human justice is a reflection of God's justice is illustrated in the use of the same formula to refer to both:

Ps. 111.2f.:   Great are the works of Yahweh . . .
full of honour and majesty are his works,
and *his righteousness endures for ever.*

Ps. 112.1–6: Blessed is the man who fears Yahweh . . .
          wealth and riches are in his house,
          and *his righteousness endures for ever* . . .
          Yahweh is gracious, merciful and righteous . . .
          It is well with the man who conducts his affairs with
               justice,
          for the righteous will never be removed.

Then again, von Rad has pursued some of the further implications of the use of righteousness within the Psalter in his important essay 'Righteousness and Life in the Cultic Language of the Psalter'. A major point of the essay is to show that righteousness is not a claim of virtue, but is concerned with a right relationship with Yahweh and the community of faith. The stereotyped form by which the claim for a right relationship was made in the Psalter was in the form of a negative, confessional list:

I do not sit with false men,
nor do I consort with dissemblers;
I hate the company of evildoers,
and I will not sit with the wicked (Ps. 26.4–5).

It is fully to misunderstand this confession to read it from a Pauline perspective as 'works righteousness' or to characterize it as a form of Pharisaism. Rather, these confessions functioned within Israel's worship as a declaration of loyalty to a prior claim. Righteousness was not earned, but proceeded from God and was conferred on a person by God. Moreover, there were not stages of righteousness. If a man was declared righteous, he was wholly, and not partially, so. The prayer of the psalmist was not a claim of self-righteousness, but an acknowledgement of something bestowed upon Israel by God. Therefore, the constant plea of the psalmist to be vindicated and declared righteous (Pss. 17.1ff.; 26.1ff.).

I return to the initial question. How does Israel's response function theologically in the context of the canon? Specifically in terms of the Psalter, the psalms function to guide Israel, both as individuals and as a community, in the proper response to God's previous acts of grace in establishing a bond. The psalmist can praise God, complain of his sufferings, plea for a sign of vindication, but through it all and undergirding his response, lies the confession that life is obtained as a gift from God. His conduct is not seen as a striving after an ideal or towards fixed ethical norms, but a struggle to respond faithfully to what God has first done on Israel's behalf. The response of the psalmist is so intense and directed so personally to God because the possession or loss of life is measured in terms of his relation to God who both 'kills and makes alive'. Although the terminology of the Old Testament psalms often differs strikingly from Paul's, the theological understanding of man's relationship to God as one of sheer grace shares much in common.

(b) *Wisdom*. How does the testimony of Israel's sages as a response serve theologically in the context of the canon?

In recent years the theological discovery of wisdom literature has been one of the more exciting aspects of Old Testament studies. During much of the late nineteenth and early twentieth centuries wisdom was thought to be a secular side of Israel's life which rested on the very periphery of the Old Testament and which had arisen in the late Persian and Greek periods. The rebirth of interest in Old Testament theology which began in the 1920s and reached it first high-point with the theologies of Köhler and Eichrodt in the 1930s also had very little interest in wisdom. The reason for this lack of attention is also clear. Theology was thought to be grounded in the great acts of God in Israel's history, and therefore it focused on the development of the traditions of election, covenant, people of God and Davidic covenant.

Interest in wisdom flagged in this period because precisely these are the elements missing from the wisdom books. For example, Proverbs is concerned not with the revelation from Sinai, but with human experiential insight. It focuses its reflection not on the covenant community, but on people in general. Increasingly, modern critical research has made it evident that wisdom cannot be identified with a secularization of religion, but its witness has its own theological integrity. Moreover, wisdom cannot be restricted to the late period of Israel's history, but extends from the earliest to the latest age, and has influenced all the other parts of the canon in various ways. Of course, there remain many other literary and historical problems which have not been fully understood, but these are questions which lie outside the scope of the present enterprise.

It is difficult to assess the theological function of wisdom within the Old Testament canon when few formal indices have been provided. The first nine chapters of the book of Proverbs do offer a certain direction for construing the rest of the book. The prologue sets out the purpose for collecting the proverbs: 'that men may know wisdom . . . and receive instruction in wise dealing.' Regardless of the originally diverse functions of individual sayings, the corpus of collected proverbs performs a didactic role. The father addresses his son, the older generation instructs the younger, and the experienced sage advises the inexperienced novice. The dominant form is the imperative. When the older nineteenth-century theologies sought to interpret the proverbs as the ethics of the Old Testament, they could at least find a certain biblical warrant in chs. 1–9. The appeal is didactic and directed toward right conduct. Yet the concern of wisdom in general cannot simply be identified with ethics, but is far broader in scope.

Recent scholarship (cf. von Rad) has emphasized the sharply different understanding of wisdom which one finds in the earlier period from that of the later. In Proverbs 10ff. wisdom appears as a rational human process of intellectual activity which sought to discern patterns of truth within experiences circumscribed by God. However, in the later period wisdom is seen more as a gift of God. When Proverbs 1–9 is read as an introduction to chs. 10ff., the effect is that the search for wisdom emerges as a subtle dialectic between its being a divine gift and an actively pursued acquisition.

The canonical shaping of the book of Proverbs took place through a protracted debate within the wisdom circles which sought to interpret and supplement a fuller understanding of the divine ordering of the world and human experience. The canonical process did not attempt to systematize the earlier proverbs but often left sharp antitheses between adjacent proverbs (26.4–5). The theological significance of the proverb did not lie in its formulation of an absolute truth, but in the ability of the wise man to use the proverbs in discerning the proper context by which to illuminate the human situation. In this respect one sees how different was the role of the sage from that of the prophet or priest in Israel.

The point has been repeatedly made that the didactic function of the biblical wisdom literature is far broader than that which is usually implied by the term ethics. When the sage challenged his pupils to pursue wisdom, it not only involved moral decisions regarding right behaviour, but was an intellectual and pragmatic activity which sought to encompass the totality of experience. Nevertheless, it is striking that the pattern of human conduct which the sage sought to inculcate overlapped to a large extent with that set as obedient behaviour within the Pentateuch and prescribed for the covenant people. In spite of the radically different starting points, both units of Hebrew tradition converge in a basically common expression of the good and faithful life. Both the Proverbs and the Law call for a commitment to God and his divine order. Both parts of the canon summon man to love justice and integrity, to care for the poor and the needy, and to accept life as a cherished gift from God. In sum, the major theological point to make is that in spite of the striking variety in theological stance, the canon has correctly recognized the profound unity between these biblical witnesses and used them both without the need for serious adjustment in order to instruct and guide God's people in the way of right response.

(c) *The Pentateuch.* I wish to pursue the same question in relation to the narrative literature, especially of the Pentateuch. How does this biblical witness to Israel's response function theologically in the context of the canon?

The difficulty of this problem cannot be easily avoided: it disturbs anyone who wishes to acknowledge the Old Testament as religious authority. How can one ever use the response of the Hebrew patriarchs as an ethical norm when their conduct is filled with flagrant immorality (cf. Bainton, 'The Immoralities of the Patriarchs')? Abraham lied and traded his wife for personal gain. Sarah was ruthless with Hagar her rival. Jacob was a cheat and Moses a murderer. Lest anyone think that ours is the first generation which was troubled with this problem, a brief review of the history of interpretation is in order.

The early Christian church, under the pressure from Greek culture, sought to overcome the ethical problems by resorting to allegorical interpretation. Particularly in the lengthy exegesis of Origen, the moral difficulties were even emphasized in order to force the interpreter to move to a higher level of spiritual exposition. The stories of the patriarchs had a different lesson to teach from that which a literal reading could discover. Of course, additional factors influenced patristic exegesis beyond this one problem, as Augustine's debate with Faustus clearly indicates (*Contra Faustum Manichaeum*, Book 22).

Classic Jewish interpretation developed a midrashic technique which assumed its fixed profile already in the Tannaite period. Basically, the midrashic approach started with a difficulty in the text and then developed a broad context in which to accommodate the problem. Usually this meant that the haggadic midrash, which found its exegetical warrant in the oral tradition, wove a new narrative context using folklore and legend to discover a different motivation, and so removed the ethical offence of the story. For example, Abraham did not betray Sarah, but rather concealed her in a box, or Moses slew the Egyptian taskmaster because he knew that he was the worst of all murderers (*Genesis* and *Exodus Rabbah*).

Christian interpreters during the mediaeval and Reformation periods developed various apologetic means to accommodate the difficulties. Usually Luther and Calvin argued that the patriarchs had been given a special dispensation to break the moral law. Luther was quick to assure his audience that the dispensation was temporary and did not apply to them. In respect to Abraham's pawning off his wife for his sister Calvin argued that Abraham was not simply motivated to protect his own life, as the biblical text appeared to suggest, but rather had a higher goal in mind when he remembered God's promise of a posterity.

The development of a full-blown apologetic to defend the ethical behaviour of the patriarchs increased greatly in the post-Reformation period and continued well into the early twentieth century in conservative, neo-evangelical writings. At times a casuistic argument was developed that the patriarchs had to choose between two forms of evil and chose the lesser evil which was, therefore, relatively right. Or they used the argument that the historical times were such that what seems evil today was more or less acceptable then. Pietistic exegesis usually allowed the patriarchs to retain their frailties as a sign that all persons stand in need of salvation. The difficulty that according to the Old Testament God commanded some of the acts was usually avoided. All these pre-critical attempts have in common the concern to portray the patriarchs as representatives of ethical behaviour and examples of morality to be imitated.

The rise of the historical-critical approach to the Old Testament brought a new set of theological options. At times it was argued that the patriarchs represented a primitive level of oriental culture with all its cruelty and nationalism, which only slowly grew into a higher, more ethical level of conduct (Mozley). Late nineteenth-century Liberal Protestant theology developed the theory of a growth in conscience. Gunkel contrasted the older, more primitive tradition of Sarah's betrayal in Gen. 12 with the later, more ethically sensitive portrayal of Abraham in Gen. 20 by the Elohist. In the 1930s both A. Weiser and W. Eichrodt developed a more theologically sophisticated approach to patriarchal morality. Weiser sought to show how a developing understanding of God broke apart the older forms of traditional morality, whereas Eichrodt traced the history of the kingship of God as it began to modify popular ancient Near Eastern culture. Variations of these theories continue to appear in most Old Testament handbooks through the 1960s. However, neither Weiser or Eichrodt really faced the theological problem of whether one could read the Old Testament as a history of morality (*Sittlichkeit*).

(iii) *Theological reflections in a canonical context*

In the light of these long-standing difficulties the present task is to explore whether a canonical understanding of the Old Testament can throw any light on the ethical problems surrounding the patriarchal response. However, before turning immediately to the narratives of the Pentateuch, where the major problems appear to reside, it seems advisable first to determine how other parts of the Old Testament canon heard these troublesome stories. Can one in this way gain a first indication of how the canon approached the subject?

(a) *The Psalter*. Psalms 105 and 106 offer an extensive interpretation of the patriarchal traditions. What is striking at the outset is the overwhelmingly theocentric perspective of these psalms. Traditions which in the Pentateuch reflect a great variety of different themes have been given almost a monolithic sound. Everything that happened to the patriarchs has been encompassed within the rubric of God's wonderful works and his mighty deeds of salvation:

Sing to him, sing praises to him . . .
Remember the wonderful works that he has done,
his miracles, and the judgments he uttered (105.2).

The patriarchs, Abraham, Isaac and Jacob, are mentioned as recipients of his covenant: 'the word that he commanded for a thousand generations'. God made a promise to Abraham, and repeated it with an oath to Isaac and Jacob. It was the gift of the promised land as an inheritance to a posterity (vv. 7ff.) Psalm 105.12ff. continues the same theme of the mighty works of God in an interpretation of Abraham's history:

When they were few in numbers, of little account, and sojourners in it, wandering from nation to nation . . . he allowed no one to oppress them; he rebuked kings on their account, saying 'touch not my anointed ones, do my prophets no harm' (vv. 12–15).

The closest parallel to the psalm text is the story of Abraham's passing off Sarah to Abimelech in Gen. 20. Only in this passage is Abraham described as a prophet. Abimelech was rebuked for the sake of Abraham, who was protected by God. It is astonishing to see the extent to which the ethical difficulties of the Genesis story are completely disregarded. The narrative is read to illustrate something entirely different, namely the faithfulness of God. Similarly, in the same psalm, Israel's despoiling of the Egyptians as reported in Ex. 12.36 is simply enumerated as another sign of divine favour.

Psalm 106 continues to deal with the theme of the mighty deeds of Yahweh, but focuses on Israel's failure to consider God's mighty works. 'They did not remember the abundance of thy steadfast love – they soon forgot. . . .' (vv. 7 and 13). The traditions of the patriarchs are recounted in order to contrast the faithfulness of God to his covenant with the people's folly, disobedience and sinfulness. In spite of Israel's blindness, God remained faithful:

He remembered his covenant, he heard their cry . . .
Blessed be the Lord . . . from everlasting to everlasting
(vv. 45–48).

The Mosaic traditions follow the same pattern of theocentric interpretation as they are rehearsed in the Psalter:

Come and see what God has done:
he is terrible in his deeds among men.
He turned the sea into dry land . . . (Ps. 66.5–6).

Psalm 81 speaks of the Law which God established in Israel, even though Israel continually refused to walk in his ways. Part of the greatness of God was that he was a forgiving God and did not requite Israel all her transgressions. Finally, the same theocentric approach can be seen regarding the Davidic tradition. In Pss. 89 and 132 the emphasis falls fully on the goodness of God and on his faithfulness to the promise.

Moreover, there is an additional feature to notice in the pattern of interpretation. Not only is God the source of great wonders on Israel's behalf, but he is also the one who calls for justice and ethical response. Psalm 76 speaks of the majestic acts of God – 'both rider and horse lay stunned' – but these deeds occurred for the purpose of establishing justice and saving the oppressed (vv. 6–9). 'He will judge the world in righteousness and everyone with equity' (98.9). The God of Israel who is exalted over all the earth is then described in ethical terms:

He loves those who hate evil (97.10).

No one who practises deceit shall dwell in (his) house . . .
No one who utters lies shall continue in (his) presence (101.7).

The way is blameless . . . (101.2).

The faithful members of Israel are constantly admonished to learn of the fear of God:

What man is there who desires life,
and covets many days . . .
keep your tongue from evil,
and your lips from speaking deceit,
depart from evil, and do good,
seek peace, and pursue it (34.12ff.).

It is not as if the theocentric emphasis made the psalmist unaware of the ethical dimension. Just the opposite. God is the source of all goodness and righteousness, who demands a response commensurate with the divine nature.

To summarize, the traditions of the patriarchs have been construed from one particular stance. They are used theologically to illustrate God's faithfulness to his promise. However, the call to an obedient response which involves honesty, charity and peace is grounded in the prior acts of God. The patriarchs are not used as models of morality, but rather to bear testimony to God who in his mercy forgave their sinfulness.

(b) *The prophets.* The references to the patriarchal traditions are fewer in the prophetic books, but the overwhelmingly theocentric interpretation is continued.

Hosea 12 uses the story of Jacob's wrestling with the 'angel' (Gen. 32) to illustrate God's indictment against Judah, and as a call to return to God by holding fast to love and justice. The prophet makes frequent use of the exodus traditions as an illustration of God's salvation which was rejected and forgotten by Israel (cf. also Amos 2.9ff.). Jeremiah moves in a similar direction in ch. 2. Then again, Ezekiel uses the Mosaic and conquest traditions to illustrate the mercy of God and the incorrigible evil of Israel's response (ch. 20). Finally, the prophet Micah calls upon Israel to remember the tradition which he construes as the means of acquiring knowledge of God:

> I redeemed you from the house of bondage,
> and I sent . . . Moses, Aaron, and Miriam . . .
> O my people, remember . . .
> that you may know the saving acts of Yahweh (6.4–5).

(c) *The histories and the writings.* A few other passages in the remaining parts of the Old Testament call for only a brief enumeration. Joshua 24 commences his recital of God's great works for Israel by recalling Terah, the father of Abraham, who was an idolater serving other gods. But God elected Abraham and gave him a promise. He sent Moses and plagued the Egyptians. Finally, he drove out the Canaanites. Then, on the basis of these redemptive acts, Joshua seeks to evoke a response of allegiance.

Similarly, Neh. 9 uses the patriarchal traditions in a long prayer, much after the form of Pss. 105 and 106:

> Thou art the Lord, the God who chose Abraham . . . and gave him the name Abraham . . . thou didst find his heart faithful before thee and made with him the covenant (vv. 7–8).

The prayer continues with reference to the Mosaic traditions and the conquest. Israel's disobedience ultimately called forth the exile. Then the writer concludes:

> Yet thou hast been just in all that has come upon us, for thou hast dealt faithfully and we have acted wickedly (v. 33).

A very similar approach to the tradition is found in Dan. 9.

In sum, the patriarchal traditions, and indeed the rest of Israel's history, are consistently construed from a theocentric perspective as a witness to God's great acts of salvation. A response is also continually evoked, but one which never functions as an ethical model. Nor is there any apologetic offered to mitigate the moral inadequacy.

(d) *The patriarchal narratives.* It is now time to turn to the narratives of Genesis, where the ethical problem regarding the patriarchs first emerged. The structure of Genesis has long been observed. The patriarchal stories are set within the framework of the primaeval history on the one side (chs. 1–11) and the establishment of the nation and Sinai on the other. The element of the promise is what now links the parts together. There is sufficient critical evidence to indicate that the promises to the Fathers, particularly respecting the land, were originally directed to the patriarchs with the prospect of imminent fulfilment. This is to say that there was nothing in the earliest levels of the tradition to suggest that an interval of hundreds of years, including slavery in Egypt, was intended until the promise of the land could be fulfilled in the conquest by Joshua.

However, within the canonical context of the book of Genesis the promises to the patriarchs have been clearly assigned a different role. This new interpretation has been realized by means of several explicit passages (cf. 15.13), and by the larger framework into which the promises have been ordered. The divine words of assurance have been set within an eschatological pattern of prophecy and fulfilment which now stretches from Abraham to Joshua. The theological effect of this new role for the ancient patriarchal stories is far-reaching. All the individual narratives concerning the patriarchs have been framed within a bracket of eschatology. The promise provides the constant element in the midst of all the changing situations of this very chequered history. In spite of the enormous variety within the individual traditions which the canonical process has retained, the portrayal of the patriarchs has been refocused about their one role as bearers of Israel's hope. Everything else has been pushed into the background.

Moreover, the theme of the bearer of the promise does not just function as a formal context, but has entered deeply into the editing of the individual stories themselves. Abraham is first called out of his country and given the promise of a land and a posterity. The two parallel stories of his betrayal of Sarah (Gen. 12 and 20) now function in strikingly different ways to make two very different points respecting the promise. In ch. 12 Abraham as the bearer of the promise is rescued from the threat of Pharaoh and returned to the land of Israel. In ch. 20 Sarah, the sole vehicle by means of whom the promised son was to come, was exposed, putting the promise in jeopardy. However, God saved both Abraham and Sarah in accordance with his faithfulness.

Again in Gen. 22, the story of Isaac's binding turns on the threat to the promise. The account comes to a climax with the divine affirmation: 'Now I know that you fear God seeing that you have not withheld your son, your only son, from me' (v. 12). All the earlier critical attempts to set this story against alleged Canaanite parallels in order to show a development of ethical consciousness in outgrowing the practice of child sacrifice have badly missed the point of the story within the book of Genesis. The narrative presents a test of Abraham's relation to the promise in which enormous tension is created when God's command to sacrifice the son seems to be pitted against the divine promise itself.

Finally, I think that von Rad's interpretation of Gen. 23, the burial of Sarah, is fully on target. Sarah, Abraham's wife, has died in Canaan, and Abraham has not yet received the promise. He remains a resident alien without land. Therefore, he purchases a piece of the very land which he had been promised, and is badly cheated in the process. However, he buries his wife in his own land, thus bearing testimony to his faith in the promise with this foretaste of his inheritance that all the land would one day be his possession.

There is one final feature of these stories to consider. It returns to the theme of the righteousness of God with which this chapter began. The story of Gen. 15 offers a programmatic interpretation of Abraham in terms of his righteousness. When Abraham could see no sign that God's promise would be fulfilled, he complained bitterly to God: 'O Lord, what wilt thou give me for I am childless and the heir to my house is Eliezer of Damascus' (v. 2). God replied: 'This man shall not be your heir; your own son shall be your heir.' 'And he brought him outside and said, look toward heaven and number the stars . . . so shall your descendants be. And Abraham believed God and God reckoned it to him as righteousness' (vv. 5–6).

To understand this narrative it is necessary to recall that righteousness is not an ideal, absolute norm, but a right relationship.

One is righteous who does justice to the claims which a covenantal relationship entails. In Gen. 15 Abraham's faith in God is declared to have established Abraham as righteous in God's sight. His righteousness is not the result of any accomplishment, whether of sacrifice or acts of obedience. Rather, it is stated programmatically that belief in God's promise alone has established Abraham's right relation to God. He has made the proper response through faith.

(iv) Summary

A summary is in order to draw out the theological implications of the question which has occupied the attention of this chapter. How do the traditions of Israel's response to God function theologically within the Old Testament canon?

First, all the apologetic attempts to explain away the immoralities of the patriarchs operate on the false assumption that the Bible's testimony to Israel's response is in terms of examples of moral conduct. This is a fundamental misconstrual of scripture which continues to be present in both conservative and liberal exegesis, and serves as a serious threat to a genuinely evangelical reading of the Old Testament.

Secondly, the Old Testament canon itself offers the hermeneutical guidelines for a theological understanding of Israel's response. The psalmists and prophets find the witness of these traditional stories to lie in God's activity. God is the source of all justice and he seeks to evoke from Israel a response commensurate with his holiness. The Psalter renders the patriarchal narratives from this perspective and thus provides a theological context which orders the original traditions into a new pattern.

Finally, a study of the narratives of Genesis reveals that the theocentric interpretation had long since begun within Israel. The stories of the Fathers are about the faithfulness of God to his word of promise. All human achievement is measured by its trust in God's faithfulness. Ultimately God is the one who reckons a human response to be righteous. As a Christian theologian, I judge that one has to await the further theological reflections of the apostle Paul to develop an understanding of the righteousness of God as an all-encompassing theological rubric under which to subsume the whole of ethics. However, the testimony of the Old Testament has already moved decisively in this direction, and the Christian can hear in its witness the Good News already sounding with clarity.

Bibliography

R. **Bainton**, 'The Immoralities of the Patriarchs according to the Exegesis of the Late Middle Ages and the Reformers', *HTR* 23, 1930, 39–49; J. **Barr**, *The Semantics of Biblical Language*, Oxford 1961; W. **Eichrodt**, *Theology of the Old Testament*, ET, II, London and Philadelphia 1967, 216–48; J. **Hempel**, *Das Ethos des Alten Testaments*, BZAW 67, 1938; A. R. **Johnson**, *The One and the Many in the Israelite Conception of God*, Cardiff 1942; J. B. **Mozley**, *Ruling Ideas in the Early Ages and their Relation to the Old Testament*, London and New York 1877; J. **Muilenburg**, *The Way of Israel: Biblical Faith and Ethics*, New York 1961; H. **van Oyen**, *Ethik des Alten Testaments*, Gütersloh 1967; J. **Pedersen**, *Israel. Its Life and Culture*, ET, I–II, Copenhagen and London 1926; III-IV, 1940; G. **von Rad**, *Old Testament Theology*, ET, I, Edinburgh and Philadelphia 1962; ' "Righteousness" and "Life" in the Cultic Language of the Psalter', in *The Problem of the Hexateuch and Other Essays*, ET Edinburgh and New York 1966, 243–66; *Wisdom in Israel*, ET Nashville and London 1972; H. W. **Robinson**, *Inspiration and Revelation in the Old Testament*, Oxford 1946, 231–61; N. H. **Snaith**, *The Distinctive Ideas of the Old Testament*, London 1944; A. **Weiser**, 'Religion and Sittlichkeit des Genesis in ihrem Verhältnis zur alttestamentlichen Religionsgeschichte' (1928), reprinted *Glaube und Geschichte im Alten Testament*, Göttingen 1961, 50–98; G. E. **Wright**, *God Who Acts*, SBT 1.8, 1952; W. **Zimmerli**, 'Zwillingspsalmen', in *Wort, Lied und Gottesspruch, FS J. Ziegler*, Würzburg 1972, 105–13.

19

LIFE UNDER THREAT

No theological reflection on the Old Testament can claim to do justice to the biblical material which has not faced the stark reality that Israel's life was lived from beginning to end under the shadow of countless threats. In fact, because these threats are so all-pervasive and extend through all sections of the Old Testament, it is a problem how best to organize the discussion. The subject is not dealt with in the Old Testament as a separate item, but intertwined with other themes and viewed from many different perspectives in the various parts of the canon.

(i) *The primaeval threat, Genesis 1–11*

There are some literary signs that the formation of the primaeval history in the book of Genesis developed secondarily to the traditions relating to Israel's election. Israel's theological reflection did not begin with the creation, but with salvation. Nevertheless, it is equally important that Israel's understanding of the nature of the covenant God soon included an affirmation of Yahweh's role as creator of the universe as well as redeemer of his people. Moreover, the final canonical positioning of the creation with its universal dimensions of cosmos, world and nations at the beginning of Israel's sacred traditions must be taken with utmost seriousness. Similarly, the inclusion of a primordial threat as an element of creation itself stands at the beginning of the Old Testament and serves as a crucial understanding of reality from which the rest of Israel's history must be viewed.

Regardless of how one translates the first verses of Genesis, whether as a superscription: 'In the beginning God created the heavens and the earth – the earth being without form and void . . .

– then God said . . .', or as a temporal clause: 'When God created the heavens and the earth, the earth was without form and void . . ., then God said . . .', the troubling presence of the chaos remains a persistent problem. God created the heavens and the earth, but at the same time, in the same breath, mention is made of an unformed entity. The various attempts to avoid the problem have not been successful, as if God could have first created the chaos of v. 2 before he ordered the world, which is a contradiction in terms. Or to suggest that there was another primordial power apart from God such as a demiurge is to run in the face of the entire Old Testament witness. Nor could God have first created the world and then allowed it to become a chaos with, say, the expulsion of Satan, which is an ancient Gnostic heresy more recently revived by the *Scofield Reference Bible.*

The intensity of the problem arises because God alone created the world in complete freedom without the use of prior material through the exercise of his full sovereignty over his creative word. Nevertheless, the biblical writer of Gen. 1 bears witness to another force, a threat to the creation which had to be overcome. Karl Barth wrestles with the subject under the rubric of 'das Nichtige' (nothingness, *CD* III/3, 209ff.). Within the Old Testament creation is set in contrast not to non-existence, but to chaos. Jeremiah speaks of God's withdrawing his hand in judgment. Significantly the world does not disappear, but returns to its primordial state of chaos:

I looked on the earth, and lo, it was waste and void,
and to the heavens, and they had no light.
I looked on the mountains, and lo, they were quaking,
and all the hills moved to and fro.
I looked, and lo, there was no man
and all the birds of the air had fled . . .
before the Lord, before his fierce anger . . . (Jer. 4.24ff.).

Of course the issue is one which has vexed theologians from the beginning. How can God be all powerful and all good at the same time? How did evil enter the world if God did not create it? The Old Testament seems to acknowledge the problem and encompass it within two parameters. On the one hand, God alone in his majestic power and absolute freedom created the heavens and the earth. He alone in his goodness brought the world into being and pronounced it good. On the other hand, there lies the mystery of a primordial threat against creation, uncreated without form and void, which God strove to overcome.

When one next turns to Gen. 3, the problem is intensified:

> Now the serpent was more subtle than any other wild creature that the Lord God had made. He said to the woman, 'Did God say, "You shall not eat of any tree . . ."? You will not die. For God knows that when you eat of it your eyes will be opened, and you will be like God, knowing good and evil' (vv. 1–4).

The serpent appears out of nowhere in the story. He is not Satan, nor a demon, but simply one of the animals that God had made. The unexpected element is the content of the serpent's conversation. How is one to account for his diabolical skill of seduction? How does he know about the tree, and why does he appear to hate God by imputing to him such unworthy motives? What at first seems to be a simple snake takes on a complex character.

Once again the problem of evil has surfaced. The snake has no power independent of God's control to whom the origin of evil could be attributed. Yet evil is not created by God, even though it erupts as a demonic force of aggressive intent. Moreover, in Gen. 3 this 'negative reality' has left the realm of mere threat to the creation to become a disruptive actuality within the world. The text of Genesis reflects the tension in bearing witness to the incomprehensibility of a reality denied existence in the creation, yet which is both active and demonic in its effect on the world.

The subtlety of the penetration of sin is depicted by the writer in the form of shame. 'Then the eyes of both were opened, and they knew that they were naked' (3.7). There is a world of difference between nudity and nakedness. The former implies the titillation of indecent behaviour. The latter reflects the profound fear of self-exposure. In the age of innocence 'the man and his wife were both naked, but were not ashamed' (2.25). They were unashamed because they were complete beings, sharing an uninterrupted harmony with God and the world. There is no shame where the self is whole. Then suddenly the Genesis writer introduces into his narrative an entirely new terminology to depict the change. Adam said: 'I was afraid, because I was naked, and I hid myself' (3.10). The sense of shame becomes the outward sign of inner dissolution. Von Rad writes with great perception:

Shame is one of the most puzzling phenomena of our humanity
... it always has to be seen as the signal of the loss of an inner unity, an unsurmountable contradiction at the basis of our existence (*Genesis*, rev. ed., 85).

It is also not by chance that the Old Testament portrays human sexuality as the mirror of the disruption. Sex is introduced in ch. 2 as part of the gracious acts of God's good creation. God said: 'It is not good for man to be alone' (2.18). God is then pictured as escorting Eve to the astonished Adam (cf. *Genesis Rabbah*). The conclusion to ch. 2 rings with joyful enthusiasm as the man and the woman are united in one flesh.

Shortly thereafter the world is filled with violence, and Lamech boasts before his several wives of his savagery (4.23f.). The divine gift of human sexuality has been twisted to become a major threat to both faith and life. The rest of the Old Testament is filled with stories of sexual abuse as the once creative drive for good is unleashed with demonic power to destroy (Gen. 38.1ff.; Judg. 20.1ff.; II Sam. 13.1ff.). Even when the distortion of the human self through homosexuality is submerged into the narrative background of a biblical text (Gen. 19.1ff.), it continues to function as a dark shadow enveloping its characters. For the prophets, a fundamental challenge to Israel's faith comes in the form of a new dimension of sexual perversion as the Canaanite cult gods lay claim on the power of sex and fertility (Hos. 2.2ff.; Jer. 3.1ff.; Ezek. 23.1ff.).

Old Testament scholars remain somewhat divided on how to interpret the canonical function of the primaeval history. On the one hand, von Rad interprets the purpose of these chapters as portraying a history of increasing alienation from God. Starting from the expulsion from Eden, sin expanded and grew until this history of sin reached its climax in the Tower of Babel, and threatened to return the whole creation to chaos. The turning point within von Rad's interpretation lies in the call of Abraham. The election of Israel provides the perspective from which the universal history of divine judgment and mercy toward human sinfulness is viewed in Genesis.

On the other hand, Westermann emphasizes that these early chapters do not move on the horizontal plane of history, but rather portray a vertical God-man dimension. Accordingly, these chapters treat the universal reality of human existence under threat which is not tied to a specific time or culture. For Westermann there is no primaeval age of innocence, nor a 'fall', but only a portrayal of the ontological problem of human existence as one of frailty and limitation (*Genesis*, 89ff.).

In my judgment, Westermann is correct in criticizing von Rad's theological subordination of creation to redemption by reading the primaeval history merely as an aetiology of Israel's election. This theological move which is grounded on the historical growth of Israel's traditions runs counter to the final canonical construal of the book of Genesis. However, Westermann's attempt to substitute an ontological interpretation of Gen. 1–11 raises a host of theological problems. There is no canonical warrant for interpreting the threat in these chapters as a description of a quality of existence which is constitutive of being human. Rather, the point of the paradisal state is to contest the ontological character of human sinfulness. Mankind was not created in alienation from God, his fellows, or himself. The theological function of a period of innocence is to testify to a harmony in God's creation at the beginning which overcame the threat of non-being in the presence of God. It also bears witness to the eschatological restoration of God's new creation in which all threats will have been conquered.

The wolf shall dwell with the lamb,
and the leopard shall lie down with the kid. . .
They shall not hurt or destroy in all my holy mountain;
for the earth shall be full of the knowledge of the Lord
as the waters cover the sea (Isa. 11.6ff.)

(ii) *Covenant and curse*

When God established his covenant with Israel, he pledged his abiding loyalty to his people: 'I will be your God and you shall be my people' (Lev. 26.12). As a result, Israel no longer needed to walk in uncertainty as if not knowing what God required of her. The pagan threat of an arbitrary, wilful and capricious deity, whose anger was revealed in fits of violence and whose will was cloaked in enigma, was removed once-and-for-all from Israel.

He has shown you, O man, what is good,
and what does the Lord require of you,

but to do justice, to exercise covenant loyalty,
and to walk humbly with your God (Micah 6.8).

However, there is another side to the covenant. On the converse-
side of the divine blessings to an obedient people lie the covenant
curses. Moses addressed all the people:

If you obey the voice of the Lord, your God . . .
then all these blessings will come upon you . . .
But if you will not obey the voice of the Lord your God,
then all these curses shall come upon you and overtake you.
Cursed you shall be in the city . . . and in the field.
Cursed shall be the fruit of your body . . . and the fruit of
the ground (Deut. 28.1ff.).

Much of the remaining narrative material in the Old Testament
bears witness that Israel succumbed to the various sins which
endangered the covenant and unleashed the threatened curses. In
the books of Exodus and Numbers the murmuring traditions occupy
a large portion in describing the complaints, rebellions and unbelief
of the people in the face of the threats from hunger, thirst and
attack. The gracious gifts of God of food, drink and protection are
all turned to dust. The psalmist describes the manna as the bread
of angels, divine ambrosia fit for gods (78.25), but Israel complained
over this 'worthless manna' (Num. 11.6), and longed for the cucum-
bers and melons of Egypt. In the end, the generation which experienced the theophany of Sinai and sealed the covenant with Moses,
perished out of unbelief in the wilderness.

The Deuteronomistic writer who has left his editorial stamp on
the historical books of Joshua through Kings uses the theme of the
covenant curse as an historical principle by which to explain the
destruction of the nation. Throughout this long history the writer
portrays the different forms of temptation and danger which Israel
faced: idolatry, corruption, assimilation, nationalism, and he often
picks up the earlier warnings from the book of Deuteronomy to
admonish against the coming disaster. Deuteronomy 8 warned of
the temptations of the land with its abundant wealth becoming a
threat:

Do not forget your God, lest, when you have eaten and are full
. . . then your heart be lifted up and you forget who delivered you

from the great and terrible wilderness. . . I solemnly warn you this day that you shall surely perish (vv. 17–20.

In a final summarizing paragraph the Deuteronomistic historian reviews the sad history of the chosen people and chronicles the working out of the curse of the covenant:

Israel walked in the customs of the nations . . . and provoked God to anger by serving idols. . . . Yet the Lord warned Israel and Judah by every prophet . . . but they would not listen. Therefore, the Lord was angry with his people and removed them out of his sight. Thus Israel was exiled from its own land until this day . . . (II Kings 17.7ff.)

(iii) *Prophets*

To experience the full dimensions of the unleashing of the divine judgment with an almost inexhaustible depiction of the divine threats one is forced to turn to the classical prophets.

Amos begins with the terrifying roar of the lion, of God against his people. There follows a relentless portrayal of awesome and terrifying images of the different manifestations of the divine anger. All the hope and comfort which faithful Israel derived from the covenant is ruthlessly stripped away. In reaction to the belief in a faithful remnant Amos cynically describes the grizzly remains of a devoured animal with only a few bits of bone left (2.12). He characterizes Israel's divinely ordained worship as causing God nausea, a racket which he can hardly endure (5.21). Even Israel's hope for the future on the 'day of the Lord' is described as a delusion. It is 'darkness and not light. . . with no brightness whatever' (5.18ff.).

Part of the disconcerting quality of Amos' portrayal of life under the divine threat is the uncertainty and sheer terror of the unexpected. Yahweh has turned into an unpredictable demon:

I sent rain on one city, and none on another,
I smote you with blight and mildew,
with pestilence like I smote the Egyptians (4.7ff.).

All the various exegetical attempts of commentators to soften the message of Amos by interpreting his attack as didactic fail utterly to grasp the nature of his judgment. The prophet is not seeking to convert Israel, but rather to pronounce a dirge over the corpse (5.1–2). For such transgressors there is no future; judgment is final.

The end has come upon my people Israel.
I shall never again pass by them . . .
The dead bodies shall be many,
and in every place they shall be cast out in silence (8.2).

Behold the eyes of the Lord are upon this sinful kingdom, and I will destroy it from the surface of the earth . . . (9.8).

Hosea addresses Israel as the rejected people – 'no kin of mine' (1.9) – who suffer from an incurable disease. As a result, even the land weeps and the animals, birds and fish are removed (4.3). Likewise, Isaiah likens the land of Israel and its people to Sodom and Gomorrah (1.10). A strange stupor, even madness, has taken hold of the nation. Society has come apart at the seams with leaders staggering in drunkenness and rulers made up of children (3.6ff.; 28.7ff.). Again, Jeremiah strikes a haunting and eerie sound. Terror descends with the enemy from the north, and the nation lies paralysed and helpless. Unable to escape or flee, it awaits in numb resignation the terrifying hordes who execute God's own fierce anger (6.1ff.).

Jeremiah also portrays life after the end, the final working out of the divine threat. The city has fallen, but some have escaped and taken the reluctant prophet with them to Egypt. The people are trapped in their own terror and superstition, and decide to worship the queen of heaven. Jeremiah can only prophesy disaster to their folly:

Thus saith the Lord, I am watching over you for evil, and not for good. All the men of Judah who are in the land of Egypt shall be consumed until there is an end of them (45.27).

One final passage from Ezekiel carries great weight. In ch. 20 the prophet reviews Israel's sad history. Each time that God intervened in gracious acts of salvation, Israel revolted and defiled herself with blasphemy and treacherous dealings. So finally God allowed his own laws which were given to engender life to be twisted and issue in death:

I gave them statutes that were not good and ordinances by which they could not have life, and I defiled them through their very gifts in making them offer by fire all their first-born that I might destroy them (20.26).

When one attempts to reflect on the prophetic message as a whole, one is struck by the enormous variety in the vocabulary of sin. The various standard lexica have sought to chart the range of terminology from sin as deviation, to sin as uncleanliness, guilt and rebellion. These word-studies are helpful up to a point, but can miss the profound intensity of the issue, especially as discussed by the prophets. To suggest, for example, that the etymology of the root to sin (*ḥṭ'*) simply denotes missing the mark does not register adequately how the word actually functions in scripture (cf. Ps. 51.4). The constant interchange of technical vocabulary along with a great range of metaphorical expressions for transgression is a characteristic of prophetic discourse and indicates the multi-dimensional attack on the subject (Isa. 1.4ff.; Jer. 3.1ff.; Ezek. 20.1ff.). Above all, sin is a wilful affront to God which opens the floodgates of universal rebellion and initiates a cosmological chain of disasters which far exceeds any human intent.

(iv) Daniel and apocalyptic

The Hebrew canon classifies the book of Daniel in the third section among the Writings, and thus separates it from the prophetic collection. In contrast, the Greek form of the canon includes it among the prophets. In content the book of Daniel shares elements of continuity and discontinuity with the prophetic corpus. Although it often functions as an extension of Old Testament prophecy, the Greek term 'apocalyptic' is useful in emphasizing a different eschatological dimension of the message which has entered into a new sphere.

Of course, prior to the final composition of the book of Daniel characteristic elements of apocalyptic writing had already been voiced by the prophets. For example, Joel describes the assembling of the nations at the last day to descend on Jerusalem. He portrays a cosmological judgment – the sun and moon are darkened – as the multitudes are judged in the valley of decision on the day of Yahweh (3.11ff; cf. Zech. 14.1ff.). Similarly, the prophecy against Gog and Magog (Ezek. 38.1ff.) far transcends the destruction of an earthly army, but is projected into a form of cosmological evil which threatens to profane God's holy name.

The book of Daniel depicts the threat under which Israel lies in bizarre, mythopoetic imagery which reaches into the sheer demonic. Nebuchadnezzar constructs a golden image, mighty and terrifying in appearance, and commands all to fall down and worship it. Or again, the king commands a fiery furnace to be prepared, heated seven times more than was wont, in order to consume the faithful. Then one reads of beasts with ten horns, huge teeth of the Antichrist, blasphemy, and 'an abomination which makes desolate' (11.31). The picture is of the faithful remnant with its back up against the wall, being overwhelmed by forces of seduction and profanation. 'Without warning', 'swept away', 'scattered' and 'seduced' – these are the terms of threat. The saints hold on by the skin of their teeth, scanning the horizon for help. It must come from God because there is no other source. How long?

(v) *The Psalms*, de profundis

Throughout the Psalter the believing and suffering community stands in between the forces of life and death. Much of the overwhelming intensity of the Psalter comes from the complaints of those who see themselves being dragged into the realm of death and Sheol. Death is the ultimate threat. It is characteristic of the psalmist to conceive of any contact with death as involving the totality of the individual. By entering into the sphere of death, one participates completely (cf. C. Barth, *Errettung vom Tode*). Any part is a manifestation of the whole. To be sick is already to experience death's reality as life oozes slowly away. To be rejected from the covenant is also to forfeit one's life.

Death as a threat is both a power and a place. It is a terrifying force which consumes life, an 'avenger' who is not independent of Yahweh but still a force of non-being which drags one out of life into death. At times the psalmist depicts a messenger of death who acts on Yahweh's behest. Yet Israel knows that God desires life for his creation. Thus there remains a mystery of death before which Israel retreats.

Death is also a place, an area of rule. It is called by many names: Sheol, land of the dead, place of no return, land of oblivion, field of thirst, the pit. As a place it corresponds exactly to the essence of death. There is no life there, but merely an existence for the 'shades'. The intensity of the plea stems from the terror before this encroaching threat:

> Thou hast put me in the depths of the Pit,
> in the regions dark and deep.
> Thy wrath lies heavy upon me,
> and thou dost overwhelm me with all thy waves. . .
> I am shut in so that I cannot escape;
> my eye grows dim through sorrow . . .
> Dost thou ever work miracles for the dead?
> Do the shades rise up to praise thee? (Ps. 88.6–10).

(vi) *Wisdom*

Finally, life under threat is portrayed in strikingly different ways in the wisdom books. Although the threat to life in the book of Job is closely allied to that of the psalms (cf. Childs, *Introduction to the Old Testament*, 536), the book of Ecclesiastes sounds a different note. Von Rad treats Ecclesiastes under the rubric of 'scepticism'. What is in doubt is not the existence of God, but rather his willingness to interfere seriously in the life of the individual. Von Rad has a theory by which to explain the threat of scepticism (I, 453ff.). Israel lost its understanding of *Heilsgeschichte* and was thus cut adrift from its moorings of faith. Whether this hypothesis adequately explains the root cause remains a moot point. Nevertheless, von Rad's description of the threat to life portrayed in Ecclesiastes has much to commend it. The sage knows that the world was created by God and that he acts unceasingly upon it. Man's calamity is that he cannot make contact with this divine action. The world remains dumb in the face of his quest for salvation. This absence of a response evokes the feeling of total insecurity. The writer of Ecclesiastes sees himself suspended over the abyss of despair. Loneliness surrounds him because not only has God withdrawn, but the world has become an alien entity outside himself which moves according to its own inexorable rules.

(vii) *The limits of the threat*

The question of whether there is a limit to the threat is one which not only engaged ancient Israel, but has suddenly become a highly existential one for modern society. Can sinful humanity actually destroy God's creation, or is there a biblical assurance given of a divine safety net?

Nowhere in the Old Testament is there a hint that human sinfulness cannot destroy mankind. When Israel as the chosen people comforted themselves with the belief that Jerusalem was inviolable, God raised up prophets to shatter the illusion. The privileges of their religion only intensified the impending judgment which was called forth by the repudiation of the covenant's demand for mercy and justice.

> You only have I known of all the families of the earth;
> Therefore I will punish you (especially) for all your iniquities
> (Amos 3.2).

It is important to see the full biblical picture. The threat to the human race does not lie simply in the proliferation of weapons or in unstable alliances. Isaiah laments:

> Woe to those who go down to Egypt for help
>   and rely on horses . . . and in horsemen because they are strong,
> but do not look to the Holy One of Israel,
>   or consult the Lord (31.1).

The problem lies in humanity itself, and no political or economic solution can resolve it. The prophets developed no comprehensive social programmes, nor did they engage their hearers solely on the horizontal plane of human history. Rather, they placed every aspect of Israel's social life under the light of divine judgment and from this perspective penetrated into every corner of political, economic and social disorder with prophetic vision. The real threat to Israel was not Assyria or Babylon, but the confrontation with the living God whom they had repudiated. Similarly, the threat to modern society from a biblical perspective lies not in nuclear weapons themselves, but in the madness to use them by a sick humanity which struggles to wrest itself free of God. For this reason, the prophets of the Old Testament remained preachers of God's righteousness and not social reformers.

In sum, the Old Testament sets no limits to the threat of final destruction. No assurance is offered that the world will survive. Yet with the ancient prophets of Israel the Christian church continues to confess that the rule of God will prevail, and that in the mystery of his will, the hope of a new creation will not be ultimately rendered void by human arrogance.

(viii) *Summary*

It does justice to the theological witness of the Old Testament to treat the subject of life under threat by itself. This chapter is not the end of the story, nor the full message to Israel. Certainly one needs also to hear the message of life under promise. Nevertheless, these two biblical testimonies are not automatically linked. Threat does not flow naturally into promise of its own accord. To pass all too quickly from threat to promise can jeopardize the overpowering reality of life under divine judgment. From the biblical perspective the threat was not a momentary phase or an introductory stage, but a recurring danger of catastrophic proportions, always present and continuously to be faced. Indeed because of its awesome and terrifying dimensions, the note of redemption, of promise and of a future life broke upon Israel as an overwhelming surprise and incomprehensible wonder:

> When the Lord restored the fortunes of Zion,
>   we were like those who dream.
> Then our mouth was filled with laughter,
>   and our tongue with shouts of joy (Ps. 126.1f.).

To translate this message into Christian terminology: unless you grasp in some measure the terror of Good Friday, you can never understand the good news of Easter.

Bibliography

B. W. **Anderson**, *Out of the Depths*, Philadelphia 1974; C. **Barth,** *Die Errettung vom Tode in der individuellen Klage und Dankliedern des Alten Testamentes*, Basle 1947; K. **Barth,** *Church Dogmatics*, ET, III/3, Edinburgh 1961, 289–368; J. **Crenshaw,** *A Whirlpool of Torment*, Philadelphia 1984; G. **Fohrer**, 'Das Geschick des Menschen nach dem Tode im Alten Testament', *KuD* 14, 1968, 249–62; H. **Haag,** *Biblische Schöpfungslehre und kirchliche Erbsündenlehre*, SBS 10, 1966; S. **Kierkegaard,** *Fear and Trembling*, ET London 1939 and Princeton 1941; M. A. **Klopfenstein,** *Scham und Schande nach dem Alten Testament*, AbTANT 62, 1972; R. S. **Kluger,** *Satan in the Old Testament*, ET Evanston 1967; N. **Lohfink**, *Gewalt und Gewaltlosigkeit im*

Alten Testament, Freiburg 1983; J. **Pedersen,** *Israel. Its Life and Culture*, ET, I–II, Copenhagen and London 1926, 411–96; G. **von Rad**, *Old Testament Theology*, ET, I, Edinburgh and New York 1962; *Genesis*, ET, rev. ed. London and Philadelphia 1972; C. **Westermann**, *Genesis* 1–11, BK I/1, 1974; N. P. **Williams**, *The Ideas of the Fall and of Original Sin*, London 1927.

20

LIFE UNDER PROMISE

(i) *The scope of the material*

Old Testament theology has traditionally concerned itself with Israel's hopes for the future by focusing attention on several classic problems. These topics fall roughly under four headings:

(*a*) For several decades, beginning in the 1950s, a heated debate has waged on the proper use of the term 'eschatology' in its relation to the Old Testament (cf. Preuss, *Eschatologie*). One group of scholars argued for a narrow definition which would restrict the term to a belief in the end of time and beginning of a new aeon. Another group defined it more broadly to include any future hope which envisioned a new element of divine intervention. The first group dated the rise of eschatology to the post-exilic age, the second to the pre-exilic period.

(*b*) Much debate has turned on the historical origins of Old Testament eschatology. Various external forces have been described such as the influence from myth, cult, or the psychological disillusionment arising from political disaster. In contrast, more conservative scholars have sought to find the roots of eschatology from inner-biblical developments, including the covenant at Sinai (Bright).

(*c*) The growth and change within Israel's future hope has also been a major subject for discussion, and different stages of development have been suggested which stretch from an early pre-eschatological period to a late full-blown apocalypticism.

(*d*) Finally, much research has been applied to the various individual topics which compromise the traditional elements of Israel's hope such as messiah, remnant, kingship of God and the after-life.

(ii) *Methodological issues*

Few topics have called forth more disagreement than the issue of Israel's eschatology. The problem lies far deeper than simply one of definition, but turns on different assessments of the theological content, which have been developed on the basis of conflicting methodological approaches. Once again the concern will be to determine whether a consistently applied canonical approach alters one's stance respecting the older issues and evokes a new set of questions for theological reflection.

Concerning the term eschatology, a canonical approach recognizes that the Old Testament makes no sharp theological distinction between God's intervention in human affairs within history or at the end of history. The issue at stake is the qualitatively new elements of the divine will at work. To force a history-of-religions definition on the biblical material is to render it largely mute. In addition, the function of canon to include the continual hearing of the biblical text by a community of faith as an integral part of the interpretative process largely relativizes the theological significance of the original temporal distinction.

Concerning the issue of the origin of eschatology, a canonical approach is critical of the rationale of seeking either to recover an extra-biblical force lying behind the text as the decisive factor, or of insisting on a single inner-biblical connection, such as covenant, whose relationship within the tradition is never understood in terms of historical source. A more suitable exegetical method would be to pursue the rich variety of ways in which theological connections are made between eschatology and Israel's tradition (cf. Amos 5.18ff.; Jer. 31.31–34, etc.) rather than to see some alleged origin of the concept.

Concerning the issue of development, a canonical approach freely acknowledges the growth within the tradition, but it focuses its theological attention on the intertextuality produced by uniting earlier and later elements (cf. Isa. 1–11) instead of concentrating on establishing an original chronological sequence within the tradition. Even to postulate a sharp distinction between eschatology and apocalypticism can obscure as well as illuminate the biblical text, especially when linked with fragile sociological theories.

Finally, concerning the treatment of various discrete subjects, a canonical approach to Old Testament theology strives to avoid attempts either to fragment the material through critical analysis or to synthesize it from a New Testament perspective which fails to hear the Old Testament's witness in its own right. The topics of messianism and the after-life are especially vulnerable to the latter danger.

(iii) *Patterns of canonical shaping*

The fundamental point to be made concerning the Old Testament's eschatological hope is that the tradition has left a major testimony in the manner by which it has construed its material within the canonical process. At times this construal has left a clear literary imprint on the material by its editors. At other times the larger canonical context functions to open up the text to a new interpretive potential without altering the shape of the original biblical tradition.

One of the clearest canonical indices is the manner by which the prophetic corpus has been edited. The pattern of first having oracles of judgment followed by those of salvation extends to the three major prophets (Isaiah, Jeremiah, Ezekiel) as well as to many of the smaller books (Hosea, Amos, Micah, Zephaniah, Haggai, Zechariah). The effect is that the great variety of prophetic material has been ordered within a unified schema which functions in the end as a message of salvation (cf. Clements, *Old Testament Theology*, 144ff.).

The canonical shape of the Psalter also testifies to a particular theological construal of this biblical material, which turns out to be eschatological in orientation. First of all, a variety of psalms reflect the traditional form of the individual complaint to which has been joined a promise of salvation (Pss. 22, 102, etc.) The effect is to render the entire hymn as a witness to Israel's future hope in God's redemption. Then again, the royal psalms (2, 45, 72, 110) have been reordered within the Psalter and suggest that at least by the post-exilic period the royal figure was being understood as God's eschatological messiah. Similarly, promises to David were soon extended to his heir (Ps. 132.11ff.). Finally, as increasingly the original cultic language of the Psalter was heard in conjunction with the prophetic message, such traditional idioms as 'waiting for God' become the vehicle by which to express the longing after God's final intervention (Ps. 130.5f.). Likewise, the theophanic language of God's appearance took on the added connotation of his coming in eschatological glory (Pss. 50, 68, etc.).

Then again, both the larger structure of the Pentateuch and the shaping of the individual books reflect a future-oriented concern with the promise. The material of Genesis has been edited into one continuous story under the keyword of promise. Various individual promises to each of the patriarchs have been picked up and used as a red thread throughout the book toward the fulfilment announced by Deuteronomy. When the apostle Paul extended the promise to Abraham (Gen. 12.1ff.) to include the inheritance of the world (Rom. 4.13), he was only exploiting an interpretative direction which had long been represented in the canonical construal of the tradition.

The structuring of the books of Numbers and Deuteronomy is strikingly different, yet both share a strong hope in Israel's future promise. Numbers has construed its material by its use of the two census lists (chs. 1 and 26) according to the pattern of the death of the old generation (1–25) and the rebirth of the new (cf. D. Olsen). Of course, for Numbers the new generation consists of those obedient Israelites poised on the brink of the promised land who realize the divine promise. Deuteronomy's testimony to the promise is quite unique in the Old Testament and comes closest to an understanding of 'realized eschatology'. Israel as the holy people of God (7.6) already experiences the reality of divine blessing (30.14) and shortly will possess the promise land. Yet Israel experiences life and blessing only as long as she constitutes a holy people. In sum, for Deuteronomy the polarity between promise and fulfilment does not lie in a temporal sequence, but in the existential tension of obedience and disobedience into which Israel has already entered. God's new and holy people has already experienced fulfilled promise, but this can be forfeited by the lawlessness which destroyed the desert generation (28.1ff.).

Finally, Israel's hope in a future promise has been reflected in the editing of the historical books. Noth, who first worked out the literary structure of the Deuteronomistic redaction (Deut.–Kings), argued that its purpose was merely to explain how Israel lost the land. However, it seems hard to deny that elements of promise have been retained (II Sam. 23.1–7; II Kings 25.27ff.), and that these elements form a theological continuity with the new vision of Israel's history which the Chronicler portrayed. The promises to the house of David have not been annulled, but a holy remnant has been preserved from the ashes of defeat to await God's final vindication of Israel. God in his great mercy has not made the final end one of judgment, but of grace (Neh. 9.31).

(iv) *Forms of the promise*

The most characteristic feature of the Old Testament promise is the enormous variety of its forms. The different images do not let themselves be joined in any highly systematized fashion, but remain incomplete and fragmentary. The very fact that Jews and Christians can use the same biblical material for such different theological purposes testifies to the lack of an overarching and unified framework within the Old Testament. The promises emerged in the context of Israel's history and continue to bear their concrete, time-conditioned features. Thus any attempt to abstract the essence of the promises into one formula (cf. Baumgärtel, *Verheissung*) sacrifices the richness of the biblical witness by reductionism.

(a) Judgment and salvation. The theme of judgment and salvation for Israel is held in common by all the prophets, but the manner in which this theological witness is made illustrates well the remarkable freedom of formulation. Amos's overwhelming emphasis on the total destruction of sinful Israel is only slightly blunted by the final chapter, and the promise of a restored people is grounded in the will of God apart from all historical contingencies. Again, Hosea's vision of an eschatological reconciliation, of a new bridegroom (2.14ff.) is grounded ultimately in the love of God who cannot abandon his child:

> How can I give you up, O Ephraim!
> How can I hand you over, O Israel . . .
> My heart recoils within me . . .
> I will not execute my fierce anger . . .
> For I am God . . . and I will not come to destroy' (11.8–9).

Isaiah 1–11 continue to juxtapose themes of eschatological judgment and salvation without clear theological links, and only slowly does the new reality of a remnant begin to emerge as signs and portent of a new people (Emmanuel, Shearjashub; cf. 8.16ff.). Yet the prophet continues to be amazed at the strange, incomprehensibility of the workings of God's will (28.21; 29.13–14). When the message of II Isaiah (chs. 40ff.) is then joined to that of Isaiah of Jerusalem, the full wonder of God's glorious future for a forsaken and blinded people emerges with tremendous force (42.18). A new Jerusalem descends which recalls the joys of paradise (62.1ff.; 65.17ff.). The role of the 'suffering servant' (41.8ff.; 42.1ff.; 49.1ff; 50.4ff.; 52.13ff.) continues to oscillate between the past and the future, the individual and the community, and the actual and the ideal. Yet the servant by his obedient suffering dramatizes the mystery of judgment and salvation within God's economy.

Jeremiah consoles the people of God whom he has condemned to judgment with a promise of a new covenant, but the exact mechanism of writing the law on the heart is left to a fresh intervention of God who forgives iniquity and forgets sin (31.31–34). Then again, one of the more radical pictures testifying to the transition from death to life is found in Ezekiel's vision of the valley of dry bones (37.1ff.). Part of the promise is that Israel will one day know the Lord:

> Behold, I will open your graves . . .
> and I will bring you home into the land of Israel . . .
> I will put my Spirit within you and you shall live . . .
> Then you shall know that I, Yahweh, have spoken . . .
> (37.12–14).

Much has been made of the discontinuity of the apocalyptic message with its vision of a new age and the breaking off of history according to a foreordained schema. Yet the theme of newness has been simply further radicalized, but in such a way as not to call into question the sovereignty of God's rule who in his time brings 'some to everlasting life and some to shame and everlasting contempt' (Dan. 12.2). God's blessing falls on those who understand and wait (12.10–12). Those modern interpreters who characterize apocalypticism as a loss of nerve have failed to grasp the nature of the promise.

(b) *The messianic kingdom and its messiah.* It has long been recognized that the term 'messiah' in its technical New Testament sense as the eschatological redeemer of Israel does not occur in the Old Testament itself, but only in the post-Old Testament period (cf. Mowinckel, *He That Cometh*, 4). Indeed, one of the important tasks of Old Testament theology is closely to describe the profile of the Old Testament witness without fusing it with that of the New Testament. What emerges in the Old Testament is the promise of a righteous king, an anointed one, from the lineage of David whose reign will be likened to the kingdom of God.

His name will be called
Wonderful Counsellor, Mighty God,
Everlasting Father, Prince of Peace.
Of the increase of his government and of peace
there will be no end,
upon the throne of David and over his kingdom
to establish it, and to uphold it
with justice and with righteousness . . . for ever (Isa. 9.6f.).

The description of the coming ruler varies greatly from prophet to prophet, and is consistently joined to contingent historical events in the life of Israel. He stands against Assyria in Micah's prophecy (Micah 5.2ff.). He is constrasted with Zedekiah as the 'righteous branch' by Jeremiah (23.5ff.). He is a 'triumphant and victorious king, but humbly riding on an ass' in Zechariah (9.9ff.). At times a messianic kingdom is portrayed with no mention of a king apart from God (Hos. 14.4ff.; Isa. 65.17), and the office appears in one place to be shared with the high priest (Zech. 6.9ff.).

In spite of the diverse and fragmentary nature of the Old Testament witness, some important theological points emerge. There is no indication that the messianic hope disappeared or grew less as Israel's political fortunes declined. Rather, the reverse movement seems likely. Increasingly the righteous king of the line of David took on roles which transcended human qualities (Isa. 9.6). Moreover, the messianic hope of the prophets seems to have influenced other parts of the canon, and provided an important means by which the royal psalms were transformed into an eschatological hope.

Still, the point must be emphasized that no one profile of the messiah emeged in the Old Testament, nor did it ever become the single dominant feature of Israel's faith. It belongs to the Christian confession when all the disparate parts within the old covenant suddenly assumed a new and unified meaning within God's promise.

(c) *The land.* At first it seems odd to include something as concrete as the possession of the land under the heading of promise. Yet the move seems to be justified by the Old Testament's own construal. Again it was von Rad's programmatic essay ('Promised Land and Yahweh's Land') which first opened up some of the important theological dimensions of the subject. He contrasted two streams of tradition in which the concept was rooted. One was the historical tradition of the Pentateuch which developed the theme in terms of promise and fulfilment. The other was a cultic tradition which described the land in terms of Yahweh's gift of his own possession with the goal of evoking purity from its inhabitants. In more recent years further studies have found a more complex traditional history than that envisioned by von Rad, but they have not broken much new ground theologically (e.g. Diepold).

Of central theological significance is the way in which the concrete possession of the land remained of fundamental importance throughout the entire Old Testament. It was never merely spiritualized. Rather, the history of Israel's encounter with the land through promise, conquest, expansion, exile and restoration formed the centre of a continual struggle to comprehend its theological significance. Within the Pentateuch the dominant manner of understanding the land fell under the rubric of promise and fulfillment. The divine promise of the land to the patriarchs coupled with that of a posterity was made to stretch even over the lengthy period of the captivity in Egypt until it was finally fulfilled in the conquest of Joshua (Josh. 11.23).

Von Rad brilliantly demonstrated that the tension between promise and fulfilment did not dissolve with the historical possession of the land, but continued to open up into newer forms of faith. Israel could possess the land, and yet not her inheritance (*naḥᵃlāh*). The land could serve as a trap and snare rather than as a gift (Deut. 8.7ff.). The writer of Deuteronomy couched the promise of the land in a conditional form. Israel was to observe the commandments in order to enter the land. Moreover, the priestly tradition of seeing the land as a sheer gift from God added a further appeal for obedience to the law in order to maintain the land's purity.

The entire prophetic corpus wrestled continuously with the theological problem of the land. Jeremiah is acutely sensitive to the impending loss of the land with the coming of the enemy from the north (5.15ff). He pictures the utter shame in being cast out of the land and the promise made void (9.19). Even the land itself mourns before the people's wickedness, and all the birds flee (12.4; 4.25). Jeremiah is of course aware that although God is not tied to the land (ch. 29), yet there can be no future hope for Israel without the land (Jer. 32.36ff.). The prophet himself then participates fully in Israel's humiliation by being carried outside the promised land to die in exile.

A major theme of the Deuteronomistic historian is to describe the disobedience of the nation as the cause of loss of the land. Israel did not understand that the land was a gracious gift of God, but practised idolatry with the fertility cults of Canaan. II Kings 24.20 summarizes the sad conclusion of the book:

> For because of the anger of the Lord it came to the point in Jerusalem and Judah that he cast them out from his presence.

There are many signs, especially in the prophetic books, that the possession of the land continued to play a central role in establishing the theological legitimacy of the returning exiles. Jeremiah had characterized the exile as the 'good figs' and those who remained in the land as the 'bad' (24.1ff.). However, those in Judah reversed this judgment and laid claim to the land as their gift from God (Ezek. 11.15f.).

Finally, the theme of the land as the promised blessing continued to assume new forms. An essential part of the prophetic hope was that the land would be restored, even to its paradisal form (Amos. 7.13). Ezekiel pictures Yahweh leading his disobedient people back to the soil ('admat) of Israel (20.42). The holy presence of God was given concrete expression in the land and the return of the 'glory' was the beginning of the eschatological reversal (Ezek. 43.4ff.). Characteristically the prophets joined their hope in a new age with a new and restored space in the land. Finally, the role of the land played a significant role in the later editorial levels of the Pentateuch. J. A. Sanders has made the important observation that according to the final redaction of the Pentateuch in the post-exilic period Israel was defined as a people of God under the Torah but still awaiting the possession of the land (*Torah and Canon*, 48–53). To the landless community of Babylonian exiles tenure of the land was not constitutive of Jewish faith, but a promise yet to be realized.

To summarize, in a real sense the theological problem of the Old Testament's understanding of the land consists in a dialectic tension which both refuses to spiritualize the commitment to the land, and yet senses that the land functions as a cipher for divine blessing which could be lost even by those living within its spatial boundaries.

(d) *Eternal life.* It has long puzzled interpreters of the Old Testament that both rabbinic Judaism and the New Testament place such stress on the resurrection from the dead and the life eternal, whereas these themes appear to play such a minor role within the Old Testament itself.

Throughout the stories of Genesis the death of a patriarch is described as his being 'gathered to his people' (25.8). There appears to be no understanding of an after-life for the individual, but the emphasis falls completely on the continuity of life in the people. The threat that assails the suffering psalmist is that in death he is cast off from the worship of God (88.10ff.). The prophets focus their attention fully on the rebirth of a new people, and only very rarely is there a veiled hint of individual after-life (Isa. 26.19; 56.5). Even the book of Job is only indirectly related to the question of an after-life, but his concern turns on his enduring relationship with God who will finally vindicate him in righteousness (10;18ff.; 19.25ff.).

Yet it is also clear that the Old Testament provided the grounds on which both later Jews and Christians developed their understanding of the after-life. The Old Testament bore witness to the power of God even over the forces of death and destruction. The psalmist in his suffering was comforted that finally nothing could separate him from the presence of God:

My flesh and my heart may fail,
but God is the strength of my heart,
and my portion for ever (73.26).

Because of his understanding of God, both of his creative power and redemptive mercy, the psalmist increasingly finds solace in his conviction that he will always be encompassed within God's watchful care.

If I ascend to heaven, thou art there.
If I make my bed in Sheol, thou art there . . .
I praise thee, for thou art fearful and wonderful . . .
When I awake, I am still with thee (139.8ff.).

Because of this understanding of God, it was not a great step before the promise of an eternal life with God who heard in the Old Testament in a manner which transcended the biblical text's original historical meaning. It is not by chance, but a particular construal of faith in God, that Christians have found a promise of eternal life in Ps. 130, which entered into the funeral liturgy as a resounding proclamation of hope for the future:

Out of the depths I cry to thee, O Lord . . .
If thou . . . shouldst mark iniquities,
Lord, who could stand?
But there is forgiveness with thee . . .
I wait for the Lord, my soul waits,
and in his word I hope.
My soul waits for the Lord
more than the watchman for the morning . . .
O Israel, hope in the Lord . . .
For with him there is plenteous redemption.

Bibliography

F. **Baumgärtel,** *Verheissung,* Gütersloh 1952; J. **Becker,** *Israel deutet seine Psalmen,* SBS 18, 1966, ²1967; *Messianic Expectations in the Old Testament,* ET Philadelphia and Edinburgh 1980; J. **Bright,** *Covenant and Promise,* London and Philadelphia 1977; W. **Brueggemann,** *The Land,* Philadelphia 1977; R. E. **Clements,** *Old Testament Theology,* London 1978, 131–54; J. J. **Collins,** *The Apocalyptic Vision of the Book of Daniel,* HTS 16, 1977; A. B. **Davidson,** *The Theology of the Old Testament,* Edinburgh and New York 1904, 356–532; P. **Diepold,** *Israels Land,* BWANT 95, 1972; W. **Eichrodt,** *Theology of the Old Testament,* ET, I, London and Philadelphia, 1961, 472–511; H. **Gese,** 'The Messiah', *Essays on Biblical Theology,* ET Minneapolis 1981, 141–66; P. D. **Hanson,** *The Dawn of Apocalyptic,* Philadelphia 1975; S. **Hermann,** *Die prophetischen Heilserwartungen im Alten Testament,* BWANT 85, 1965, 472–511; W. C. **Kaiser,** *Toward an Old Testament Theology,* Grand Rapids 1978, 71–261; J. **Lindblom,** 'Gibt es eine Eschatologie bei den alttestamentlichen Propheten?', *StTH* 6, 1952, 74–114; reprinted in Preuss, *Eschatologie,* 31–72; M. **Noth,** *Überlieferungsgeschichtliche Studien,* I, Halle 1943, partial ET, *The Deuteronomistic History,* Sheffield 1981 (cf. pp. 1–110); D. T. **Olsen,** *The Death of the Old and the Birth of the New: The Literary and Theological Framework of the Book of Numbers,* Diss. Yale University 1984; H. D. **Preuss,** *Eschatologie im Alten Testament,* WdF 480, 1978; G. **von Rad,** 'The Promised Land and Yahweh's Land in the Hexateuch' (1943), in *The Problem of the*

Hexateuch and other Essays, ET Edinburgh and New York 1966, 79–93; J. A. **Sanders**, *Torah and Canon*, Philadelphia 1972; T. C. **Vriezen**, 'Prophetie und Eschatologie', *SVT* I, 1953, 199–229; W. **Zimmerli**, *Man and His Hope in the Old Testament*, ET, SBT II. 2, 1968; 'Land and Possessions', in *The Old Testament and the World*, ET Atlanta and London 1976, 67–79.

INDEX OF AUTHORS

INDEX OF BIBLICAL REFERENCES